Dramatic Movement of African American Women

Dramatic Movement of African American Women

The Intersections of Race, Gender, and Class

By
Yuvraj Nimbaji Herode

Anthem Press
An imprint of Wimbledon Publishing Company
www.anthempress.com

This edition first published in UK and USA 2023
by ANTHEM PRESS
75–76 Blackfriars Road, London SE1 8HA, UK
or PO Box 9779, London SW19 7ZG, UK
and
244 Madison Ave #116, New York, NY 10016, USA

© Yuvraj Nimbaji Herode 2023

The author asserts the moral right to be identified as the author of this work.

All rights reserved. Without limiting the rights under copyright reserved above, no part of this publication may be reproduced, stored or introduced into a retrieval system, or transmitted, in any form or by any means (electronic, mechanical, photocopying, recording or otherwise), without the prior written permission of both the copyright owner and the above publisher of this book.

British Library Cataloguing-in-Publication Data
A catalogue record for this book is available from the British Library.

Library of Congress Cataloging-in-Publication Data
A catalog record for this book has been requested.
2023933061

ISBN-13: 9781839988257 (Hbk)
ISBN-10: 1839988258 (Hbk)

This title is also available as an e-book.

CONTENTS

Acknowledgments		vii
Foreword		ix
Chapter One	Introduction to Dramatic Movement of African American Women	1
	General History of African Americans	1
	Rise and Development of Dramatic Movement of African Americans	8
	Major African American Dramatists	13
	Dramatic Movement of African American Women	21
	Major African American Women Dramatists	23
	Works Cited	38
Chapter Two	Alice Childress	41
	Life Sketch and Works	41
	Florence	43
	Gold through the Trees	52
	Trouble in Mind	58
	Wedding Band: A Love/Hate Story in Black and White	64
	Wine in the Wilderness	73
	Works Cited	81
Chapter Three	Lorraine Hansberry	83
	Life Sketch and Works	83
	A Raisin in the Sun	85
	The Sign in Sidney Brustein's Window	94
	Les Blancs	100
	The Drinking Gourd	109
	What Use Are Flowers?	116
	Works Cited	121
Chapter Four	Suzan-Lori Parks	123
	Life Sketch and Works	123
	The America Play	126
	Venus	132
	In the Blood	142

	Fucking A	152
	Topdog/Underdog	160
	Works Cited	167
Chapter Five	Conclusions	169
	Works Cited	177

Bibliography   179

Index   185

ACKNOWLEDGMENTS

This book is based on my research work which was carried out under the supervision of Dr. Kashinath Ranveer, Professor and Head (Retired), Department of English, Dr. Babasaheb Ambedkar Marathwada University Aurangabad. I am sincerely grateful to him for his constant, inspiring, scholarly, and constructive guidance whose wide-ranging knowledge and critical acumen have led to many improvements in this endeavor.

I would like to express my sincere love and respect for my mother, Mrs. Sanghmitra Herode and father, Mr. Nimbaji Herode, who sacrificed their every happiness to see me rationally on the rise as an academic. I would also like to express my heartfelt reverence and high regard to my mother-in-law, Mrs. Jaya Gole and father-in-law, Mr. Bhaurao Gole, for encouraging and cheering me to move on the supreme ladder of higher education.

I owe a special debt of gratitude to my aunts and uncles, Mrs. Goukarna and Mr. Vasudeo Herode, Mrs. Shila and Mr. Arun Herode; my brothers and sisters-in-laws, Mrs. Vaishali and Mr. Sunil Herode, Mr. Pradip Herode, Mrs. Priyanka and Mr. Mahadeo Herode, Mrs. Minal and Mr. Harshanand Ingle, Mrs. Anita and Deepak Morey, Mrs. Subatta and Siddharth Herode; my sisters and brothers-in-laws, Mrs. Deepmala and Mr. Vijay Wankhade, Mrs. Ankita and Mr. Dipak Damodar, Mrs. Kavita and Mr. Rajesh Athawale, Mrs. Sadhana and Mr. Mangesh Gawai, Mr. Prasenjit Gole, Mr. Mahendra Herode, Mr. Kirtiratna Herode, and Miss Arati Herode for their uncompromised support.

I would like to convey my earnest adoration to my beloved wife Mrs. Sonal Herode for being with me in critical circumstances in my life and reliable backing to reduce the heavy burden of the work. I would also like to express passionate affection to my little angels Miss Rinzen and Miss Ritvika who have a worth mentioning portion in the success of the book. Moreover, I would like to thank the entire team of editorial board at Anthem Press who has supported me directly or indirectly in this pursuit of mine.

FOREWORD

African American women are one of the oppressed groups of humanity who suffer from triple jeopardy. They suffer because of their race, gender, and class. As they are black, they suffer because of their race and have been forced to believe that if you are white, you are right, if you are black, stay back and have been discarded from the mainstream life in the United States even today. Moreover, they have been forced to believe that this is the man's world and the woman's place is in home.

In her book, *The Second Sex* (1949), Simone de Beauvoir has written about humanity. She has written, "humanity is male and man defines woman not in herself but as a relative to him, she is not regarded as an autonomous being …. He is the absolute, she is the other …. Man sets himself up as the essential as opposed to the other, the inessential, the object" (16–17). This kind of objectification or commodification of women is being created by men so that they can enjoy the upper hand over women.

African American women are the victims of racism, sexism, and poverty. Moreover, they were also denied to have access to knowledge and knowledge-generating enterprises because of their race, gender, and poverty. The African people were brought to America as slaves and were sold on auction blocks to the highest white bidder. As they were sold as slaves, their humanity was taken away from them. The position of enslaved African women was worse than that of men as every kind of liberty was taken with them by the white masters.

However, after the abolition of slavery and the passage of the thirteenth, fourteenth, and fifteenth amendments made to the constitution of the United States, they started gaining their humanity and access to knowledge and knowledge-generating enterprises. As a result, they started to read and write whatever they wanted to read and write in their own limited capacity. In due course of time, they also started to write autobiographies, poems, short stories, novels, and plays too. The autobiography was one of the basic literary forms which was handled by both African American men and women. Though late, plays were also written by them in due course of time.

Alice Childress, Lorraine Hansberry, and Suzan-Lori Parks are some of the well-known women playwrights who are the famous ones and highlight the social, economic, political, and cultural predicaments of African American people in general and African American women in particular. The present book entitled *Dramatic Movement of African American Women: The Intersections of Race, Gender, and Class* written by Dr. Yuvraj Nimbaji Herode is one of the attempts to study in detail the plays written by these three African American women playwrights.

Dr. Yuvraj Nimbaji Herode has attempted to study and analyze the language, styles, techniques, images, similes, symbols, metaphors, myths, miracles, fables, legends, folksongs, and folklores used by these three major African American women playwrights to turn down the dominant ideology and cultural hegemony of the white people who are powerful and have created different systems to perpetuate their power against the powerless African American people, especially the African American women.

The book is divided into five chapters. In the very first chapter, Dr. Herode has given a full-length introduction to the background of African American people, including their social, economic, political, and cultural life, and a detailed history of the dramatic movement of African Americans in general and African American women in particular.

In the second, third, and fourth chapters, he has dealt with the plays written by Alice Childress, Lorraine Hansberry, and Suzan-Lori Parks, respectively. In the end, in the fifth chapter, he concluded the study with his major observations and arguments about these playwrights.

The book written by Dr. Yuvraj Nimbaji Herode is one of the best additions to the study of African American women playwrights and their plays. I am sure it would be of great help to scholars and especially to all those who want to study African American women playwrights and the world of their plays.

Dr. Kashinath Ranveer
Professor and Head (Retired)
Department of English
Dr. Babasaheb Ambedkar Marathwada University
Aurangabad, Maharashtra-431004, India

Chapter One

INTRODUCTION TO DRAMATIC MOVEMENT OF AFRICAN AMERICAN WOMEN

General History of African Americans

African Americans are the citizens or residents of the United States who have origins in any of the black populations of Africa. However, the term refers to a racial group, most often to the people whose ancestors have experienced slavery in the United States. The genesis of African Americans was the result of forced detention and transport of Africans from their homeland across the Atlantic Ocean. In the 1400s, European traders plundered the west coast of Africa for slaves. The Portuguese, Dutch, French, and British became active players in the theft and the sale of African human beings for profit. Africans were brought to the United States against their will to work on the plantations owned by the white in the South. The permanent settlement of Africans and the regular slave trade between Africa and the English North American colonies began in 1619. Therefore, the history of black slavery emerged in 1619, when a Dutch man brought twenty Africans in America, and sold them at Jamestown in Virginia.

The first shipload of colonists to Charleston in 1670 brought three enslaved Africans with them and the next year, Sir John Yeamans, an English colonial administrator and planter who served as Governor of Carolina from 1672 to 1674, brought more Africans to South Carolina. Over one lakh Africans were being brought in America each year. Merchant shippers from New York and New England imported Africans as usual commodities for the planters of Maryland, Virginia, and Carolina. Both laws and customs defined all Africans in the colonies as slaves by 1670. The enslaved Africans were gradually employed on the growing rice plantations in South Carolina from the 1690s, because numerous slaves were required to cultivate the plantations. From 1619 to 1700, the African in colonial North America increased from sixty to almost twenty-eight thousand.

During more than three centuries of the slavery era, an estimated fifteen million Africans were captured and shipped to the New World where they were sold into slavery. The majority of slaves went to the plantations in the Caribbean and South America. During 1700–1750, thousands of enslaved Africans were shipped to the American colonies each year. By 1776, the colonies had a slave population of more than five lacks. The majority of these enslaved Africans lived in the south of Maryland.

The African Americans were first brought as slaves and they have been systematically and deliberately kept in a position of inferiority for a long period. Many blacks were brought from the West Indies, but the largest numbers were brought directly from Africa, especially the Gold Coast and Gambia. In South Carolina, the status of African Americans was that of a slave. They saw the black slavery as it was "a means of breaking a luckless 'savage' people to gainful domestic use" (Farley 97). The deep Southern states of Mississippi, Alabama, Georgia, and South Carolina have the largest African American population. These states have been recorded not only for the oppression of the enslaved Africans but also for economic and social backwardness, because they had less wealth and less expenditure in education and social services.

The African Americans were economically and socially backward due to the imposition of slavery. They were pauperized and were forced to be the member of the servant class. The economic and political restrictions placed on them have been closely associated with social prejudice. At the time when they were brought across, they were "considered and treated as though they were horses" (Brodhead 139). The cotton plantations of the south needed human hands in a great number and the enslaved Africans filled the need most conveniently. Some masters treated their slaves quite well, but some did not. The slaves who were used as personal house servants were like the members of their masters' families. Unlike, the majority of the slaves who were employed on the plantations were working under the brutal overseers.

The black slavery system laid the foundation of the American economy in three ways: as a basic commodity, as the workers producing agricultural commodities for the market, and as a property. They were prohibited to acquire money beyond their wages. They were not allowed to accumulate property. If any property would be accumulated by them, it would belong to their white master. The black fathers had no moral responsibility to bring up their children and maintain their family. It was a white master who was the godfather of the black family. In Louisiana, the black slave "can do nothing, possess nothing, nor acquire anything but what must belong to his master" (Tannenbaum 74).

African Americans were not only the victims of political disfranchisement and educational discrimination but also suffered humiliation in the form of racial segregation, lynching, and the convict-leasing system launched by the state to secure cheap labor. The enslaved Africans in America were allowed no human dignity; hence, their cultural past was entirely ignored. They supported the superstructure of slavery in America, because they were the living proof of racial superiority of white people in America. They constituted the labor force and gave tremendous political power to the white people.

The enslaved Africans in colonial South Carolina were permitted the freedom of movement and economic initiatives that were to be unthinkable to later generations. Some enslaved Africans were held as bonded servants rather than the slaves who were able to possess property after serving their terms. "In South Carolina and Virginia free blacks were allowed to vote until the second decade of the 18th century" (Thernstrom 9). There were laws to prohibit intermarriage between whites and blacks which indicate not only the growth and codification of racist fear but also the existence of considerable interracial contact. These colonial laws prescribed that the condition of slaves was for their lifetime and that it was transferred to their children through the mother.

The major factor shaping the life and culture of slave was cotton, followed in the order of importance by tobacco, sugar, and rice. Nevertheless, a large number of slaves worked in urban areas, two-third of them as craftsmen, stevedores, draymen, barbers, house and hotel servants, and common labors. Although, the south was still tremendously rural and agricultural, most of the slaves were employed in factories, mines, and other industrial occupations. They made the hemp bags used to pull cotton from the fields, dug coal and iron in Appalachia, gold in the piedmont, lead in Virginia and Missouri, and salt in western Virginia, Kentucky, and Arkansas. These industrial slaves were hired from the urban plantation owners and some were owned by the companies that employed them. The conditions for these slaves were probably worse than on the plantations. Most of them were men who were often housed in barracks away from their families. They generally worked for longer hours and had less leisure than their rural counterparts. The shelter of plantation slaves was probably inadequate than their clothing. Some slaves continued to live in windowless one room huts about 10–15 square feet with dirty floors.

In 1778, Virginia becomes the first state prohibiting the import of the slaves. The cotton boom, which began after the invention of Eli Whitney's cotton gin in 1793, created a greater demand for slaves to work on the new lands opened up in the southern and south western United States. The Cotton gin makes picking cotton much quicker and cost-effective. As the demand for southern grown cotton rises, slavery becomes an institution of the south. During the Great Migration, more than three lacks African Americans moved to northern cities from southern rural areas in search of better opportunities. The African American population of Washington, DC, New Orleans, Baltimore, Philadelphia, and New York City each swells to more than five lacks. The urban life proves difficult for the African Americans who find limited work and housing opportunities for their living. Many African Americans were forced to pay high rent to live in the overcrowded, unsafe slums where crime rates soon increase despite the creation of social agencies to support African American families.

The slaves outnumbered the white settlers in the south. In the North, the slaves make a much smaller percentage of the population. As the African American population grew in numbers, they began to outnumber the white race in the southern states. This led to a fear on the part of the whites about the slave rebellion. As the slave number grew, the whites began to fear slave insurrections, and throughout the eighteenth century, there were rumors, plots, conspiracies, and outright insurrections (Farley 98). In 1711, South Carolina was kept in great terror and fear by the activities of few slaves who were led by an African American named, Sebastian. They had robbed and plundered some plantations. The news from Charleston in 1793 implies the fear:

> The Negroes have become very insolent, in so much that the citizens are alarmed and the militia keeps a constant guard. It is said that the St. Domingo Negroes have sown these seeds of revolt, and that a magazine has been attempted to be broken open. (Farley 101)

In 1800, Gabriel Prosser, a literate enslaved blacksmith, plans the first major slave uprising in Richmond, Virginia. The violent rainstorms wash out local roads and bridges, preventing the revolt, but it increased the fear among the white population of the south. In 1791, slave riot in Haiti frightened American slave owners.

However, the era of racial subjugation seems to have begun with the freedom of the United States from the British Empire in 1776. The Southern whites who were in favor of slavery dominated the Constitutional Convention of 1787. As a result, the slavery and the slave trade were legitimatized under the newly framed constitution. The first quarter of the nineteenth century seems to have witnessed a new climate of tension in American race relations. In 1810, in defiance of the Fugitive Slave Acts, Quakers and the other antislavery groups established the underground rail roads to help slaves escape from the south to the Free States in the North. In 1812, Louisiana gained statehood, and its sugar plantations created additional demand for slave labors.

The forceful torture of the African Americans resulted into protest ranging from subtle insubordination to the slave insurrections. The less violent forces formed antislavery societies and raised their voice of protest through speeches, pamphlets, periodicals, and newspapers such as *Freedom's Journal, The Coloured American, The North Star, The Liberator, The National Era, The Frederick Douglass Paper,* and *Walker's Appeal.* Sojourner Truth, a former slave, becomes an outspoken activist for the abolition of slavery and women's rights movement in 1827. Frederick Douglass, Peter Williams, Maria Stewart, David Walker, Sarah Mapps Douglass, and Henry Highland Garnet were famous abolitionist orators. They form the public opinion against the inhumane treatment of the slavery that meted out to the African Americans in the country.

In 1850s, the Reverend Stephen Elliott of Georgia, the Reverend James A Lyon of Mississippi, and Edward A. Pollard of Virginia led a movement for slavery reform. Their demands included the sanctioning of slave marriages, the prevention of the separation of families, the education of slaves, the sheltering of slaves from cruelty and inhumanity, and the admission of African American's testimony against whites in courts of law. However, the whites thought that granting the slaves the basic human rights would destroy the foundation of the institution of slavery.

The abolitionists were getting more and more violent in their campaign against slavery and the federal government's enforcement of the Fugitive Slave Act in 1850. Harriet Tubman, a former slave and abolitionist, was known and greeted in the North as "Black Moses" (Allen 11) because, like Moses in the Bible, she had led many African Americans out of slavery. In 1849, she escaped from slavery and helped other African Americans to escape via underground rail road. After her escape, she went back again and again to guide other slaves to freedom. She said, "I have heard their groans and sighs, and seen their tears. And I would give every drop of blood in my veins to free them" (Allen 13). The slaveholders in the south offered rewards of thousands of dollars to catch this black woman who was furious about the slavery. She wanted to save all men, women, and children who were enslaved. She says, "There was one of two things I had a right to liberty, or death. If I could not have one, I would have the other, for no man should take me alive. I should fight for my liberty as long as my strength lasted" (Allen 23).

Harriet Tubman was never frightened of the threats of white slave masters. She was fully convinced that the only way to end the slavery was an armed rebellion by slaves and ex-slaves against slave masters. The rebellions turned out to be the prominent cause to demolish black slavery. John Hope Franklin, in *From Slavery to Freedom: A History of Negro Americans*, said:

> During the Civil War, increasingly large numbers of slaves practiced the most widespread form of disloyalty [...] desertion because it could hardly be called running away in the sense that it was before the war. Between 1861 and 1865 Negroes simply walked off plantation, and when the union forces came close, they went to their lines and got food and clothing. In Arkansas, whenever federal forces appeared, most of the able-bodied adult Negroes left their owners and sought refuge within the Union lines. [...] In August 1862, a Confederate General estimated that Negroes, worth at least a million dollars, were escaping to the federals in North Carolina. (216–17)

The racial slavery came to an end in America in 1863 legally, when Abraham Lincoln, the president of the United States, declared the Proclamation of Independence and set the African Americans free. In 1863, the Emancipation Proclamation declared all the slaves in confederate controlled areas forever free. In 1865, Congress approved the 13th Amendment to the Constitution of the United States to abolish slavery. In 1868, the African Americans got the citizenship of America, but they did not get civil rights.

In 1870, Congress adopted the 15th amendment to the constitution granting suffrage to the adult African American males. Though the right to vote in political elections was given to them in 1870, the southern politicians imposed severe literary tests and poll testes to keep African Americans from voting. The African Americans had no property; therefore, they were deprived of this political right. The southern states passed many laws and kicked the African Americans into economic and social slavery. Though the African Americans were legally free, the new forms of racial harassment were devised to trouble them. The segregation laws were enacted by various states. These laws did not allow equal access to African Americans on public transport and various facilities like schools, churches, hospitals, graveyards, and so on.

In 1881, Booker T. Washington, a former slave, founded Tuskegee Institute in Tuskegee, Alabama, to educate African Americans. He urged African Americans to obtain education and vocational training from this institution. In 1885, W. E. B. DuBois became the first African American to receive a PhD from Harvard University. He opposed Booker T. Washington's position on race relations (friendly relations with white men) and pronounced that African Americans should fight for equal rights.

At the beginning of the twentieth century, the social, economic, and political condition of the African Americans in the United States was miserable. During 1914–1917, despite *Jim Crow* segregation policies, African Americans obtained benefits from educational programs and educational training and found work as laborers in the manufacturing industry. In his collection of essays, *The Souls of Black Folks* (1903), DuBois lamented not only the denial of social justice and education to African Americans from the material richness of America, but also the "sense of always looking at one's self through the eyes of others and the malaise of measuring one's soul by the type of a world that looks on in amused contempt and pity" (qtd. in Thernstrom 21). DuBois was proud of his African American heritage:

> There is no true American music but the wild-sweet melodies of the Negro slave; the American fairy tales and folklore are Indian and African; and, all in all, we, black men seem the sole oasis of simple faith and reverence in a dusty desert of dollars and smartness. (qtd. in Thernstrom 21)

The Harlem Renaissance (1920–1940s), also known as the New Negro Movement, created an environment where African American music, art, dance, and writing could flourish. In the 1920s, African Americans migrated from the Southern states to the Northern states. Many African American colonies came into existence in northern cities, because they were not allowed to dwell in the colonies of white Americans. They used to work in factories and were becoming educated. Moreover, they were also recruited in the army. Due to this economic and educational development, a new intellectual African American middle class came into being. They were able to think about their problems. They started thinking about equal status as white Americans. In 1946, the Supreme Court ruled that a Virginia State law allowing segregation of blacks and whites on interstate buses as unconstitutional.

The Civil Rights Act of 1960 reinforced African Americans the right to vote. The Emancipation Proclamation of Abraham Lincoln in 1863, the president of America, was the great inspirational light of hope to millions of black slaves. They had been burnt in the flames of crushing injustice in the hands of white people. It was a joyous daybreak to end the lengthy darkness of their slavery. But one hundred years later, the black people were not still free. The life of African Americans was still crippled by the restraints of segregation and the chains of discrimination. They had been living still in poverty in the vast material prosperity in American society.

In 1963, on August 28, almost 250,000 people march in Washington, DC to demand full civil rights for African Americans, an end to segregation, the prevention of discrimination in employment and education, and an end to federal funding of discriminatory packages. Standing on the steps of the Lincoln memorial, Martin Luther King, Jr. declared:

> I have a dream that one day, down in Alabama, with its vicious racists, with its governor having his lips dripping with the words of interposition and nullification, one day right there in Alabama little black boys and black girls will be able to join hands with little white boys and white girls as sisters and brothers [...]. (20)

His dream of a country where blacks and whites can live in equality inspires millions around the world.

In 1965, Malcolm X, a Muslim leader, who articulated the concepts of Black Pride and Black Nationalism, was assassinated in Harlem. In 1966, Huey Newton and Bobby Seale found the Black Panther Party at Oakland in California. Its purpose was to patrol black ghettoes to protect the African American residents from the acts of police brutality. During 1977–1990, the educated and talented African Americans moved into the upper-middle and wealthy socioeconomic classes, though poverty, crime, and the disintegration of the family took their tax on the millions of African Americans living barely out of poverty. Although discrimination is against law, African American professionals and executives were prevented from advancing because of racial prejudice.

At the beginning of the twenty-first century, there are 34.3 million African Americans living in the United States. Barack Obama, a member of the Democratic Party, became the first African American president of the United States. He served as the 44th president of United States from 2009 to 2017. Despite equal opportunity laws that guarantee equal rights in voting, education, and housing, many African Americans continue to experience prejudices up to the present time. George Floyd, a forty-six-year-old African American, was killed in Minneapolis during his arrest for seemingly using a bogus bill on May 25, 2020. A white police officer knelt on his neck for almost nine minutes, while he was shackled and lying face down in the street begging for his life. His death in police custody has exploded a nationwide protest against the police killings of African Americans.

All human beings are born equal and free, but there is inequality on the basis of race, gender, and class in the American Society. Race, gender, and class are the factors which bring inequality and injustices in American society. American social life was divided into black life and white life, male and female, and upper class and working class. In these binary oppositions in the American society, one group is dominant and the other a subservient. In America, the white people were the masters, while the blacks were the slaves. The white men were superior in the social hierarchy followed by the white women. The black men were the slaves and the black women were the slaves of the slaves. Therefore, the black women are doubly marginalized in the American society. At the same time, those who have the means of material production at their command constitute the upper class and those who lack the means of material production are at the mercy of them. As the servants, they had economic, political, and social restrictions.

The African American women were brought to America to please the lust of the white master. They suffered humiliation, sexual exploitation, and lynching. They were deprived of human dignity and their cultural past was entirely ignored. Their task was to bear the burden of the double standard of whites. This double standard allowed premarital and extramarital sexual expression of white men and denied it to their women. Thus, the purity of white women was preserved completely. But for years, the sexual subjugation of African American women was perpetuated.

African American women had to work either in the house or on the plantation of their white masters. The women who were working in the house were forced into cohabitation. In the pregnancy and childbirth, they had no release from labor. They were forced to cultivate a strong dislike toward their children. Moses Grandy, a former slave, wrote about the treatment of African American women by the overseer:

> On the estate I am speaking of those women who had sucking children, suffered much from their breasts becoming full of milk […] the infant being left at home […] the overseer beats them with rawhide. So that the blood and milk flew mingled from their breasts […]. (qtd. in Frazier 168)

African American women gave birth to white masters' infants. They loved much and cared more for their white masters' children, though they had children of their own. The black woman became mammy of white masters' children. Her rape by white brutality is melancholic. She had no ability to protest the brutality and her black man could not protect her.

The slavery as a system had many consequences in the social, economic, political, and cultural life of the African Americans. They lost their self in the slavery. In America, African Americans forgot their language, religion, culture, and customs absolutely. Their color and defiled bodies mere remained there. They were forced to learn their master's language and accept their master's religion. They were entirely thrown away from African history and culture. Their family system and marriage system were destructed, because black slaves, their wives, and their children could not live together in the possession of one master. The white masters sold their wives to one, and their children to another. Their honor was grabbed away from them. The black slaves were the tools of material production. Hence, the black slavery became economic institution in America.

The black slavery was rooted in race and color. The African Americans are black by color. Consequently, the slavery system depended on face and body of the blacks. They cannot hide their faces and bodies because it is hereditary. This black skin cannot be thrown away. So, the black color was the stigma on the black race. And this stigma is adhered thoroughly on them till today. The black people could not change their color and also cannot give up their bodies. Therefore, there is the feeling of hatred in the minds of black people about their color and body. However, after getting education, they started saying black is beautiful and glorified their blackness.

This general history of social, economic, political, and cultural life of African Americans is given here, because according to Marxist tenet:

> Literature is basically a creative reproduction of reality. The writer born in a particular period of society has certain experiences and those experiences make him study the underlying reality of the social events and interpret it in his individual way [...]. Since the writer presents that reality by creating a world of imagination which is not quite different from the world we live in. (Sinha 93)

Thus, there is a tragedy hidden in the overall experiences of African Americans. The black women put their experiences in the form of different arts and especially dramas written by them that dominate African American theater.

Rise and Development of Dramatic Movement of African Americans

The dramatic movement of African Americans refers to the plays written and performed by African Americans to portray African American experience. It comprises the plays written by, for, and about African Americans in the United States. It opened the door of theater to all African Americans who were denied the access to it. This dramatic movement is a medium where African Americans recognized themselves as human beings with the ability to think, speak, and analyze their own values of life. It speaks the language of revolt, protest, liberation, and revolution that affirms the existence of African Americans who had the right to live, to speak, and to condemn everything that was oppressive. African American dramatists were firm to abandon their silenced position and voice with energy and power. They were determined to destroy the prejudice and simplicity of stereotypes created by white society and to show the complexity of their real selves.

The rise of African American dramatic art has been marked at the beginning of the nineteenth century. The origin of African American theater is traced back to the slave trade and the continuation of African performance traditions. In 1820, The African Grove Theatre has been established in New York. This theater played a role as an inspiration in the development of African American theater. In fact, African American theater has been evolved through the African American folk drama. African American theater has its roots in oral stage performances as well as in dance drama that the African Americans brought with them as slaves from their mother country. Elizabeth Brown-Guillory, an African American theater scholar, observed that "black playwriting in America is directly linked to African theatrics and oral drama was transferred to American soil by enslaved Africans" (Dakorwala 32–33). Gradually, African American theater took its form through African Folk culture and folk drama.

The American professional theater rejected African American performers. The African American playwrights were restricted of opportunities in the professional theater in the United States, because of the social, economic, and cultural circumstances. Darwin Turner writes about the African American playwrights and their recognition on American stage as follows:

> The first play by a black American was not written until 1858. No Afro-American had a full length serious drama produced on a Broadway Theatre in New York City until 1925, and only ten additional plays written totally or partly by Afro-American were produced on Broadway from 1926 until 1959, when Lorraine Hansberry's *A Raisin in the Sun* began its longest run on Broadway ever experienced by a play on Afro-American Authorship. (113)

There was no play written by a writer of African ancestry in America until the end of the nineteenth century. A play entitled, *The Drama of King Shot Away*, fashioned by African Americans, was produced for the first time in New York in the African Grove Theatre in 1821. The African Grove Theatre was developed out of Mr. William Henry Brown's tea garden under the leadership of the leading actor James Hewlett. This theater has made its contribution to the genesis of African American theater and drama. The first black play, *Miralda* or *The Beautiful Quadroon* (1855), was written by William Wells Brown. However, it was never produced. In accordance with Brown-Guillory:

> Though the African-American theatrical tradition had begun with *King Shot Away*, the first African-American playwright of record is William Wells Brown, whose play, *The Escape: or A Leap for Freedom*, written in 1858, marks the impetus from dramatic oral tradition to formal playwriting. (qtd. in Dakorwala 34)

The Escape is a melodramatic closet drama. Brown-Guillory further says about the play that, "It levels an indictment against slavery and is the first attempt in the line of protest plays that would dominate early Black plays and that made an appeal for justice for African-Americans" (qtd. in Dakorwala 34). Pauline Hopkins (1859–1930) is one of the earliest African American woman playwrights whose musical play entitled *Slaves' Escape: Or the Underground Railroad* (1879) was performed by the Hopkins' Colored Troubadours at the Oakland Garden, Boston, in 1880. It focuses on how the Underground Railroad was instrumental in assisting slaves in their flight to freedom.

The nineteenth century, thus, provided a necessary context for the emergence of African American theater and drama, which appeared from the beginning of the twentieth century. W. E. B. DuBois outlines four fundamental principles of African American theater as "Real Negro theatre: About us, By us, For us, and Near us" (134). His play, *The Star of Ethiopia* (1913), was staged in major American cities for African American audience. This play made the African Americans aware of the spectacular history of the achievements spanning continents.

In first decade of the twentieth century, two events marked a revolution in African American theater and drama and ushered in the Harlem Renaissance. First was the publication of *The Crisis* magazine edited by W. E. B. DuBois in 1910, and the second was Ridgely Torrence's New York Production in 1917 of three plays for a Negro theater which included *Granny Maumee*, *The Riders of Dreams*, and *Simon the Cyrenian*. However, this period is remembered more for the successful Broadway production of African American plays.

A very few African American dramatists got recognition till the 1930s. The Harlem Renaissance of the 1920s and early 1930s was the first significant event in the history of the dramatic movement of African Americans. It plays a vital role in the growth and development of the African American theater and drama. Until the nineteenth century, the role of African American characters in American theater appears to be limited to minstrel, burlesque, and the musical. The African American characters began to emerge as an ordinary human being with everyday actions in written plays in this period. The Harlem Renaissance resonates with such names as W. E. B. DuBois, Alain Locke, Langston Hughes, Claude McKay, and Zora Neale Hurston.

African American drama came to Broadway with Willis Richardson's one act play *The Chip Women's Fortune* (1923). Garland Anderson's *Appearances* (1925) was the first full-length play by an African American to be produced on Broadway stage. Doris Abramson says, "It was so didactic, so filled with Anderson's personal belief in new thought and healing by faith, that it provided only glances at the Negro problems of his or any other day" (27). Another play by African American playwrights appeared on the Broadway was William J. Rapp and Wallace Thurman's *Harlem* (1929), which shows African American life with realism. Both the plays were well received by Broadway audience and by the majority of critics.

Thus, the Harlem Renaissance seems to have provided a pleasant background for the flourishing of the African American playwriting. The African American playwrights used the drama as a medium to speak against racial injustices in America. The African American theater in the Harlem Renaissance dealt with the issue of racial oppression as experienced by African American people. Even during the economic depression of the 1930s, African American playwrights were active both in the downtown theaters and in the community theaters.

The Negro Theatre Guild staged Augustus Smith's *Louisiana* in 1933 which depicts religious forces in the African American community in south. In the same year, Hall Johnson's *Run, Little Chillun* was produced by the Federal Theatre in Harlem. The Federal Theatre tried to develop African American playwrights to write the realism in the life of African Americans. The 1930s was the decade of protest for the African American dramatic and theatrical movement. Langston Hughes's *Mulatto* (1935), an explosive protest play, began the longest Broadway run of any play by an African American dramatist before Lorraine Hansberry's *A Raisin in the Sun* (1959). His another play in the tradition of protest was *Don't You Want to be Free?* (1937).

The period between 1940 and 1960 was marked by realism in the African American dramatic and theatrical movement. The urban social reality was observed in African American theater through *Native Son* (1941), a Broadway run protest drama, written by Paul Green and Richard Wright based on Richard Wright's novel *Native Son* (1940). The play presented the realistic picture of the African Americans who live in the ghettoes in the city. Theodore Ward's *Big White Fog* appeared on Broadway in 1940 and ran for sixty-four appearances. It depicts an African American man's frustrations and tragic experience more bitterly. Theodore Ward's another play, *Our Lan*, appeared on Broadway in 1947 which describes the attempts made by the African Americans to gain freedom after the civil war. The play focuses on the United States' betrayal of the freed slaves who were thinking of the Promised Land—escape from slavery. They were forced to give up their rights to the land of freedom and were driven off by union troops.

In 1940, American Negro theater came into existence which worked hard to develop African American dramatic art. In the 1940s, African American theater took a new form, that is, the form of caricature. It worked properly for caricaturing the tendencies of the African American bourgeois. Abraham Hill's drama, *On Strivers Row* (1940), is a mockery about a black bourgeois in Harlem. The playwrights of the1940s were aware that the strength of their art would lay in exploring the inner linguistic resources of their culture as a way of correcting the misconceptions about them created by the whites. Their objective was "to break down the barriers of black participation in the theater, to portray Negro life as they honestly saw it, to fill in the gap of a Black theatre which did not exist" (Bigsby 376).

The 1940s provided an appropriate transition for a fresh upsurge of the African American drama in the 1950s and early 1960s. The African American professional theater came on Broadway during 1950s. Louis Peterson's *Take a Giant Step* (1953) ran for seventy-six performances. The play tells the story of educated Northern African Americans in Philadelphia. It is concerned with the problems that an African American boy faces in growing up in a white neighborhood. The play implies that the African Americans should grow alone and should not try to imitate the cultural values of the whites. The play highlights the plight of African Americans in 1950s.

Loften Mitchell's *A Land beyond the River* appeared in 1956 in New York Off-Broadway. The play conveys the courageous efforts of Mr. Dulane, a minister in South Carolina, to help African American children to enroll in schools reserved for white children. He succeeded, but was forced to save his life by escaping from a community of whites who were resentful of changing the conditions. Lorraine Hansberry achieved success with her first play, *A Raisin in the Sun* (1959), which became the first play by an African American woman to be produced on Broadway and to win the New York Drama Critics Circle Award for 1959–1960. Hence, Loften Mitchell, in his book, *Black Drama*, points out that "the 50s was a millennium in the development of black drama" (qtd. in Shyama 222).

The Civil Rights Movement that began with the bus boycotts of 1956 and the sit-ins of 1960 gave birth to a socially committed African American theater. During this period, the majority of African American dramatists wrote for ethnically diverse audience and used the traditional forms of naturalism, melodrama, and farce to convey their racial concerns. The 1960s produced many new African American dramatists who brought to the theater the intimate inside vision of the African American life and the roles that the African American women play in it. The main thrust of the African American theater in the 1960s, as the emphasis of the Civil Rights Movement, is shifted to the north. The theater tackles directly the realities and myths of African American life. A racially conscious, racially derived, and racially directed African American theater saw itself as the cultured arm of black power movement. The African American theater saw the protest and anger against racism in the 1960s. As Robert J. Willis said:

> Protest [...] is implicit in most of the contemporary plays of Black American dramatists. While not forgoing artistry, dramatists such as Lorraine Hansberry, Imamu Amiri Baraka (LeRoi Jones), and Jimmy Garrett are replacing the stereotype "nigger" image of buffoonery and low comedy with angry characters designed to forge Black consciousness into a literature that speaks not only for the Black man but also for the underground experiences of all Americans. (213)

In the mid of 1960s, the African American theater began to be divided into two clear directions: first, the Negro Ensemble Company and second, the New Lafayette Theatre. Douglas Turner Ward, Lonne Elder III, and Adrienne Kennedy were the representatives of the first group. Douglas Turner Ward stressed the need of a permanent black repertory company, a theater concentrating on the lives of black people. According to him,

> Black Revolutionary Theatre is the name given to that special Black American Strain of theatre, film, and agitprop public activity that originated in the Black Arts Movement, in the Black religious and spiritual sects, and in Third World Revolutionary Cultural and Political societies. (qtd. in King 122)

The Negro Ensemble Company describes a school of African American theater in the early 1970s which has special revolutionary strain. There are the growing numbers of plays by contemporary African American writers like Imamu Amiri Baraka and Ed Bullins who present their plays as black revolutionary theater. Ed Bullion was the most prominent playwright of the New Lafayette Theatre in Harlem. The African American playwrights during the 1960s turned to the resources of native culture derived from African roots for theater.

In the 1970s, the African American theater experienced the Black Arts Movement which opposed to any concept of the African American artist that separates him from African American community. They advocated a cultural revolution in ideas and arts and tried to destroy the cultural values which do not tackle toward African American culture. Emamu Amiri Baraka represents the most advanced aspects of the Black Arts Movement. He was the prime motivator of the African American theater, a revolutionary theater for him, which forces to change the black victimization. He enlightened the African American audience to understand that they are the brothers of victims of the racism. Hence, they must resist the oppression of African Americans in the hands of the whites.

During the 1970s, the nationalistic zeal created by African American dramatists, especially Emamu Amiri Baraka and Ed Bullins, continued with the younger playwrights like Ntozake Shange and others. One feature of African American drama of the 1970s was that it was shared by both men and women. Gerald Wales saw in the African American drama a counter to the hopes of the African American community. He remarks, "During the 1970s pattern of play-going among Blacks changed. In increasing numbers, they began to attend the commercial theatres in large cities" (qtd. in Dakorwala 52). This indicates that the African American drama has crossed the restricted space and has joined the main stream American theater.

In the 1980s, African American theater suffered financially due to the lack of support from the community as well as from the funding agencies. Instead of this financial problem, the African American theater continued to survive and do the revolutionary work. In his essay, *A Look at the Contemporary Black Theatre Movement*, Peter Bailey says:

> Talented, committed, imaginative, and resourceful theatre artists, and directors, playwrights [...] and a host of outstanding actors, actresses, choreographers, technicians, and administrators will keep contemporary Black Theatre on a steady course forward. (qtd. in Dakorwala 52)

The history of dramatic movement of African Americans, thus, shows that though there are many ups and downs in the development of the African American theater, it has the continuity of a revolutionary spirit that protests against the injustices of racism, sexism, and classism.

Major African American Dramatists

The African American playwrights were slowly to emerge, because of slavery and racism. When they began to write the plays, their plays were rarely published. In his *Foreword to Black Theatre USA*, Ted Shine writes:

> Black characters appeared in American dramas as early as 1767, beginning with Raccoon in Andrew Barton's (Thomas Forrest's) *The Disappointment: or, The Force of Credulity*. With few exceptions the plays that followed used blacks mostly for comic relief or as "contented" servants. This stereotyping was sustained and climaxed by the minstrel show, which sprang up in the early 1840's. Not until 1852, when Harriet Beacher Stowe's novel, *Uncle Tom's Cabin*, was adapted for the stage, was there a major attempt in American drama to treat black characters and the problem of slavery with sympathy. (ix)

The African American drama of the twentieth century has some contexts in the nineteenth century. William Wells Brown wrote *The Escape; or, A leap for Freedom* in 1858. This melodrama in five acts is centered on two slaves, Glen and Melinda, who, unknown to their masters, are married.

Ira Aldridge, an abolitionist, was an actor and playwright in the middle of the nineteenth century. His first play, *The Black Doctor* (written in 1847; first published in 1870), tells the story of Fabian, a former slave, who becomes an eminent doctor. He saves Pauline Raynerie, the daughter of his former master and falls in love with her and elopes with her. But he is caught and sent to the prison, and consequently he goes mad. When he is released from the prison, he sacrifices his life to save his beloved Pauline. The play depicts a society that acknowledges his skills, but does not accept his marriage to a white woman. At the end, pity, terror, and moral resentment are evoked again, when a gunman aims to shoot Pauline, and Fabian, rushing forward, received the bullet and dies. Bernard Peterson identifies Aldridge's *The Black Doctor* as the "second recorded play in English by a black American Playwright" (qtd. in Carter 5). Aldridge's second play, *Titus Andronicus* (unpublished) is an adaptation of Shakespeare's play of the same title.

William Easton, an African American dramatist, wrote two plays, entitled *Dessalines* and *Christophe*, which were about some leading African American revolutionaries against Napoleon. In 1901, Joseph Cotter published a full-length play entitled *Caleb the Degenerate* in which he contrasted the economic philosophy of Booker T. Washington with the backwardness of the African Americans. W. E. B. DuBois opposed Washington's notion of economic independence for African Americans, in his play, *The Star of Ethiopia* (1913).

Willis Richardson is the first African American playwright to have his play, *The Chip Woman's Fortune* (1923), produced on Broadway. It is Richardson's most successful folk play which centers on the need for black self-help and cooperation. He tackles African Americans' issues such as gender, class discrimination, marriage, family problems, exploitation, racial solidarity, unemployment, and requirements for the advancement of African American race. In *The Deacon's Awakening* (1920), Richardson deals with the issue of women's rights as Deacon Dave Jones and his friend Sol try to discourage women members of their church from voting. *A Pillar of the Church* (written in the 1920s), deals with a woman's right to receive education of her choice. *The Broken Banjo: A Folk Tragedy* (1925) highlights the need for black unity and family solidarity. Matt Turner and Emma Turner constantly quarrel about the time Matt spends playing the banjo. Sam and Adam in a fight break the banjo. The breaking of the banjo leads to the breaking apart of a family through betrayal.

Compromise: A Folk Play (1925) depicts the difficulties the African Americans experienced in obtaining justice in the post-emancipation period. Ben Carter, a white man, shot Joe Lee who was hiding in a tree, escaped by paying only $100. When Ben Carter's son, Jack, impregnates Annie Lee, her mother wishes that he should pay for her children, Alec and Ruth, go to school. His play, *The Flight of the Natives* (1927), is about the myth of contented slave. Luke, the mulatto slave, brings the news that the Fugitive Slave, Slim, has been captured, because of Jude's betrayal who is fugitive slave of Marse.

The slave Mose threatens to beat Jude for his action, but is dissuaded by his wife, Pet, who fears that Marse will sell Mose down to river.

The Idle Head (1929) is a folk play about a black man who, refusing to grin and cringe before white people, is unable to obtain employment. He stands with dignity and does not want to compromise his self-respect. *Mortgaged* (1924) concerns the field's brothers. One is a landlord of slum property, who makes money by exploitation of other black people by charging high rents. The other brother is a research scientist who seeks to uplift the black race through science. *The House of Shame* (1929) tells the story of the shady deals and sharp practices of Mr. John Cooper.

Another significant African American dramatist is Arna Bontemps whose play entitled *St. Louis Woman* (written in 1933; published in 1973) centered on Little Augie, a jockey who believes that he will always have a good luck at the track and elsewhere. He is led to believe that good luck has left him after he becomes romantically involved with Della, and he is accused of murdering Biglow, Della's former boyfriend.

Langston Hughes, a prominent figure in the Harlem Renaissance, has a significant place in the history of African American theater. His play, *Cross: A Play of the Deep South or Mulatto* (1935), based upon the theme of the tragic mulatto, is a "hoary tale of lust, revenge and miscegenation in the early 20th century south" (Dakorwala 40). It was taken to Broadway in 1935 and became the longest running play by an African American. In this play, Hughes transformed the black man's submissive nature into aggressiveness. In *Little Ham* (1935), he transformed carefree primitive into a Harlem sporting man. Thus, in these plays, Hughes created positive images of the African Americans. His *Don't You Want to Be Free?* and *Jericho Jim Crow* are two experimental plays.

Hughes Allison, an African American playwright, wrote *The Trial of Dr. Beck* (1937), which was produced by the Federal Theatre. The play centers on Dr. Beck, a handsome mulatto, who was accused of murdering his wealthy black wife, Amanda. The play unfolds through the evidences at trial in New York City. After the successful production of *The Trial of Dr. Beck*, Allison wrote *Panyared* for the Federal Theatre which portrays the origin of black enslavement. It is a dual tragedy of both the enslaved and enslavers. Allison concerns with the African American roots in his plays.

Theodore Browne wrote for Federal Theatre. His play, *Natural Man*, first presented as a folk opera, was produced by the Federal Theatre in 1937. The play portrays the transformation of a brute African American into a black revolutionary hero. John Henry is an escaped convict and has murdered a white man. He fights back and ultimately chooses death rather than submission to white exploitation. His philosophy of human dignity, justice, and freedom for all is superior to the hypocrisy and double standards of his oppressors. Theodore Browne's play, *Go Down Moses*, is another example of such transformation. The play is based on the life and exploitation of Harriet Tubman, who is an escaped slave. She ran an Underground Railroad up to the civil war, and then scouted for the union army. She has all the characteristics of the vicious and revengeful female stereotype and was capable of any act of violence necessary to insure the safety of the slave passengers. She hated her slave masters with burning passion. She was considered dangerous enough to the slave system. She was like Moses, a giant among women and architect of African American freedom.

Randolph Esmonds established the stereotype of a brutal African American. His play, *Bad Man*, written in 1934, represents an important step in total transformation of a brutal African American. In *Bad Man*, Maybelle, the sister of a sawmill worker, wheedles into the mill shanty to get a look of Dugger, whose reputation as a bad man is guaranteed to attract any innocent. She believes that Dugger is really a good man at heart who would not kill in cold blood. He is affected by her trust and spares his attacker, a fellow worker with a gun. But soon after white men found a poor white man dead. They are fully convinced that he must have been murdered by a black. The white men threaten to burn down the shack unless the guilty black comes out and surrenders. No one of these black was guilty. But it becomes clear that one black would be lynched or all would be burned in the shack. Dugger emerges from the shack full of terrified blacks and marches toward the white mob. He gives himself up with all nobility.

Theodore Ward is a significant African American playwright. His *Big White Fog* was one of the best plays in the 1930s. He was one of the founders of Negro Playwrights Company. His aim was to foster the spirit of unity between the races, provide an outlet for creative talents of Negro artist, and supply the community with the theater reflecting the historical reality of the life of the Negro people (Bigsby 3: 378). His next play, *Our Lan* (1941), is set in post-bellum America and projects a newly freed slave who prepares to receive the promised benefits of emancipation. Joshua Taint, a slave, had planned to revolt against his white master. Moreover, he prepares to challenge the forces of the United States. Joshua is the epitome of the resisting spirit who organized the group of slaves into a community. One senses his sincerity and warm-heartedness which seems to blind him to others in deep, sympathetic accord.

> Indeed, he is an expression or symbol [...] of the best trait of his people. There is a sure sense of dignity about him and his very physical strength bespeaks something of relentlessness and courage which characterizes the bulk of the vilified black men of the period. (Bigsby 3: 379)

Owen Dodson (1914–1983), an African American playwright, director, and poet, provides insight into the twentieth-century African American experiences. His *Divine Comedy* (1938) explores the stories surrounding Father Divine. It is a verse drama that exposes a type of evangelical fraud man. *Bayou Legend* (1946), set in Louisiana, is a reimagination and adaptation of *Peer Gynt*, a five-act play in verse by the Norwegian dramatist Henrik Ibsen. *The Ballad of Dorie Miller* (1943) depicts the heroic African American sailors who shot down Japanese planes during the attack on Pearl Harbor. *Everybody Join Hands* (1943) deals with the resistance of Chinese people against their Japanese oppressors. *Garden of Time* (1939), a reworking of *Medea* set in Greece and post–civil war North America, deals with race relations. *New World A-Coming: An Original Pageant of Hope* (1944) recognizes the contribution of African Americans to the war efforts. Dodson's other plays include *The Shining Town* (1937), *Doomsday Tale* (1941), *Amistad* (1939), *Gonna Tear Them Pillars Down* (1942), *The Third Fourth of July* (1946, with Countee Cullen), *The Decision* (1947), *Medea in Africa* (1963, with Countee Cullen), *The Story of Soul* (1978), and *Freedom, the Banner* (1984).

Louis Peterson is best known for *Take a Giant Step* (1953–54), which is set in a middle-class white community. Spencer, the protagonist, is the young African American adolescent boy. The play demonstrates the difficulties of growing of Spencer in a white middle-class neighborhood in New York. He also confronts the insidious racism of his teacher and his classmates. When Spencer questions his teacher's knowledge of slavery and civil war, he is expelled from the school for two weeks. The play also focuses on Spencer's loss of his grandmother, his humorous and unsuccessful encounter with a prostitute, and his sexual initiation with a caring and lonely widow. His innocence enables the playwright and the audience to reexperience the realities of racism.

> His realism in the portrayal of his protagonist and in the depiction of the racial division of the country [...] gives the message to the black dramatist that in order to be authentic he/she must use local elements without any romantic exaggeration through primitivism or exotic fancy. (Dakorwala 42)

His second play entitled *Entertain a Ghost* (performed in 1962) is a semi-autobiography and the story of an interracial couple. *Crazy Horse* (performed in 1979) explores an interracial marriage in the 1950s between an African American journalist and a white woman. It is about the disapproval of marriage by parents of both sides. *Another Show* (1983) is a story of a college student who commits suicide and the effects of his death on the people closest to him.

Loften Mitchell's *Star of Morning: Scenes in the Life of Bert Williams* (produced, 1965) portrays the early dramatic career of Bert Williams, the great West Indian comic artist. *Tell the Pharaoh* (produced, 1967) celebrates Harlem as the hub of African American culture. It traces the history of Harlem from its origins as Dutch Harlem to which a road was built in 1920 by eleven African slaves. *Bubbling Brown Sugar* (produced, 1975) transports a young African American couple, Jim and Ella, and a white man, Charlie, from the 1970s to an earlier era in the century. His other plays include *Shattered Dreams* (1938), *Blood in the Night* (1946), *The Cellar* (produced, 1952), *A Land Beyond the River* (produced, 1956), *The Phonograph* (produced, 1961), *The Final Solution to the Black Problem in the United States; Or, The Fall of the American Empire* (produced, 1970), *Sojourn to the South of the Wall* (produced, 1973), *Cartoons for a Lunch Hour* (produced, 1978), *A Gipsy Girl* (produced, 1982), and *Miss Waters, To You* (produced, 1983).

William Blackwell Branch's first play, *A Medal for Willie* (1951, unpublished), is about the ironies of a memorial service and presentation ceremony for Willie Jackson, an African American Corporal in United States army who has been killed in a battle. The play points to the irony of the African American soldier fighting for the freedom of others in another country, but he is being denied the same basic freedom and rights in his own country. In his next play, *Baccalaureate: A Drama in Three Acts* (1954, unpublished), Branch addresses the issues of feminism, civil rights, and family relationships. The play focuses on the struggles of Angela, a young African American woman, her attempts to gain advancement through education, and her battle for self-fulfillment. His other play, *In Splendid Error* (1954, unpublished), takes place in the home of Frederick Douglass. The play reflects on slavery by presenting two dominant personalities and their perspectives on how this horrible system can be abolished. John Brown believes that the freedom can only be attained through guerrilla warfare, while Frederick Douglass believes that freedom must be attained through a national mandate.

Although James Baldwin is better known as an essayist and novelist, he is the author of two plays. His first Play, *The Amen Corner*, written in 1952 and produced in 1965, is set in an African American community church. It presents "a private struggle for meaning and identity" (Bigsby 388) from racial to sexual sphere. In this drama, he traces an African American church-woman's path from a theology of hell fire to a theology of love and sufferance. He depicts, in *Blues for Mr. Charlie* (1964), a southern town before and after a young African American man is shot dead by a white shop owner. The play is influenced by the murder of the civil rights worker Medgar Evers in 1963. Both plays fail badly in theater because of complicated and too many subplots.

Douglas Turner Ward's *Happy Ending* (1965) is a farce in which an enlightened African American woman is given a lesson by her aunts. They work as domestics and artfully exploit their employers. His *Day of Absence* (1965), a comedy, is set in a southern town which is paralyzed when its African American citizens disappear one day. His *The Reckoning* (1969) presents a battle of wits between a southern governor and his blackmailing African American mistress. *Brotherhood* (1970) is about neighboring black and white families who go through the motions of integrationist brotherhood.

Lonne Elder III came under the influence of Ward. He is more interested in rendering the smoothness of African American life. In *Ceremonies in Dark Old Men* (1969), he imparts a naturalistic view of social and psychological tricks of African Americans to keep their self-respect. The play is set in a shop of a barber in Harlem. It is a detailed account of a family's tragedy.

Joseph A. Walker is affiliated with Negro Ensemble Company. His *The River Niger* (1972) is a generational play that covers a father who is shattered by his inability to provide for his family, his son to whom he passes his thwarted dreams, his octogenarian grandmother who tolerates no dreams, and his wife dying of cancer who supports her husband's flight from reality. The play is anchored in the African American experiences.

Imamu Amiri Baraka, formerly LeRoi Jones, has been a major spokesman for African Americans' anger since the 1960s. He encourages African Americans to adopt a separatist stance and supports communism. His *Dutchman* (1964) is set in a subway train and describes as "the flying underbelly of the city" (Bigsby 397), a world which is rich in myth. It is a ritualistic work in which a white slut taunts a middle-class African American man for refusing to admit his sociopolitical rage. A white woman, Lula, sexually provokes the African American man, Clay, yet he does not rape her. Then he is knifed by Lula and his body is thrown off the train by the white passengers. Another African American enters the compartment and she begins the same cycle again. *The Baptism* (1964) deals with a boy who has committed a sexual sin and seeks redemption. The minister wants the boy to be a savior for his people. When the boy rebels against this, the entire congregation decides to sacrifice him. Then the boy kills the entire congregation to free himself. Thus, the boy's baptism into manhood is through the mass shedding of blood instead of through the sin of sexual procreation.

The Toilet (1964), is set in a high school restroom. It centers on the secret offstage affair between Ray who is the well-built, physically fit leader of an African American's gang and Karolis, a skinny, unattractive, well-spoken white boy. *The Slave* (1964) is set at the moment of a literal revolt. It is concerned with a revolution the leader of which is in essence a slave. The play revolves around Walker who is dressed as an old field slave. He is a black freedom fighter accused of murder. He has left his white wife and two children and gone to join a black army preparing for revolution. The slave wishes to destroy the ideas and values of the white world. Both *Dutchman* and *The Slave* present racial tension. His *S-1* (1976) was aimed at an actual piece of proposed legislation which threatened a numbers of constitutional rights. *The Motion of History* was an attempt to reclaim the past as a prelude by seizing the present and determining the future. *A Black Mass* (1966) and *Slave Ship* (1967) indicate the African American consciousness.

Charles Fuller brings historical resonance to plays about African American's struggle for social justice. His play *The Village: A Party* (1968) is a play of racial conflict among racially mixed couples. *The Brownsville Raid* (1976) is an adaptation of 1906 incident in which all the enlisted men in a regiment of African American soldiers were discharged without trial for shooting up the town of Brownsville, Texas. *Zooman and the Sign* (1979) focuses on a murder of a young black girl by a black boy. Charles Fuller is recognized for *A Soldier's Play* (1981) for which he received Pulitzer Prize for Drama in 1982. The play is about the murder of a psychic African American army sergeant during World War II. It is an investigation of not only a murder but also the psychopathology of racial hatred. Thus, Fuller is an angry African American playwright.

Phillip Hayes Dean, like Fuller, touches the African American history with a talented finger. In *The Sty of the Blind Pig* (1971), he delineates a portrait of the African American life at the dawn of the civil rights movement. Through the character of a blind street-singer, Dean insinuates both the past and the future into their temporal lives. The singer symbolizes the historical condition of being African American in white American. In *Paul Robeson* (1978), the portrayal of Robeson simplifies some of the facts of the African American actor's life and softens some of his extremist positions.

Charles Gordone (1925–1995) is the first African American playwright to gain the Pulitzer Prize for his play *No Place to Be Somebody* in 1970. He opposed the racially oriented theater and spent much of his life to the recreation of multiracial American theater and racial unity. His play, *No Place to Be Somebody* (1969), achieves this purpose on a grand scale. The play is set in a Greenwich Village bar patronized by both the blacks and the whites. It is an ensemble play with a wealth of subplots, a range of moods, and sudden burst of anger, violence, and humor. *Gordone Is a Muthah* (1970) and *The Last Chord* (1976) reflect Gordone's expansive approach to the African American theater.

Ossie Davis (1917–2005) is a distinguished African American actor, director, civil rights activist, and a dramatist. His *Purlie Victorious* (1961) is a folk comedy lampooning the old south that served to ease the African American experience on Broadway. It is the story of an African American preacher who tries to establish an interracial church in a South Georgia community.

Thomas Covington Dent (1932–1998) was an author, a playwright, a poet, an essayist, a civil rights activist, and an oral historian. He was a leading member of a group of African

American writers who during the 1950s merged artistic expression with explorations of African American identity. The Free Southern Theatre staged the work of African American playwrights throughout the South, including Dent's plays *Negro Study No. 34A* (1969), *Riot Duty* (1969), *Snapshot* (1970), and *Features and Stuff* (1970). In 1976, his play, *Ritual Murder*, became a classic of the Southern African American theater.

Ed Bullins (1935–2021) is the most prolific of contemporary African American playwright of Black Arts Movement. He started his dramatic career as a revolutionary playwright with focus on the separateness of African Americans and on their struggle of self-expression. He also focuses on the issues, which were general in nature in the context of the situation of African Americans in the American cultural mosaic. As an exponent of separatist theater, he, as an editor of *Black Theatre* and in association with the New Lafayette Theatre, produced the *Electronic Nigger and Others* (1969). These plays touch the innermost conscience of African American race. His plays are straightforward about the blacks who are trying to recognize themselves in the context of white society.

His play, *How Do You Do* (1965), is about a stereotypical African American assimilation and an African American whore with a prediction for white men. The third character is a young African American man who urges them not to submit to the white man but to "kill him in the mind" (Bigsby 404). In *The Gentlemen Caller* (1969), a young African American man calls on a rich white woman, Mrs. Mann, where living room is decorated with the mounted heads of an African American man. Bullins' *Clara's Ole Man* subtitled *A Play of Lost Innocence* is set in the 1950s in a slum kitchen in Philadelphia. It is a play of frustrated dreams and distorted characters. As Weales remarks,

> Perhaps most representative of his dramas are those plays—*In New England Winter* (1967), *In the Wine Time* (1968), *Miss Marie*, *The Duplex* [which form the] part of a projected cycle of the twenty in which, through recurring characters, he explores African American society, celebrating the vigor of the people and at the same time showing their acquiesence in their own situation. (Dakorwala 46)

Samuel L. Kelly's *Pill Hill* (1995) is about a group of African American mill workers living in Chicago who meet over the years and compare how well they have done in life since they quit the mill. His play, *The Blue Vein Society* (1988), is about an African American man who is marrying a light-skinned woman of slavery times. The play reveals the superior attitude of light-skinned African Americans who would not socially accept an African American person whose skin was too dark to have visible the blue vein on the wrist. Another play, *White Chocolate* (1999), is about a middle-class African American family in which the father is about to be considered for a tenured position at his university. His teenage daughter is dating a white boy. The play dramatizes a dilemma among members of the African American bourgeoisie as how far into assimilation they can move without using their own sense of self-worth.

His *Thruway Diaries: Driving While Black* (2000) is a realistic depiction of what happens to an African American family that is stopped on suspicion of carrying drugs, although their only crime is being African Americans. His latest drama entitled *Faith, Hope, and Charity: The Story of Mary McLeod Bethune* (2002) highlights the life story of one of the most influential African American women of the twentieth century.

Ron Milner (1938–2004) is an African American playwright whose play, *Who's Got His Own* (1966) portrays the troubled relationship of a mother, son, and daughter after the death of an overbearing father. In his play, *What the Wine-Sellers Buy* (1973), Milner focuses on the pimp culture and of easy money on intercity youth. *The Warning: A Theme for Linda* (1969) examines African American manhood in the context of women's experiences. In *Checkmates* (1987), Milner compares a retired African American couple with a young upwardly mobile African American couple to show the intergenerational shift in values. His recent play, *Urban Transition: Loose Blossoms* (2002), revisits the consequences of drugs and money on the African American family.

Charles F. Gordon (1943), professionally known as OyamO, is an African American playwright and professor. His play, *I am a Man* (1995), is based on some historical events in America. The play reenacts the Memphis Sanitation Strike of 1965, which culminates in massive riots and the assassination of Martin Luther King, Jr. His *The Resurrection of Lady Lester* (1981) is inspired by the life of Lester Young, the famous saxophonist. In *Fried Chicken and Invisibility* (1988), William Price and Winston McRutherford, the protagonists, discuss their experiences as African Americans. William Price is convinced that blacks should adopt invisibility as a means for survival. *In Living Color* (1992) celebrates song and dance and focuses on Gullah-speaking African Americans. The play explores the African American people's attempt to evolve without losing their culture.

His play, *Let Me Live* (1971), dramatizes the lives and crimes of eight African American prisoners. The prison system becomes a reflection of real world with all its negative conditions and social injustices for African Americans. *Famous Orpheus* (1991) is based on the legend of mythical lovers Orpheus and Eurydice and the film adaptation of the story Black Orpheus. The play blends myths with reality to dramatize the story of the lovers. His other dramatic works include *Chimpanzees* (1970), *Last Party* (1970), *The Negroes* (1970), *Outta Site* (1970), *The Thieves* (1970), *Willie Bignigga* (1970), *The Advantage of Dope* (1971), *The Lover* (1971), *The Breakout* (1972), *His First Step* (1972), *Juice Problem* (1974), *Mary Goldstein and the Author* (1979), *The Place of the Spirit Dance* (1980), *Distraughter and the Great Panda Scandal* (1983), *Old Black Joe* (1984), *Every Moment* (1986), *An Evening of Living Colors* (1988), *Return of the Been-To* (1988), *Singing Joy* (1988), *The Stalwarts* (1988), *One Third of a Nation* (1991), and *Angels in the Men's Room* (1992).

Dramatic Movement of African American Women

African American women are the female human beings of African descent living in the United States. They were the subject of extreme abuse and oppression based upon the racist perception of inferiority by the white oppressors. African American women, throughout the history of America, have encountered brutality and repression. They suffered a lot, because they were subjected to racial enslavement, patriarchal social order, and labor force in America. The African American women suffered as colored, enslaved humans, and as women who were struggling to survive in a brutal white social order. Their struggle stemmed from their black race. These women proved their triumph because of their strong spirit and love to life. They fought for their survival which is something actively linked to their African heritage. The American mainstream society does not acclaim their dignity and the autonomy under the supremacy of the white materialistic norms.

The African American woman's history is the account of oppression and struggle. In the history of the United States, when the rights of women and African Americans began to be asserted, the African American women emphasized the intersection of race and gender. Anna Cooper wrote, "The colored woman of today occupies, one may say, a unique position in this country …. She is confronted by both a woman question and a race problem, and is as yet an unknown or an unacknowledged factor in both" (45). However, the African American women became united to fight against the inhuman treatment meted out to them in the hands of the white superiority. They engender the solidarity by generating a harmonious bond among themselves to subvert the notion of their subjection and otherness.

This history of oppression has united them to create an exclusive position for redefining themselves. African American women continue to play significant roles from their struggle as slaves through the middle passage in America. Their hardship, leadership, motherhood, womanhood, intellect, and artistic expressions have enhanced the African American community which has been exhibited in African American drama and theater. The historical oppressions and the power of struggle have been exposed by African American dramatists, both male and female, with a difference. They have exposed their agonizing roles through their dramas.

The African American women's theater is a dramatic movement of African American women who write the plays to protest against racism, sexism, and classism. It challenges the oppressive ideology of white patriarchy and African American male dominance. It is an expression of African American feminist consciousness with pride in African American communities and in themselves that had been plundered by white society. African American women playwrights, using their personal experiences, widened and completed a simplistic view and broke with the old stereotypes observed in the male playwrights' works. They manifested a double consciousness that embraced their cultural background as well as their gender. The female characters depicted in the plays written by African American women playwrights incorporated new components, creating a world in which the personal became political. The African American womanhood reflects and reclaims power, voice, and choice over the African American female body through the African American women's theater.

In the nineteenth century, few plays were written by African American women. Sojourner Truth (1797–1883) is the first African American feminist. She had been assumed as an ideal of African American womanism during the slavery period. Her speech, entitled *Ain't I a Woman*, is addressed to the 1851 women's rights convention. She communicated an undeniable truth—being both African American and a woman she was not viewed as a human being but used as both beast of burden and producer of free labor. She said:

> Look at me! Look at my arm! I have ploughed, and planted, and gathered into barns, and no man could head me! And ain't I a woman? I could work as much and eat as much

as a man–when I could get it–and bear de lash as well! And ain't I woman? I have borne thirteen children, and seen 'em mos' sold off to slavery, and when I cried out with my mother grief none but Jesus heard me! And ain't I a women? (Burke 85)

She used her own life as text to seek and speak for change. Hence, she is one of the mothers of African American feminist drama.

In 1916, African American women actively engaged in writing serious plays for the nonmusical theater. Elizabeth Brown-Guillory notes that "African American women were able to turn theaters in nurseries where the black race [was] given roots, nurtured, tested, healed and provided with the sprit to survive" (qtd. in Gray 245).

Major African American Women Dramatists

Between 1916 and 1935, the African American women playwrights like Angelina Weld Grimke, Alice Dunbar-Nelson, Georgia Douglas Johnson, May Miller, Mary Burrill, Myrtle Smith Livingstone, Ruth Gaines-Shelton, Eulalie Spence, and Marita Bonner captured the realities in the lives of the African Americans. They wrote about various issues like lynching, poverty, disenfranchisement, miscegenation, racial pride, revolution, and women's rights. They detached from the widespread images of African American women as mammies, maids, and whores by constructing credible and distinguished portrayal of African American women. They presented the feminine point of view in American theater through their plays by virtue of race and gender.

Angelina Weld Grimke (1880–1958) contended against racism and patriarchy. Her *Rachel* (1916) was the first significant play by the African American woman and was performed publicly by African American actors. It is both propaganda and protest drama. *Rachel* focuses on an unmarried African American woman, Rachel Loving, and her decision not to marry and bear children. It was "the first attempt to use the stage for race propaganda in order to enlighten the American people relative to the lamentable condition of ten million of colored citizens in this free republic" (Burke 87). *Rachel* revealed the gross prejudice that educated African Americans faced in seeking meaningful employment. Even with a college degree, Rachel's husband-to-be can find job as a waiter only. *Rachel* is a dramatic investigation of lynching and its consequences and focuses on the Loving family—Mrs. Loving, a widow and her two children—son Tom and daughter Rachel. Through *Rachael*, Grimke breaches the male discourse of lynching to demonstrate its effects on African American women. Thus, the play designates that African American women were not only physically lynched but also psychically and metaphorically, because of the death of their men. Hence, lynching ceases to be "a crime against black men" (Gourdine 535) and becomes a crime against all members of the African American race. Grimke, thus, opened the door for African American women playwrights to step over the threshold and began creating different images of African Americans.

Mary Burrill (1879–1946), an early twentieth-century African American woman playwright, departs from genteel tradition of Grimke. Her race dramas feature the characters who are suffering from poverty as well as racism. She has written two one-act plays, namely *They That Sit in Darkness* (1919) and *Aftermath* (1919). Both the plays deal with the social concerns. The play *They That Sit in Darkness* was first published in *Margaret Sanger's Progressive Birth Control Review*. *They That Sit in Darkness* is a typical tragedy of African American Women which clarifies that the mother's death was the result of bearing too many children because the law of the land had denied her to get information about birth control. It focuses on a young black girl who must abandon her hope of obtaining education by attending the African American Tuskegee Institute when her mother dies after the birth of a tenth child. As the eldest child, the daughter must remain home to take care of her brothers and sister. The poverty in the Jasper Family is caused by African American women's inability to stop bearing the children. They live in a badly maintained house. The play reveals the causes of Jasper Family's poverty, including lack of information about birth control, economic inequalities, racial discrimination, and prohibition of education.

Burrill speaks about the birth control issue in African American community which was the leading problem in the early twentieth century. In devoting this issue to "the Negroes need for birth control, as seen by themselves" (Burke 91) to control their destinies, she sought to empower the black women. The play illustrates the intersection of race, gender, and class. Poor African American women are oppressed and limited by the fact of their race, gender, and income status. They do not have access to health care and information concerning birth control. In her *Aftermath* (1918), a decorated African American serviceman returns to his rural southern home from the war in Europe to find that his father has only recently been lynched by a white gang. Burrill's plays reflect the experiences of African Americans in the first quarter of the twentieth century.

Georgia Douglas Johnson (1880–1960) wrote history, race, folk, anti-lynching, Africans, and brotherhood plays. In *A Sunday Morning in the South* (1925), an innocent young African American man is taken from his family on a Sunday morning and hanged by a white mob that suspects him of flirting with a white woman. In *Blue Blood* (1926), the complications of miscegenation are considered. A marriage is prevented before few hours of ceremony when the young African American couple learns about their parentage. The respective mothers discover that their children have the same white father.

Her *Plumes* (1927) features a mother who must choose between giving her ill daughter the remote chance of a cure and putting that money into a grand funeral for her child. Johnson underscores the high mortality rate among African American children in the racist world bounded by poverty. In *Safe* (1929), an African American woman about to deliver her first child is traumatized by hearing the shouts of a lynching mob and its seventeen-year-old victim calling for his mother. Maddened by what she has heard, she strangles her new born son while muttering repeatedly: "Now he's safe–safe from the lynchers! Safe!" (Burke 95). *William and Ellen Craft* (1935) features the escape of the self-enslaved protagonists to freedom in the North. Through this history play, Johnson symbolizes the self-assurance that is associated with freedom. Johnson's dramas brought to attention the issues of lynching, rape, miscegenation, and the theft of human dignity of the African Americans.

May Miller (1899–1995) was an African American poet, playwright, and educator. She was known as the most widely published female playwrights of the Harlem Renaissance.

She used the history and tradition for her plays. Her history plays feature African, Haitian, and African American protagonists. *Harriet Tubman* (1935) presents one of Tubman's nineteen trips from Canada to Maryland to free her fellow African Americans through the Underground Railroad. In *Graven Images* (1929), Miller exposes sexism as well as racism. While worshiping the golden bull, the boys taunt the girls telling them the bull "does not like girl children ... he does not want women to speak [and they] must bow lower than we for [they] are girls" (Burke 94). *Riding the Goat* (1930) deals with a clash of values within the black community. Miller's dramas inculcated a sense of pride in its heritage in the black community. Her history plays instructed young people creating for them a usable past. In 1986, Miller received the Mr. Brown Award for excellence in the drama and poetry from the National Conference of African American theater.

Marita Bonner (1899–1971) focused on the restrictions placed on the colored women. She calls for revolution. Brown-Guillory observes that Bonner depicts "Poor and middle class black women who defend themselves against gender-based, societal constraints" (Christy 8). In *The Pot Maker* (1927), an African American man is killed by his wife for his emotional battering for her. The play reflects Bonner's concerns with resisting the romanticization of the South, portraying poverty and immorality, and dramatizing the devaluation of women. Her next play, *Exit, An Illusion* (1927), is about jealousy of an African American man, Buddy, for a white, Exit Mann, who he believes is in love with Dot, a half-black, half-white woman.

The Purple Flower (1928) won the 1927 Crisis Prize for the best play. It is the radical response to the question of what can be done about white racism. It is the most explicit in criticizing discrimination and in portraying anti-white sentiments. It condemns the "white devils" and "their intrusion on the black community and its beliefs" (Gray 249). Marita Bonner and all the other women of the Harlem Renaissance wrote about more than their race. They challenged the conventions in the social philosophy and brought into the drama authentic representation of African Americans. As feminists, they dared to question the "naturalness" (Burke 98) of race relation erected on an assumption of the African American inferiority.

Beah Richards (1920–2000) is primarily known as an actress, but she is also a playwright. Her best known work is *A Black Woman Speaks* (1950). She created *A Black Woman Speaks* out of the history of her race and her life as a woman. Richards addresses white woman seeking to forge an alliance against the white patriarchy and seeks to make black and white women as one. She asserted that the purity of white womanhood is a notion promulgated by white supremacist and sustained on the flesh of the African American women whom the white men rape. She informs white women that they too are slaves; in spite of the fact that "the difference is degree" (Burke 124).

Alice Dunbar-Nelson's *Mine Eyes Have Seen* (1918) focuses on a young African American man who has an obligation to serve his country in time of war despite his father's lynching by a white mob in the South. In Maud Cuney Hare's *Antar of Araby* (192 [?]), audience learned of African American warrior and hero. Ottie Graham's *Holiday* (1923) features a woman who passes as white so she can further her stage career. On finding her actress mother years later, hurt by her mother's abandonment, she commits suicide.

Dorothy C. Guinn's *Out of the Dark* (1924) presents images of the blacks in Africa as slaves and as a freed people.

Zora Neale Hurston's *Color Struck* (1925) concerns a woman who is distressed with the darkness of her complexion and so jealous of light-skinned women. She drives away the man who loves her. In Frances Gunner's *Light of the Women* (1925), actors portray notable women in African American history who appear on stage to address the audience. Myrtle Livingston Smith's *For Unborn Children* (1926) concerns the choice of a young African American man who must make his engagement to a white woman. Though he loves her, he breaks off the engagement, because his unborn children will not have to contend with ostracism and the problems of mixed parentage. At the play's close, he exits his cabin and offers himself to the waiting white lynch mob.

These African American women playwrights have paved the way for the succeeding generation of African American women playwrights of the twentieth century. They were fully involved in the African American theater's protest against conditions of the African Americans. The 1950s observed the appearance of the most talented African American women playwrights like Alice Childress, Lorraine Hansberry, Adrienne Kennedy, and Ntozake Shange. They formed a link in the development of African American women playwriting in America from the 1950s to 1980s.

The Civil Rights Movement of the 1960s produced many new African American women playwrights who brought to the stage the intimate inside vision of African American life and the roles that African American women play in it. Regardless of the great difficulties, the African American women playwrights from Angelina Grimke to Lorraine Hansberry have raised their voices to document and celebrate the lives and experiences of African American people in general and African American women in particular. The African American women playwrights have emphasized their voices in making the feminist dialogue one of the central intertwining cords of African American discourse.

Alice Childress (1920–1994) is the reigning African American woman dramatist. She wrote the following: *Florence* (1949), *Just a Little Simple* (1950), an adaptation of Langston Hughes's *Simple Speaks His Mind*, *Gold through the Trees* (1952), *Trouble in Mind* (1955), *Wedding Band* (1966), *Wine in the Wilderness* (1969), *String* (1969), *Mojo* (1970), and *The African Garden* (1970). *Florence* (1949) centers on a discussion between an African American woman and a white woman who happens to meet in a railroad station in the South. A railroad station waiting room which is divided into the colored and the white sections apparently proposes the race superiority. This enforces separation of races that leads African Americans to anger, fear, and hatred. *Gold through the Trees* (1952) is a dramatic revue with music that takes place in Africa prior to colonization and after. It explores the history of African slavery from 1619 to the Civil Rights Movement of the 1950s in Africa as well as America in three fragments.

Trouble in Mind (1955) voices about the difficulties faced by African American actors. It is about a play rehearsal during which Wiletta Mayer, an African American actress, rebels at unconscious stereotyping by a self-consciously liberal director. She struggles for her desire to be an actor and the inaccuracy of her role that of a mother who sends her son to face a lynch mob. Challenging the white director by asking if he can send his son to be murdered, she leads him into exposing his bigotry. *Wedding Band* (1966) concerns the 10-year love affair of Julia and Herman, who are forbidden from marrying by South Carolinas anti-miscegenation law. Childress spurns the myth of African American matriarchy but proffers a vision of African American women who refuse to be less strong than the world demands. In *Wine in the Wilderness* (1969), Childress highlights the fusion of racism, sexism, and classism in drama that presents in its protagonist Tommy a vibrant, independent African American woman who demands the dignity due to her. Tommy dreams of finding a man who will love her. She loves Bill Jameson, a young African American middle-class artist. Tommy Marie is an evolving African American woman.

Lorraine Hansberry (1930–1964) is the first African American woman and the youngest playwright to win the New York Drama Critics Circle Award in 1959. *A Raisin in the Sun* (1959) is an attempt to transform the experiences of her early years in Chicago into a drama and those experiences which capture the deferred dreams of her race. The play obviously illustrates her detailed knowledge of south side Chicago. The development of the major theme reveals how Hansberry uses her personal experiences. *The Sign in Sidney Brustein's Window* (1964) offers Hansberry's objectivity toward her subject to be dealt with. It has only one African American character, and he is guilty of an act of profound personal betrayal. It is a lament for human imperfection by a woman. *To Be Young Gifted and Black* (1969) emphasizes Hansberry's political views, especially her conviction that racism is rotten and must be eliminated. To Hansberry, aggressive political action was necessary to bring about racial equality. She concerns the human condition as blacks have experienced. She anguished over blacks entrapped by poverty and the ghetto. She wept for those who were tired, from years of struggle.

Les Blancs (1972) has a strong sense of universal womanhood in which black and white women collectively fight against the black women's oppression in Africa under white colonial rule. *The Drinking Gourd* (1972) is an insightful exploration of racial slavery based on the economic exploitation of the African Americans. It dramatizes the devastating psychological and physical impact of the slave institution on both the master and the slave. The play transcends popular literature as a fair, balanced treatment of slavery. *What Use Are Flowers?* (1972) is a short play about hermit who returns from holocaust and decides to civilize the savage children and chooses those aspects of civilization to continue the human race and necessary for their spiritual and intellectual growth.

Vinnette Carroll (1922–2002), an actress, director, and playwright, was the first African American woman to direct a production on Broadway. Her first play, *Trumpets of the Lord* (1963), a musical, is based on the work of poet James Weldon Johnson. *Don't Bother Me, I Can't Cope* (1972) is the hit gospel show for which she became the first African American woman to direct on Broadway. As the first successful African American woman playwright, Carroll's work served as a stepping stone for future aspiring directors and attracted greater audiences. However, she is known for the reinvention of song play, which has been revitalized in many of her theater works. The expression of identity through gospel music in the African American theater experience is very clearly delineated in the development of the song play as shaped and realized by Carroll. Her main interest was to give voice to the African Americans or minority communities that have been culturally and artistically silent. Her other plays include *Agamemnon* (1948), *The Little Foxes* (1948), *Deep Are the Roots* (1949), *Caesar and Cleopatra* (1950), *A Streetcar Named Desire* (1956), *The Grass Harp* (1956), *Small War on Murray Hill* (1957), *The Crucible* (1958), *Moon on a Rainbow Shawl* (1958), *Jolly's Progress* (1959), *The Octoroon* (1961), *Black Nativity* (1963), and *The Prodigal Son* (1965).

Adrienne Kennedy (1931) was raised in a racially mixed suburb of Cleveland, Ohio. She grows up in an integrated neighborhood enjoying the rich cultural activities of Italians, African Americans, Jews, Poles, and others. Adrienne Kennedy describes her plays as "states of mind" (Shafee 83). Her plays "strongly insinuate probably unconsciously the sensibility of the African continuum," because for her "Blackness is an obsessive theme" (Shafee 83). Her characters walk the line between dream and consciousness as well as reality and the surreal fantasies of the subconscious. Her plays reflect "an acquaintance with oppression that is germane to the existence of black people everywhere" (Shafee 83). Her *Funnyhouse of a Negro* (1964) focuses on a sensitive young girl named Sarah whose confused identity is linked with her ambiguous feelings toward her white mother and black father. The contrast between the African and the European experience of Kennedy herself forms the background for this play. The play focuses on identity crisis and confusion of a sensitive young African American woman.

The Owl Answers (1966) explores the desperate attempts of Clara to resolve her uncertain emotions about black and white. The drama testifies to Kennedy's lifelong fascination with film, film stars, and fame. It also graphically presents the mystery of the representation of the minorities. Clara's life is the subject and she narrates her own drama in a unique manner. Kennedy's protagonist remains subsumed by the white majority. *A Rats Mass* (1969) was rooted in her brother's injuries in an automobile accident and subsequent death. Kennedy bases the play on a dream that she had while on a train from Paris to Rome. In the dream, she was pursued by red-blooded rats. Haunted by this image, she finally captured it in *A Rats Mass*. In the play, the love that brother and sister have for each other is juxtaposed to their previous adoration for the white and beautiful "descendent of the Pope and Julius Caesar and the Virgin Mary" (Wilkerson 151).

Kennedy's *A Beast's Story* (1969) practices the same mode of psychological expressionism and dividing combined characters in an African American girl's fantasia of unbridled sexual alarm. *The Alexander Plays* is a quartet centered on the character of Suzanne Alexander, a writer. The first play, *She Talks to Beethoven* (1989), is set in Ghana. Suzanne anxiously awaits the arrival of David, her husband, who is vanished two days before. *The Film Club* (1992) and *The Dramatic Circle* (1992) deal with David's later disappearance. The first is Suzanne's monologue and the second its dramatization. *The Ohio State Murders* (1992) enlarges into a restaging of Suzanne's memories of her undergraduate days. Kennedy's own pain at the prejudice, she experienced living in a dormitory, is present in Suzanne's story. Kennedy's dramas challenged the two pillars of racism and sexism on which patriarchy is based. Thus, Kennedy explores the interior reality of her own self.

In the 1970s, issues of racial identity tended to defer to questions of sexual identity. Ntozake Shange (1948–2018), the African American woman playwright, is mostly associated with change of emphasis. Her works reveal the stark facts of African American life with a splendid fusion of imagination and reality from an African American woman's perspective. *For Colored Girls Who Have Considered Suicide/When the Rainbow Is Enuf* (1976) has been described by Shange as, "a young black girl's growing up, her triumphs and errors, our [her] struggle to become all that is forbidden by our [the] environment, all that is forfeited by our [her] gender, all that we [they] have forgotten" (Bigsby 411). Shange's feminist play, *For Colored Girls* ... strongly advocates that women bond together to protect themselves from the enemy men. The evolving African American women speak of brutal treatment by their own men. Shange emphasizes their struggle to rise above from the bondage and their success at coping in a world where "Being alive, being women and being colored is a metaphysical dilemma" (Brown-Guillory 212). For Shange, *For Colored Girls* "introduced feminist thought-in-action to theatre" and played a social role in "moving our theatre into the drama of our lives" (Burke 184–85). The twenty poems in *For Colored Girls* ... chronicle the African American women's progress from enduring death in life through learning African American history, experiencing a joyful sexual initiation and knowing the pains of betrayal, rape, and abortion.

Her play, *Where the Mississippi Meets the Amazon* (1977), expresses the experiences of growing up an intelligent and sensitive African American woman in a man's world. In *Boogie Woogie Landscapes* (1978), Layla, an African American woman in her 20s, returns from a disco and reviews her life through the guises of her "night-life" companions, who enter through her bedroom walls and represent her "dream-memories" (Burke 187). The play concerns with the plight of women, more especially African American women. It is a lament for the forces which conspire to limit the freedom of women, to deform their sensibility, and to damage their spirit. In *Spell #7* (1979), Shange criticizes the manner in which representation works to make African Americans invisible.

Thus, Shange's dramas represent the tortured moment of emergence and discovery. She illuminates the recesses of racism and sexism. Her drama describes African American characters overcoming oppression and learning to love them. She presents African American women's experiences with a new intimacy. Her dramatic works make a powerful impact on the literary circles that they made everybody look at the African American literary tradition afresh from an altered perspective.

Sonia Sanchez (1934) is an African American professor, poet, dramatist, and one of the foremost leaders of Black Studies Movement. Her dramatic works occupy an apex space in the development of African American theater. She has written six plays: *The Bronx Is Next* (1968), *Sister Son/Ji* (1969), *Dirty Hearts* (1971), *Malcolm Man Don't Live Here No Mo* (1972), *Uh Huh, But How Do It Free Us?* (1974), and *I'm Black When I'm Singing, I'm Blue When I Ain't* (1982). Jacqueline Wood says, "Sanchez's Plays, like her poetry, both embraced and transformed the political and social issues at the Black Power Movement and the Black Arts Movement" (49). Her first play, *The Bronx Is Next*, focuses on the impact of American racism and racial response of the African American community to the racist oppression. The central focus of the play is an examination of the frustrated anger brewing in the isolated and impoverished African American communities and the militant vision that recognizes these communities as places for fostering revolutionary change.

Sister Son/Ji offers a more concentrated study of the women in the militant community. The memories of Son/ji, an aged female character, are representative experiences of African American female militants. Sanchez directly addresses the issues like militant activism and a search for African American female identity. In *Dirty Hearts*, she explores various oppressions and the stances of power that work within conquest and domination. Oppression is characterized through the power of imperialism, military domination, racial difference, and gender bias. Her next play, *Uh Huh, But How Do It Free Us?*, has three groups of characters. Group I is an examination of the negative impact of polygamy as a social experiment informed by African traditions within the militant community. Group II presents the impact of hedonism and violence upon certain African American communities during 1960s and 1970s. Group III examines degrading force upon African American women in the movement. In group III, Sanchez warns about the dangers threatening the growth and welfare of African American community. Sanchez's *I'm Black When I'm Singing, I'm Blue When I Ain't* offers a relevant approach to issues in the African American community. The play confronts urban life in terms of racist, economic, and social oppressions and their debilitating effects on the mental health of a young African American woman, Reeha.

The late twentieth-century African American women playwrights explored the issues like racism, sexism, classism, poverty, unemployment, drugs problem, health, and identity. They also write about social, economic, political, and technological changes taking place in the American society. They were the playwrights like Kia Corthron, Joan California Cooper, Barbara Molette, Aishah Rahman, Pearl Cleage, Anna Deavere Smith, Kathleen Conwell Collins, and Suzan-Lori Parks.

Barbara Molette (1940–2017) was an award-winning African American playwright and university professor. Her plays treat the impact of white values on African American society with middle-class characters in urban atmosphere. In *Rosalee Pritchett* (1970), the main characters are middle-class African Americans portrayed with negative images. The African American wives and husbands in the play are characterized as assimilationists, because they have middle-class values. They try to deny their African American identity. The women, Rose, and her friends, Doll, Belle and Dorry, are portrayed with negative images, because they are destroying racial pride. They separate themselves from African Americans who are less fortunate than they are and make negative comments about them. The play attacks the African Americans who do not associate themselves with the lower class African Americans and consider the poor African Americans far inferior than themselves.

In other plays, Molette expresses the idea of African American consciousness. The characters are middle-class African Americans who live in an urban locale in the south. *Dr. B. S. Black* (1970), set in a southern city, deals with a con artist. In *Booji Wooji* (1971), an African American attorney attempts to make the system work for African American people. The play details the difficulties he encounters with both the whites and the blacks. In *Noah's Ark* (1981), Noah is a college professor and a pacifist. His son, Daniel, is to be inducted in the army during a period of wars in Africa. Noah wages his own nonviolent war. *Fortune of the Moor* (1995) is based on a part of the last line of *Othello*. The story line is that a baby boy was born to Othello and Desdemona and raised by nuns following the death of his parents. There is a battle for the custody of the boy between Desdemona's powerful family and African-born Othello's noble Moorish family. The play makes political and social statements pointing toward cultural differences, religion, and slavery.

Kathleen Collins (1942–1988) was an African American playwright, writer, filmmaker, director, civil rights activist, and educator. She wrote and directed *Losing Ground* in 1982 which was the first feature-length drama directed by an African American woman. *Losing Ground*, set in New York, tells the story of a marriage of two remarkable people, both at a crossroads in their lives. Sara Rogers, an African American professor of western philosophy, is embarking on an intellectual quest to understand ecstasy just as her painter husband Victor sets off on a more earthly exploration of joy. She struggles against becoming the stereotypical tragic mulatto. She is orderly, straightforward, practical, and logical. Victor is passionate, disrespectful, and vulgar. She knows that her husband is a flirt and engages in extramarital affairs. In the marriage, her stable, rational personality acts as a buffer to her husband's more instinctual artistic approach to life. Feeling limited by this too intellectual definition, Sara goes in search of happiness and winds up on a student movie set. Collins wrote many other plays and screenplays, but her two most well-known theatrical plays are *In the Midnight Hour* (1981) and *The Brothers: A Play in Three Acts* (1982).

Themes frequently explored in the works of Collins are issues of marital dissatisfaction, male dominance and impotency, freedom of expression and intellectual pursuit, and the un-glorified plight of the African American middle class. Her protagonists are cited as typically self-reflective women who move from a state of subjugation to empowerment. *In the Midnight Hour* (1981) is an unusual drama with a twelve-hour time span. Set in 1962, Harlem, New York, the drama focuses on the Daniel's family members and their own personal dreams. Each family member—Ralph, Lillie, Anna, and Ben—wishes to paint a canvass with his or her memories and hold forever with his or her good times in the family parlor where they have talked, danced, and entertained.

The Brothers (1982) is a complex drama which centers on the Edwards men but focused on the Edwards women. The Edwards brothers, Lawrence, Franklin, Jeremy, and Nelson, and the one sister, Marietta, were reared to be proud of their blackness. They were coached by their cruel father to pursue whiteness and white dreams. The women take center stage and are involved in all the play's action. The brothers are central and essential in the women's lives. The conversations, actions, and attitudes of the wives and the sisters are restricted to the brothers' needs, wants, and dispositions.

Her screen play, *The Cruz Brothers and Mrs. Malloy* (1980), is about the struggle of three Puerto Rican brothers to survive in a small country town. *The Reading* (1984) is a one-act play about the conflict between the white and black women. She also penned *Begin the Beguine* (1985), a play about the first African American aviatrix, Bessie Coleman. *Conversations with Julie* (1986), screenplay, is about a mother and daughter coming to terms with separation. Her other plays include *Only the Sky Is Free* (1985), *While Older Men Speak* (1986), and *Looking for Jane* (1986).

Pearl Cleage (1948) is one of the foremost African American women dramatic voices in contemporary African American theater. She is an African American feminist and conscious of being both African American and female. Each of her plays combines the struggle against racism and sexism. She uses specific historical moments to engage her audience in a moment in the African American history. Her plays provide clear delineation of her African American feminism. She says,

> I am writing to expose and explore the point where racism and sexism meet. I am writing to help myself understand the full effects of being black and female in a culture that is both racist and sexist. (Anderson 17)

In her plays, she addresses the issues like violence against women, domestic violence, abortion, reproductive rights, depression, stress, drugs addiction, parenting, and prostitution. She also reimagines historical periods like Exodus of 1879, the Harlem Renaissance of the 1920s, and Civil Rights Movement of the 1960s in which racial and women's issues encompass. In her *Artistic Statement*, Cleage says,

> As a third generation nationalist and a radical feminist, the primary energy that fuels my work is a determination to be a part of the ongoing worldwide struggle against racism, sexism, classism and homophobia. I approach my emotional response to oppression, since no revolution has ever been fuelled purely by intellect, no matter what the boys tell you; second, as a way to offer analysis, establish context, and clarify point of view; and third, to incite my audience or my readers to action. (46)

Her *Puppet Play* (1981) is the most significant play in terms of national recognition. It is about a young woman's devastating love relationship. Cleage presents the woman's psychic distress by splitting her into two characters: woman one and woman two. Her play *Hospice* (1983) features two female characters: Alice Anderson and her daughter Jenny. At the beginning of the play, it becomes clear that the play is impending birth and imminent death. Jenny's body bulges with the infant to whom she is about to give birth at any moment. At the same moment, Alice's chemotherapy-induced ball head attests to her impending death from cancer. Each woman has sought her own private hospice in the solace of the family home. Alice is uncomfortable to find Jenny in the house, because it has been twenty years since she abandoned the then ten-year-old Jenny to the care of her husband and departed to Paris to pursue her dreams of being a poet. Jenny sees their chance encounter as a possible opportunity to recover what she believes is missing from her life—her mother's wisdom. But even as she approaches her death, Alice remains a woman who refuses to comply with societal dictates of motherhood.

Chain, a one-act play, is about a young Puerto Rican family whose daughter, Rosa Jerkins, a sixteen-year-old girl was a crack addict. As a last resort, the parents had chained her in the house, resulting in their being arrested. Rosa is lying in the heap in the middle of an apartment living room. She is attached to the radiator by a long thick chain. The chain is significant as a metonym for slavery in conjunction with an African American body. Rosa is enslaved by crack cocaine. Toward the end of the play, her parents have removed the chain as a reward for her progress. But as she struggles with her craving for drugs, at the end of the play, she takes the chain again, because she is aware of the safety the chain offer.

Cleage wrote *Flying West* (1992), a two-act historical melodrama. It tells the story of four African American women pioneers: seventy-three-year-old Miss Leah; two sisters, Fannie Dove, age thirty-two, and Minnie Dove Charles, age twenty-one, and an adopted sister miss Sophie, age thirty-six. The play is about the conflicting marital life of the youngest sister Minnie with her mulatto husband Frank. He physically abuses and terrorizes his pregnant wife by means of a severe beating. His intention is to sell the land of inheritance from his deceased slave-owning father to white entrepreneurs. The adopted sister, Sophie, throughout the play, is the most comfortable with a rifle in her hand to shoot Frank. To protect Sophie from certain imprisonment, the women decide to kill Frank with a poisoned apple pie made by elderly Miss Leah.

Her *Blues for Alabama Sky* (1995) is the story of four Harlem residents in 1930: Angel Allen, a singer and a former prostitute; her gay friend Guy Jacobs, formerly a male prostitute but now a dress designer; Delia Patterson, a social worker and family planning activist; and Dr. Sam Thomas, a doctor at Harlem Hospital. They are joined by a recently arrived widower from Alabama, Leland Cunningham, whose eventual attraction to Angel fatefully involve him in the lives of the four Harlemites and drives the play into a tragic ending. For the first time, Cleage has created more male roles than female allowing for multiple explorations of sexual politics, reproductive rights, and homophobia in this explosive drama.

Her last play, *Bournbon at the Border* (1997), set in a Detroit neighborhood, takes place in 1995, but the roots of the story go back to the Freedom Summer in Mississippi in 1964. During the fateful summer, Charles, a student activist at Howard University had recruited May for the ride to Mississippi to help register African American folks to vote. They were, while there, captured by racist police, who threatened to rape May if Charles did not whip her. When she was beaten within inches of her life, they still raped her so savagely in front of him that she was never able to conceive children. After May returned home, Charles was recaptured and tortured for two weeks. He emerges with his leg broken in three places and his mind compromised. Feeling alienated from their families and friends, they clung to each other, eventually marrying and moving to their apartment on the border of Canada.

Aishah Rahman (1936–2014) was an African American dramatist, author, essayist, and professor. She was recognized for her valuable contribution to the Black Arts Movement. In her plays, she reveals various aspects of black life. She centers her plays on the complex intersections of race, gender, class, and spirituality. Through her plays, she documents the vibrancy of African American culture. She draws attention to the unique plight of African American women in American society. Her play, *Unfinished Women Cry in No Man's Land While a Bird Dies in a Gilded Cage* (1977), concerns the African American women, motherhood, and freedom. Through the play, Rahman gives voice to those women of lower status who are triply marginalized by race, gender, and class.

Rahman's play, *Lady Day: A Musical Tragedy* (1972), challenges the myths surrounding legendary jazz and blues singer Billie Holiday's life. Sexual violence and exploitation robbed her childhood. The play depicts sexual and economic oppressions of women through Holiday's relationship with her lover and business manager. In *Tale of Madame Zora* (1985), Rahman shifts her attention to novelist, playwright, and anthropologist

Zora Neale Hurston. The play is located in Hurston's hometown. Rahman establishes a vivid and dynamic environment in which she honors Hurston by staging rich folk culture. The play is retelling of black histories as a restored behavior that helps to reconstitute the community. *Mojo and the Sayso* (1987) is an examination of lives profoundly affected by racial profiling. Linus, a son of Awilda and Acts, was killed by a policeman who mistook him for a thief. Three years after the tragic event, Awilda and Acts are still trying to make sense of their lives. Linus's death has ripped the family apart, sending each member running in a different direction to seek comfort.

Another play, *Only in America* (1997), is a commentary on the power of voice. The play reinterprets a controversial moment in African American and American history: The Clarence Thomas/Anita Hill Hearing. The play offers a traditional African American feminist critique of the intersectionality of African American women's oppression and their unique angle of vision on American culture. Cassandra works with a voice coach, Lilli, who encourages Cassandra to assimilate and become a part of the mainstream culture. *Chiaroscuro: A Light and Dark Comedy* (2000), her unpublished play, refers to the practice of colorism within African American community. The light-skinned African Americans, especially women, are seen as more attractive than dark-skinned African Americans. The play sets on a fantastical cruise ship, placing three light-skinned African American women and three dark-skinned African American men in an environment in which their prejudices can collide.

Glenda Dickerson (1945–2012) was an iconic director, folklorist, adaptor, writer, choreographer, actor, African American theater organizer, and educator. She was known throughout the American theater as a promoter of African American womanism in the theater. Her plays center on folklore, myths, and African American legends. She adapted numerous vehicles for the stage from various dramatic and nondramatic sources, including the miracle plays *Jesus Christ, Lawd Today, Owen's Song, The Unfinished Song, Rashomon, Torture of Mothers, Jump at the Sun,* and *Every Step I Take.* She performed in her one-woman shows, *Saffron Persephone Brown, The Flower-Storm of a Brown Woman, Spreading Lies,* and *The Trojan Women: A Tale of Devastation for Two Voices.*

Her play *Re/Membering Aunt Jemima: A Menstrual Show* (1996) is about a big strong capable woman who came from Africa to guide journey through bondage. The play explores the connection between images of African Americans and the construction of African American identity. The play does not only deconstruct and reconsider the iconic figure of Aunt Jemima, the woman on pancake box; it also looks at other African American myths and stereotypes. The play connects the personal history of Aunt Jemima with the historical struggles of African American women in America. Aunt Jemima's thirteen daughters represent significant female figures from African American history. These women share with all African American women in America a collective identity constituted by a common heritage of struggle for survival. The subtitle of the play, *A Menstrual Show*, underscores the significance of gender which focuses on African American women and their concerns. Her *Eel Catching on Setauket: A Living Portrait of a Community* is a creative performance project which makes use of African American's rich oral history to document the lives of the African American Christian Avenue Community in Setauket, a designated place on the North Shore of Long Island in New York.

Elizabeth Brown-Guillory (1954) is a playwright, performing artist, and former professor of English. Her plays are published in *Black Drama: 1850 to the Present* including *Somebody Almost Walked off with All of My Stuff* (1982), *Bayou Relics* (1983), *Marry Me, Again* (1984), *Snapshots of Broken Dolls* (1987), *Mam Phyllis* (1990), *Saving Grace* (1993), *Missing Sister* (1996), *La Bakair* (2001), *The Break of Day* (2003), and *When the Ancestors Call* (2003). *Bayou Relics* (1983) is about senior citizens in a nursing home in southwest Louisiana who envy the youth of young people. *Mam Phyllis* (1990) focuses on love, ambition, and ageing in Louisiana. *Marry Me, Again* (1984) is about a newly married couple making adjustments in their relationship. *Snapshots of Broken Dolls* (1987) is about the three generations of Louisiana women who are waiting for the birth of the fourth generation.

Kia Corthron (1961) is an African American playwright, activist, television writer, and novelist. In *Wake Up Lou Riser* (1992), four sisters, aged twelve to twenty-four in the 1990s, learn directly how alive and well arbitrary racial violence still is when their teenage brother is lynched. The young women choose eye-for-an-eye revenge: dressing in African American Klan robes and preparing to lynch a Klan member, they presume to be responsible. *Cage Rhythm* (1993) is about the relationship between two women in prison finding tenderness, love, and occasionally a magical way out. *Come Down Burning* (1993) deals with a disabled woman who moves around on a cart and her emotionally paralyzed sister struggles against poverty, prejudice, and unwanted pregnancy.

In other plays, she has examined the land mine issue, female gangs, prisons, capital punishment, youth violence, and disability. In *Life by Asphyxiation* (1995), Jojo has company after thirty years on death row: Nat Turner in the next-door cell on one side, Crazy Horse in the next-door cell on the other. His execution date is approaching, and he bides these days chatting with his best-friend prison guard and with the ghost of his ever-present victim. *Seeking the Genesis* (1996) is about a young urban mother overwhelmed by her first-grade son's hyperactivity and by her struggle to keep from losing her teenage son to the streets is pressured, in both cases, to address the situation pharmaceutically. *Splash Hatch on the E Going Down* (1997) is about Thyme, a fifteen-year-old Harlem girl who is conscious of environmental issues and of the placement of the racial, economically disadvantaged in risky areas. She is also married and pregnant. Her eighteen-year-old husband, Erry, is awkward and sincere, and gradually ill. A journey punctuated by a dirt-eating pregnant friend, a knockdown drags out between hugely pregnant girls and a water birth.

In *Digging Eleven* (1999), Ness, a twelve-year-old orphan girl in a rural town, directs the changes in her life: local tensions regarding the possibility of a strike at the factory that employs her older brother and family breadwinner; the love developing between that brother and a coworker who is a family friend and married man; and her own helplessness as a girl growing into womanhood while her sole female family member, her grandmother, daily slips further away from clarity and from Ness. *Breath Boom* (2000) tells the story of Prix, the leader of a violent girls' gang, who makes booms on the street and loves booms in the sky, fireworks. But her destructive everyday world is gradually turned upside down by actions of her mother and her sisters, and by confrontations with the consequences of her past. *Force Continuum* (2002) deals with the struggle between the race and occupation of an African American police officer. In *The Venus De Milo Is Armed* (2003), an upper-middle-class African American family in a Southern city is shaken by the sudden appearance of land mines all over the country.

Her shorter piece *Safe Box* (2004) centered on an industry that dumped cancer-causing chemicals into the air and water. *Light Raise the Roof* (2004) centers on Cole, a homeless man and self-taught architect and builder who is commissioned by other homeless to design and construct houses for them out of scraps around New York City. He struggles with all the obstacles challenging the most economically disadvantaged community. In *Slingshot Silhouette* (2004), Malik suffers a terrible accident, the result of a negligent manufacturing defect. In a nation where litigations have been equated with greed, how can Malik's father, Gid, attain compensation, and justice? In the play, two twelve-year-old girls, an African American and a Somali immigrant, are suddenly living together and fighting sometimes with fists through twin competitiveness and personal loss.

In *Sam's Coming* (2005), Beedee has worked at her small-town big department store for eighteen years and loves it, or thinks she does. But the utopia slowly begins to disintegrate, and even visitations from Sam Walton cannot prevent the crash. In *Trickle* (2009), five women of various ethnicities and economic classes, during the 2008 financial crisis, gradually discover that the trickle-down theory is most applicable to poverty. Corthron's latest play, *A Cool Dip in the Barren Saharan Crick* (2010), concerns Abebe, an African preacher-in-training who arrives in a drought-stricken rural American town intending to further his studies in religion and water conservation. He has come to live with an African American family. His village was submerged with the building of a dam. He befriends a small white boy who is struck mute by witnessing violence in his own home, and gradually comes to see how his host family still live with their own death-by-water ghosts. Hosted by a mother and daughter haunted by tragedy, he takes an interest in a young orphan starved for guidance—all the while maintaining an infectious optimism in the face of his obstacles. Fearless, Abebe determines to fight—by any means necessary—the personal and political forces that threaten the ecology of his new home.

Megastasis deals with nineteen-year-old Tray who loves his grandfather and loves caring for his infant daughter, hoping one day to marry the baby's mother. But in the War on Drugs, a joint at a party becomes a major military provocation, and Tray unknowingly falls into a black hole of perplexity, rearranging his plans and his life. *Moot the Messenger* is about a young journalist and her soldier brother who separately wind up in Iraq. Their Vietnam grandfather compares notes with the younger generation, and Abu Ghraib hits very close to home. *Poor La Patrie* is about a librarian and her father, a former Panther and victim of government surveillance. They suffer too much when they and those closest to them are targeted during the early days of the Patriot Act. *Tap the Leopard* is a three-act epic stage representation of the historical African American colonization of Liberia, from slavery in the United States through immigration and appropriation to the twenty-first century civil war and life in Africa on an American-created modern plantation.

Suzan-Lori Parks (1964) is a contemporary African American woman playwright. As an African American born in the second half of the twentieth century, she belongs to an innovative generation of African American artists who have developed a new awareness of blackness. Her first history play entitled *Imperceptible Mutabilities in the Third Kingdom* (1986–1989) is essentially about the problem of history, specially the problem of the self in relation to history and the problem of identity. It exposes the connections between African American literary and historical figures in several hundred years in two continents. *Death of the Last Black Man in the Whole Entire World* (1989–1992) deals with the Black Woman, widow of the last Black Man, tries to bring return her husband. But he is killed again and again—falling off a building and a slave ship, electrocution, hanging, lynching—only to be resurrected again and again.

Parks, in *The America Play* (1990–1993), manipulates representations by casting her characters in paradoxical roles. An African American protagonist in the guise of Abraham Lincoln subverts the legend of historical figures. The play questions about American history and removes identity of African Americans from reality. In *Topdog/Underdog* (2001), Parks concerns with history, social injustice, and tension between necessity and freedom. The play also looks at the concept of social and theatrical identity. It explores the plight of African American males in the circumstances of family interruption, urban poverty, and socioeconomic oppression. Lincoln and Booth, two brothers, bring up some characters in their conversation which indicate their relationship. But no character has real relationship with any brother. They lack the social and family bonds as well as community relations.

In *Venus* (1997), Parks revises the story of the historical Saartjie Baartman, turning the protagonist into a self-conscious woman instead of a mere victim of European colonialism. Her body is a main attraction of the audience in England and France. She is objectified by the European colonialist policy. *In the Blood* (1999) is about Hester La Negrita, a homeless, illiterate African American woman who independently raises her five bastard children. Throughout the play, she encounters a chain of characters that often sexually use her and discard from their life. *Fucking A* (2000) portrays a woman named Hester Smith who is reprimanded by people for her socially strange routine. She works for and with the enemy in society where women are alienated from their own bodies and expected to be the tools of production.

Thus, in the tradition of African American women playwrights, the pioneers like Angelina Grimke, May Miller, Georgia Johnson, and Mary Burrill have laid the foundations for African American women's theater, and Alice Childress, Adrienne Kennedy, Ntozake Shange, Lorraine Hansberry, and Suzan-Lori Parks have built their plays on those foundations. Their plays reveal the predicament of the African American people in general and the African American women in particular. The African American women dramatists recount the social, economic, cultural, political, and educational problems of African Americans and particularly the African American women in the racist white society. These dramatists captured the African, African American, and especially African American women's experiences in their dramas. They highlighted their existential troubles to reveal African and African American life, history, and culture.

Therefore, in the forthcoming chapters, the selected plays of Alice Childress, Lorraine Hansberry, and Suzan-Lori Parks are interpreted in the illumination of a crux of intersections of race, gender, and class.

Works Cited

Abramson, Doris. *Negro Playwrights in the American Theatre: 1925–1959*. New York: Columbia University Press, 1969. Print.
Allen, Thomas B. *Harriet Tubman: A Secret Agent*. Washington, DC: National Geographic Society, 2006. Print.
Anderson, Lisa. *Black Feminism in Contemporary Drama*. Urbana and Chicago: University of Illinois Press, 2008. Print.
Bigsby, Christopher William Edgar "Black Theatre." *A Critical Introduction to Twentieth-Century Drama (Beyond Broadway)* Volume 3. Ed. Bigsby, Christopher William Edgar Cambridge: Cambridge University Press, 1985: 375–415. Print.
Brodhead, Peter. *Life in Modern America*. London: Longman Group Limited, 1970. Print.
Burke, Sally. *American Feminist Playwrights: A Critical History*. New York: Twayne Publishers, 1996. Print.
Carter, Linda M. "Ira Aldridge." *African American Dramatists: An A to Z Guide*. Ed. Emmanuel S. Nelson. Westport: Greenwood Press, 2004. Print.
Christy, Gavin. *African American Women Playwrights: A research Guide*. New York: Rutledge, 2011. Print.
Cleage, Pearl. "Artistic Statement." *Contemporary Plays by Women of Color: An Anthology*. Eds. Kathy A. Perkins and Roberta Uno. New York: Routledge, 1996. Print.
Cooper, Anna Julia. "The Status of Woman in America." *In Words of Fire: An Anthology of African American Feminist Thoughts*. Ed. Beverly Guy-Sheftall. New York: The New Press, 1995.
Dakorwala, Nanubhai K. *Contemporary African-American Drama: From Cultural Nationalism to the Poetics of Resistance*. Jaipur- India: ABD Publishers, 2004. Print.
DuBois, W. E. B. "Krigwa Players Little Theatre." *Crisis* 32. 2 (1926).
Farley, M. Foster. "A History of Negro Slaves Revolts in South Carolina." *Afro-American Studies* 3. Ed. Richard Trent. London: Gordon and Breach Science publishers Ltd., 1972. Print.
Franklin, John Hope. *From Slavery to Freedom: A History of Negro Americans*. 5th ed. New York: Knopf, 1980. Print.
Frazier, Franklin. "Motherhood in Bondage." *Black History*. Ed. Melvin Drimmer. New York: Doubleday and Company, 1968. Print.
Gourdine, Angeletta. "The Drama of Lynching in Two Black Women's Drama, or Relating Grimke's *Rachel* to Hansberry's *A Raisin in the Sun*." *Modern Drama* XLI. 4. Toronto: University of Toronto Press Incorporated, 1998. Print.
Gray, Christine R. "Discovering and Recovering African-American Women Playwrights Writing before 1930." *The Cambridge Companion to American Women Playwrights*. Ed. Murphy Brenda. Cambridge: Cambridge University Press, 1999. Print.
King, Martin Luther Jr. "I Have a Dream." *Speeches That Changed the World*. Ed. Alan J. Whiticker. Mumbai: Jaico Publishing House, 2015. Print.
King, Woodie Jr. "Black Theatre: Present Condition." *The Drama Review* 12 (Summer 1968).
Shafee, Syed Ali. "Probing the African-American Psyche: A study of the Protagonists of *Funnyhouse of a Negro* and *Les Blancs*." *Indian Journal of American Studies* 24. 2. Ed. David Harrell. Hyderabad: A. S. R. C., Summer 1994. Print.
Shine, Ted. "Foreword to Black Theatre U. S. A." *Black Theatre U. S. A.: Forty-Five Plays by Black Americans 1847–1974*. Eds. Hatch, James V. and Ted Shine. New York: The Free Press, 1974. Print.
Shyama, D. P. "Black Symphony: A Study of Lorraine Hansberry's Plays." *Critical Essays on American Literature*. Ed. Bal Chandra, K. New Delhi: Sarup & Sons, 2005. Print.
Sinha, M. P. *Research Methods in English*. New Delhi: Atlantic Publishers and Distributors, 2004. Print.
Tannenbaum, Frank. "The Negro in the Americas." *Black History*. Ed. Drimmer, Melvin. New York: Doubleday and Company, 1968. Print.

Thernstrom, Stephan. *Harvard Encyclopedia of American Ethnic Groups.* Cambridge, MA: Harvard University Press, 1980. Print.

Turner, Darwin. "The Black Playwright in the Professional Theatre in the U. S. A., 1858–1959." *The Black American Writer.* Ed. Bigsby, Christopher William Edgar. Florida: Everett/Edwards, 1969. Print.

Wilkerson, Margaret. B. "From Harlem to Broadway: African-American Women Playwrights at mid Century." *The Cambridge Companion to American Women Playwrights.* Ed. Brenda, Murphy. Cambridge: Cambridge University Press, 1999. Print.

Willis, Robert J. "Anger in Contemporary Black Theatre." *Negro American Literature Forum* 8. 2 (Summer 1974).

Wood, Jacqueline. "Shaking Loose: Sonia Sanchez's Militant Drama." *Contemporary African American Women Playwrights: A Casebook.* Ed. Collin, Phillip C. New York: Routledge, 2007. Print.

Chapter Two

ALICE CHILDRESS

Life Sketch and Works

Alice Childress (1920–1994) was born on October 12, 1920, in Charleston, South Carolina. She moved from Charleston to Harlem in 1925, where she lived with her grandmother Eliza Campbell who became her legal guardian. She grew up in Harlem, New York City, where she was raised by her grandmother who was the daughter of a former slave. Childress was inspired to write at an early age by her grandmother who would sit with her at the window and encourage her to make up stories about the people who walked by. She attended two years of high school but left before receiving a degree.

Accompanying her grandmother, she used to visit regularly the Church where she listened to the poor people's troubles and witnessed the social ceremonies of the African American community. During those notable references, the poor people told their plights which Childress kept in mind for her future writings. She attended Public School, The Julia Ward Howe Junior High School, and then Wadleigh High School for three years, before dropping out when both her grandmother and mother died in the late 1930s. She was encouraged by her grandmother to use her imagination. Furthermore, due to her grandmother's instinctive love for arts, Childress visited periodically museums, art galleries, libraries, concert halls, and drama shows.

At the age of nineteen, she married Alvin Childress, an actor, who was renowned for his role as Amos in the controversial television show, *Amos and Andy*. In 1957, Alice and Alvin were divorced due to differences in their ideologies. Alvin left her alone with their only daughter Jean, but she got married to her friend and the company composer Nathan Woodard in the same year. He was a musician who composed music for many of her plays. Childress and Woodard were too dedicated and absorbed artists in theater, but kept a close space of intimacy between them which lasted for the end of their life. Childress died of cancer on August 14, 1994, in New York City.

Childress is indebted so much for her grandmother in her teachings and the art of storytelling. In her recent essay, *Knowing the Human Condition*, Childress makes the following statement:

> My great grandmother was a slave. I am not proud or ashamed of that; it is only a fact [...]. I was raised in Harlem by very poor people. My grandmother, who went to fifth grade in the Jim Crow school system of South Carolina, inspired me to observe what was around me and write about it without false pride or shame [...]. (10)

Further, Childress was extremely influenced by the dramatic works of William Shakespeare. In 1941, Childress joined the American Negro Theatre in Harlem, where she worked as an actress, playwright, and director for the next twelve years. She got widespread recognition for her first performance in the play, *Anna Lucasta* (1944), by Philip Yordan. She wrote, *Florence* (1949), her first play to be produced, and took the leading role in it. The play was reviewed for *Freedom* by Lorraine Hansberry who called Childress a "leading black woman playwright" and characterized her as "our first" and "our best" (Burke 145). She wrote: *Just a Little Simple* (1950), adaptation of Langston Hughes's *Simple Speaks His Mind*, *Gold through the Trees* (1952), *Trouble in Mind* (1955), *Wedding Band* (1966), *Wine in the Wilderness* (1969), *String* (1969), *Mojo* (1970), and *The African Garden* (1970).

Childress also wrote many other plays with music such as *The World on a Hill* (1968), *The Freedom Drum* (1969), later re-titled as *Young Martin Luther King* (1969), *Sea Island Song* (1979), *Gullah* (1984), and *Moms* (1987), which was based on the life of comedienne Moms Mabley. Among her other writings were *Like One of the Family* (1956), a compilation of her newspaper pieces written from the perspective of a domestic worker; the young adult novel *A Hero Ain't Nothin' But a Sandwich* (1973), for which she also wrote the screenplay; and the adult novel *A Short Walk* (1981).

She was the recipient of numerous awards and distinctions, including a Tony Award nomination for her performance on Broadway in *Anna Lucasta*, the Obie Award for the best Off-Broadway play *Trouble in Mind*, and a Pulitzer Prize nomination for her novel *A Short Walk*. She was awarded a two-year Harvard appointment at the Radcliffe Institute for Independent Study. She graduated from the program in 1968, and in 1984 she received a Radcliffe Alumnae Graduate Society Medal for Distinguished Achievement. Moreover, she was awarded the first Paul Robson Medal of Distinction from the Black Filmmakers Hall of Fame in 1977 and a Lifetime Career Achievement Award from the Association for Theatre in Higher Education in 1993.

Childress's *Gold through the Trees* (1952) was the first play by an African American woman to be professionally produced on the American stage. With the production of the play on Broadway, Childress occupied a profoundly important place in the history of American theater. Her most controversial plays were *Wedding Band* (1966) and *Wine in the Wilderness* (1969). These two plays brought Childress widespread reputation in the literary arena, because of their critical themes of interracial love and sexism. She bears the merit of being one of the most creative and dynamic figures in the history of African American theater. Her plays address the difficulties of the struggle against racism and sexism which are the legacies of the white patriarchy that doubly subjugate the African American women. In her essay entitled *A Woman Playwright Speaks Her Mind*, Childress writes:

> The Negro woman has almost been omitted as important subject matter in the general popular American drama, television, motion pictures and radio [...]. The Negro woman will attain her rightful place in American literature when those of us who care about truth, justice and a better life tell her story, with the full knowledge and appreciation of her constant, unrelenting struggle against racism and for human rights. (qtd. in Barlow 469)

Her play *Trouble in Mind* (1955) makes Childress the first female playwright ever to have won the 1956 Obie Award for the Best Original Off-Broadway play. In the play, an actress struggles over between her desire to be an actor and the inaccuracy of her role that of a mother who sends her son to face a lynch mob. She has done something grand in the theater by confronting the hypocritical white director. Donald T. Evans wrote:

> *Trouble in Mind* [...] begins with the hassle of the black artist. She [Childress] shows the difficulty of working in the man's theatre and maintaining one's integrity and identity. She shows why the Black Arts Movement had to come about. (Burke 147–48)

Her play, *Wedding Band* (1966), set in South Carolina in 1918, is about interracial marriage, as a result, it was controversial and the television broadcast was banned by a number of stations. Another controversial work, *Wine in the Wilderness* (1969), addresses the issues of socioeconomic and gender conflict within the African American community. It takes place in the apartment of Bill Jameson, an artist who is painting a triptych on African American womanhood. The play is a critique of narrow definitions of the 1960s slogan, "Black is beautiful" (Wilkerson 146).

Childress is most widely acknowledged for her novel, *A Hero Ain't Nothin' But a Sandwich* (1973), written for a young adult readership, about a young drug addict. It examines the issues of teenagers' addiction. The novel was a National Book Award nomination in 1974. It was widely acclaimed for its power and realism and was named one of the Outstanding Books of the Year by the *New York Times Book Review*. But it was also controversial and was banned by the Long Island school district as obscene. In 1978, a movie adaptation of *A Hero Ain't Nothin' But a Sandwich*, the screenplay written by Childress, was released by New World Pictures. Her last published work, *Those Other People* (1989), is a young adult novel about a boy coming to terms with his homosexuality.

Childress was a pioneering dramatist, actress, director, novelist, and activist. She paved the way for other African American female playwrights such as Adrienne Kennedy, Lorraine Hansberry, and Ntozake Shange. She addressed the hopes and lives of middle-class African Americans in their conflict against racism and sexism as well as their quest for social and political justice.

Florence

Alice Childress's first one-act play, *Florence*, was written in 1949 and first published in *Masses and Mainstream* (1950), a Communist Magazine which was used to publish African American literature. Childress has given her mother's name as the title of *Florence*. In fact, Childress was the first African American woman to have her play, *Florence*, produced on the professional American stage. The play centers on Florence Whitney, who never appears on the stage. Racism lies at the focus of the play which prevents blacks and whites from crossing the boundary lines which separate them. Racism is very dominantly seen in the American South during the 1940s and 1950s. The law of the land and social customs maintain racial discrimination in the American South.

At the opening of the play, Mama, a middle-aged African American woman, walks onto the stage, crosses to the Colored side, and sits on a bench in the railway station waiting room. A moment later, Marge, the younger daughter of Mama, who is twenty-one years old, follows her. She also crosses to the Colored section and rests the suitcase at her feet. Marge comes to the railway station to drop her mother, Mama, who is going to New York City to bring home her elder daughter, Florence, a young widow who has moved to New York to find success as a dramatic actress. Florence fled to Harlem with the ambition of being an actress. She has not felt right about living in the south when Jim, her husband, was murdered while he tried to vote. Her husband was an abolitionist and was fighting the injustices caused by racial slavery. Mama and Marge sit in the "Colored" section of the train station, while Mama awaits a train to Harlem to convince Florence to come back home to the south.

Marge is convinced that Florence will fail because she is an African American woman who attempts to make it in a business dominated by whites in a racially segregated society. Although Mama seems to have a little bit more faith in Florence, she still wants to convince Florence to come back home. They even have a check ready to pay for her trip home which is causing them to be late on their rent. This reveals to us that they are willing to sacrifice a little in order to prevent Florence from possibly failing in her quest for success. As Marge speaks to her mother, she reveals her mind in regard to Florence's situation. Before Mama's conversation with Mrs. Carter, she feels Florence will not make it as an actress. After realizing that a racist white woman feels the same way, Miss Whitney reevaluates her reasons for wanting Florence to come home. Realizing her reasons that were not much different, she felt the best thing to do is to encourage Florence to follow her dream no matter how hard it may be to achieve, rather than making her believe it was impossible, just as the white society wanted her to believe.

The play focuses on a confrontation between two women, one black and the other white, in a Jim Crow train station waiting room in a very small town in the south. The waiting room is divided into two sections to separate the blacks from whites. As the stage direction indicates,

A railway station waiting room [...] is divided in two sections by a low railing. Upstage center is double door which serves as an entrance to both sides of the room. Over the doorway stage right is a sign "Colored," over the doorway stage left is another sign "White". Stage right are doors [...] one marked "Colored Men" [...] the other [...] "Colored Women". Stage left two other doorways are "White Ladies" and "White gentlemen." There are two benches, one on each side. (Childress, *Florence* 110)

This division is emphasized by hanging written boards such as "Colored Women" and "Colored Men" as well as "White Ladies" and "White Gentlemen" over the restroom doors. Racial segregation is very much visible in the use of the words "Ladies" and "Gentlemen" designated for whites. These words suggest that whites have a rich culture, wealth, and royalty. On the contrary, these words do not appear on the restroom doors for the African Americans. The words "Colored Women" and "Colored Men" represent the ordinary people of low ranks; this implies that colored men and women are inferior to the white ladies and gentlemen. This suggests that the black and white passengers are not on par with each other; one group is inferior while the other is superior. The play of words such as White Ladies and Black Women implies that colored women are not ladies. The label "ladies" has a special social status which does not confer on black women. In an aristocratic society, the word "Lady" has a higher social position. The word "Lady" denotes a woman of refinement, of social position, and of manner. The word "Woman" simply designates a person of the female gender, a person having feminine biological features.

The division of females as "Ladies" and men as "Gentlemen" takes one further step of humiliation for Mama, when Porter tells her that "If you go to the rest room, use the Colored Men's ... the other one is out of order" (Childress, *Florence* 114). According to Porter, the bathroom for the colored women is out of order, so Mama must use the colored men's bathroom. She is not permitted to use the restroom labeled as "white ladies." Here, Mama faces the worst humiliation where a woman, as a biological female gender must use the bathroom of biological male gender instead of white female gender. It hints that for colored women, there is no room for rest. And if any black man enters the bathroom, there will be an invasion of female gender's privacy. This is the worst grade of racism expressed in *Florence*. This unequal treatment is given to Mama because the white women are superior to African American women. It is a degrading experience for Mama for her emergency physical need.

This play teaches us to be more open-minded as well as not being a hypocrite. The discussion between Marge and Mama clarifies the grief of Florence in the south:

> MARGE. Listen, Mama ... she won't wanna come. We know that ... but she gotta!
> MAMA. Maybe we shoulda told her to expect me. It's kind of mean to just walk in like this.
> MARGE. I bet she's livin' terrible. What's the matter with her? Don't she know we're keepin' her son?
> MAMA. Florence don't feel right 'bout down here since Jim got killed.
> MARGE. Who does? I should be the one goin' to get her. You tell her she ain't gonna feel right in no place. Mama, honestly! She must think shes white! (Childress, *Florence* 112)

Florence does not accept the racial discrimination in the south that the African American people have been forcefully enduring for so long. She challenges this coerced oppression of the blacks in the south by searching the opportunity like the whites in the north. She thinks that the south is too restricted for black women who are desirous to improve their lifestyle. As a spirited black woman, she is willing to take risks. She is an evolving black woman who strives to survive in a hostile world. She dreams of becoming a successful actress and to fulfill the dream, she chooses to move to New York. In the beginning, she has not acquired much success. Several times, she finds the role of a maid servant in the play. It is observed in the conversation between Marge and Mama:

> MARGE. Well, you got to be strict on her. She got notions of a Negro woman don't need.
> MAMA. But she was in a real play. Didn't she send us twenty-five dollars a week?
> MARGE. For two weeks.
> MAMA. Well the play was over.
> MARGE. It's not money Mama. Sarah wrote us about it. You know what she said Florence was doin.' Sweepin' the stage!
> MAMA. She was in the play!
> MARGE. Sure she was in it! Sweepin'! Them folks ain't let her be no actress. You tell her to wake up. (Childress, *Florence* 112)

Florence acts as a sweeper in the play. It is a racist white society which does not recognize her talent and capabilities of being an actress. Marge is fully convinced that Florence will never play as an actress because she is an African American woman. Still, Florence is determined to find a way to make her name in the theater. Jullie Burrell rightly observes:

> *Florence* [...] masterfully conveys the complex physical and psychological barriers that prevent interracial understanding. One major stumbling block, the play reveals, is the stereotypical depiction of black women, which ranges from the tragic mullatta character to the presumption that all black women are maids. (Burrell 310)

Her attempts prove to be useless in theater career which is dominated by the whites in a racially segregated society. Elizabeth Brown-Guillory states:

> Florence is a positive image of black womanhood: she refuses to use racism as an excuse for not trying to improve her lifestyle. She represents those black women who refuse to despair in the sight of seemingly insurmountable obstacles. Instead of applying for public assistance, she sets out to become self-sufficient in a profession that she considers dignified. It is her determination to success after her husband's death which makes her a character truly to be admired. (236)

Marge, the sister of Florence, thinks that Florence must accept her place as a black woman in the segregated south. She wants Florence to give up her dream of succeeding in a dramatic career and return to the south. Since Florence moved to New York, Marge has been helping her mother to raise Florence's child. But now she says that the child needs its mother.

> MARGE. I got to get back to Ted. He don't like to be in the house by himself ...
> MAMA. You'd best go back .... You know I think he misses Florence.
> MARGE. He's just a little fellow. He needs his mother. You make her come home! She shouldn't be way up there in Harlem. She ain't got nobody there. (Childress, *Florence* 111)

She thinks that Florence will not be happy living away from home. She does not understand Florence's fight against a system of white oppression. She forces her mother to convince Florence to accept the rules of the south that define black people as less human being. She thinks that Florence is foolish for acquiring a career as a dramatic actress which is open only to the whites.

The play depicts the struggles of an ordinary African American family against oppression and racism. Childress says, "I choose to write about those who come in second, or not at all …. My writing attempts to interpret the ordinary because they are not ordinary" (qtd. in Barlow 470). Such ordinary people and events are the substance of convincing Florence. Mama is an ordinary African American woman who does not make any heroic sacrifices. She just sacrifices what the ordinary people must do to survive. She is an ordinary mother who is willing to sacrifice to see her daughter a successful actress. She will not be able to pay the rent on time because she is using the money to take the train to New York. She is a strong African American woman who is not frightened either by Marge or by the white woman, Mrs. Carter, who considers herself a liberal and tolerant woman.

The play explores the visible and invisible symbols of racism that oppress African American women in the 1940s. Segregation is very much evident in the play. The law of the land does not offer equal opportunities and basic rights to the African Americans. The African Americans were not free to travel, take shelter in hotels, and eat at restaurants. The public transformations were also segregated to the African Americans. They were forced to sit in the back of a bus or offer their seats for the comfort of standing white passenger. The segregation denied these freedoms to Mama in *Florence*. Mama Whitney and Mrs. Carter sit on opposite sides of the color line in the segregated railway station. The low railing creates two separate areas within the room, one for white passengers and another for colored passengers. The artificial division is a barrier which keeps white and black passengers separate in the room.

Racial discrimination is so prevalent in *Florence* when Mama brings a sack of lunch on train, because she, being an African American, is not allowed to enter in the dining car. Marge, placing the lunch box on the bench informs to Mama, "Don't forget to eat your lunch …. Buy yourself some coffee when the man comes through. You need something hot and you can't go to the dinner" (Childress, *Florence* 111). Marge reminds Mama to eat the lunch that was packed for her. She also advises her to buy coffee for her lunch before she boards the train, because when the train begins, she is not permitted to enter the dining car. This segregation is observed on the train dining room where African Americans are not allowed to enter and have food from it.

Mrs. Carter is introduced in the play as a "White woman … well dressed, wearing furs and carrying a small, expensive overnight bag" (Childress, *Florence* 114). She is on her way back to New York City. She thinks herself as being beyond the racist state of the south. But her racist mentality is exposed when she speaks, referring to the Porter, a fifty-year-old black man, her first word, "Boy" (Childress, *Florence* 114). This word focuses on the harsh effects of racism and stereotyping images of the African American men.

The play is realistic in nature which depicts the prejudices that the white people had about African Americans. Mrs. Carter tells Mama that her brother is a novelist who has written a novel about African Americans. But the novel has been reviewed very badly by the critics, because it is an artificial view of the African American people. Mrs. Carter's brother has written the novel based on stereotypical images of African Americans. Consequently, he is discouraged that he is not able to write any more novels. Mrs. Carter has encouraged him to write more novels. He has struggled much to catch the lives of the black people. Mrs. Carter boasts her brother's novels as:

> MRS. CARTER. The review came out on his last book. Poor fellow.
> MAMA. I'm sorry mam ... Mrs. Carter. They didn't like his book?
> MRS. CARTER. Well enough ... but Jeff's ... well, Mr. Willey is a genius. He says they missed the point! Lost the whole message! Did you real ... do you ... have you heard of. Lost My Lonely Way?
> MAMA. No, mam. I can't say I have.
> MRS. CARTER. Well, it doesn't matter. It's profound Real .... You know. (Stands at the railing upstage) It's about your people.
> MAMA. That's nice.
> MRS. CARTER. Jeff poured his complete self into it. Really delved into the heart of problem. Pulled no punches! He hardly stopped for his meals .... And of course, I wasn't here to see that he didn't overdo. He suffers so with his character. (Childress, *Florence* 115)

Mrs. Carter projects her brother as a genius who writes about the reality of black life. But the critics could not understand his point of the novel. He thinks that the critics have missed the importance of the subject matter of the novel, which is the contemporary reality of African American life. He is troubled with the delineating of the characters. Zelma, a colored woman, is a perfect character in the novel. When Mama questions about the plot of the novel, Mrs. Carter tells her that the novel is about a beautiful and talented mulatto woman who commits suicide, because she wants to be like whites.

> MRS. CARTER. Well ... she's almost white, see? Really you can't tell except in small ways. She wants to be a lawyer ... and ... and well, there she is full of complexes and this deep shame you know.
> MAMA. (*Excitedly but with curiosity*) What shame has she got?
> MRS. CARTER. It's obvious! This lovely creature ... intelligent, ambitious, and well ... she's a Negro! (Childress, *Florence* 115)

She almost delineates her as white except in small ways. She is also delineated as intelligent, ambitious, and willing to become a lawyer. But she killed herself, because she was a black. She is ashamed of being black, so she does not want to live her life. She constantly hates herself. Thus, it was inevitable for her to die, because there was no other way. She stands on the bridge in the moonlight, takes a mirror from her purse, and looks at her reflection in the glass and then jumps down from the bridge. Mrs. Carter describes the last word of the black woman as:

> MRS. CARTER. Tears roll down her cheeks as she says ... almost! Almost white ... but I'm black! I'm a Negro! And then ... she jumps and drowns herself!
> MAMA. Why?
> MRS. CARTER. She can't face it! Living in a world where she almost belongs but not quite .... Oh it's so ... so ... tragic. (Childress, *Florence* 116)

But Mama does not agree with the reason of the suicide of the black character in the novel. She articulates that it is a myth that black people kill themselves for wanting to be like whites. Mama offers some examples of black people who have lived healthy and normal life without self-hatred to support her argument. She rises in anger and says:

> MAMA. "That ain't so! Not one bit it ain't! .... I know it ain't! Don't my friend Essie Kitredge daughter look just like a German or somethin'? She didn't kill herself! She's teachin' the third grade in the colored school right here. Even the bus drivers ask to sit in the front seats 'cause they think she's white! ... an' ... an' ... she just says as clear as you please ...." "I'm sittin' where my people got to sit by law. I'm a Negro woman!"
> MRS. CARTER. But there you have it. The exception makes the rule. That's proof!
> MAMA. No such thing! My cousin Hemsly's as white as you! ... an' ... an' ... he never .... I just meant Hemsly works in the colored section of the shoe store .... He never once wanted to kill his self! .... (Childress, *Florence* 116)

Consequently, Mama says that the novel is not true about the black people. Mrs. Carter's brother does not know the reality of black life, because he cannot identify the black world which he has never experienced. He relies on the stereotypes in the black community which he has heard from a black man to construct the character of black woman in his novel. Mama views that the fictional character of the black woman is not based on the reality of black life. But Mrs. Carter rejects the examples offered by Mama, because she has learnt the black life from the cultural stereotyping. She thinks that black women are satisfied to work as domestic servants and housekeepers as she has employed them. She firmly believed in the stereotypes that define black women as less talented.

Mrs. Carter is caught between anger and reason of Mama. She laughs nervously and apologizes for discussing the controversial subject with Mama. She is uncomfortable for the discussion with Mama. She tries to brush away the tension between them. She seems to be a racist white woman, but she tries to defend herself to Mama that she is not a racist:

> MRS. CARTER. You know I try but it's really difficult to understand you people. However .... I keep trying.
> MAMA. (*Still tight*) Thank you, Mam.
> MRS. CARTER. Last week ... why do you know what I did? I sent a thousand dollars to a Negro college for scholarship.

MAMA. That was right kind of you.

MRS. CARTER. (*almost pleading*) I know what's going on in your mind … and what you're thinking is wrong. I've … eaten with Negroes …. And there's Malcom! If it weren't for the guidance of Jeff he'd never written his poems. Malcom is a Negro. (Childress, *Florence* 117)

Mrs. Carter pretends to be an open-minded, generous, and tolerant white woman because she has given money to an African American college for a scholarship and eaten with blacks. These expressions show surface tolerance because mere eating with blacks does not mean someone is tolerant, and helping African American college financially does not mean to be generous and open-minded. Racism is beyond the surface actions and overt expression. It is deeply rooted and more systematically inherent in the minds of white people. When Mama explains to Mrs. Carter that her daughter is hardworking to make her living on stage, Mrs. Carter assumes that she is a singer. She says to Mama, "You people have such a gift. I love spirituals …." "Steal Away" "Swing Low, Sweet Chariot" (Childress, *Florence* 117). Here, Mrs. Carter refers to Florence as "you people," which clearly indicates her discriminating attitude toward the black people.

Mrs. Carter does not think of Florence as an individual with the talent of acting, but stereotypically defines the black people on the basis of the gift of music and singing. Mrs. Carter's prejudiced unawareness about black art indicates that she is a racist white woman. She herself thinks as liberal and tolerant but her mind reveals that racism is deeply ingrained in her thinking. Mama pronounces that Florence wants to become a dramatic actress. She has been in a colored moving picture and a big show for two weeks on Broadway. Mrs. Carter responds that Florence's aspiration of becoming a dramatic actress is pathetic:

MAMA. She been in a colored moving picture, and a big show for two weeks on Broadway.

MRS. CARTER. The dear, precious child! …. But this is funny … no! It's pathetic. She must be bitter … really bitter. Do you know what I do?

MAMA. I can't rightly say.

MRS. CARTER. I'm an actress! A dramatic actress …. And I haven't really worked in six months …. And I'm pretty well-known …. And everyone knows Jeff. I'd like to work. Of course, there are my committees, but you see, they don't need me. Not really … not even Jeff.

MAMA. Now that's a shame.

MRS. CARTER. Now your daughter … you must make her stop before she's completely unhappy. Make her stop!

MAMA. Yes 'm …. Why?

MRS. CARTER. I have the best of contacts and I've only done a few broadcasts lately. Of course, I'm not counting the things I just wouldn't do. Your daughter … make her stop. (Childress, *Florence* 118)

Mrs. Carter reveals that she is an actress who has not worked in the last six months. She is a recognized white woman actress having so many contacts in theater profession;

however, she is workless for the last six months. That is why she assumes that Florence will have no success in acting on stage. Mrs. Carter advises Mama to stop Florence from what she is doing, because it is difficult even for herself to get work as an actress. But Mama argues that a drama teacher had told her that she has a real talent for acting. Her talent is her strength which encourages her to stick to acting. Mrs. Carter states that there are lots of corrupt whites up there giving such opinions who cannot be trusted to be honest in assessing the talent of Florence. Mama states that it was a colored dramatic teacher who has assessed the talent of Florence. Mrs. Carter views that Florence as a black woman cannot have the talent to succeed as an actress. On the contrary, Florence wants to have the opportunity as white woman to prove her talent. Mrs. Carter cannot imagine that a black woman could have talent that can bring her success on the stage as an actress.

Mama asks Mrs. Carter, having well-known and many contacts with people in the dramatic/theater profession, to help her daughter in any way. Mrs. Carter quickly says that she can help Florence by giving work with a woman, Melba Rugby, who is the most versatile woman writer and director. Mama is so excited that Florence will get help from a white woman who is a writer, director on the stage:

> MRS. CARTER: She's [Melba Rugby] in California, but she's moving East again … hates California …. A most versatile woman. Writes, directs, acts … everything!
> MAMA. That's nice, mam.
> MRS. CARTER. Well, she's uprooting herself and coming back to her first home …. New York … to direct "Love Flowers" …. It's a musical …. She's grand … helped so many people … and I'm sure she'll help your … what's her name.
> MAMA. Florence.
> MRS. CARTER. (*Turns back to bench, opens bag, takes out a pencil and an address book*) Yes, Florence. She'll have to make a place for her.
> MAMA. Bless you, mam.
> MRS. CARTER. (*Holds handbag steady on rail as she uses it to write on*) Now let's see … the best thing to do would be to give you the telephone number …. Since you're going there …. (*writing address on paper*) Your daughter will love her … and if she's a deserving girl …. (Childress, *Florence* 119)

The above conversation explores that Mama is very happy by finding a ray of hope in the form of Mrs. Carter by showing her intention to help Florence. She gives blessings to Mrs. Carter, but very soon she realized that Mrs. Carter is willing to help Florence to find a position as a domestic. Mama infuriates when she finds that Mrs. Carter is willing to find Florence the position of her friend's maid, not an actress. She clutches Mrs. Carter's wrist pulling her off balance. She soon realizes how tight she's clutching her wrist and releases her wrist. Mrs. Carter is frightened by the anger of Mama who sits quietly, staring in front of her. She looks at the address for a moment and tears the paper into little bits and lets them flutter to the floor. She, then, opens the suitcase, takes out a notebook, an envelope, and a pencil. She writes Florence the message "Keep trying" (Childress, *Florence* 121). She sells back her train ticket and sends the money to Florence. She asks Mr. Brown to put a stamp on it and mail it to Florence. She explains her revolutionary thinking to Mr. Brown, "She [Florence] can be anything in the world she wants to be! That's her right. Marge can't make her turn back" (Childress, *Florence* 120).

"Keep trying" is a powerful message for Florence. Mama realized that a racist white woman thinks that Florence cannot become an actress. Mama reevaluated the reasons of Mrs. Carter's thinking which is racially prejudiced and finally resolves to encourage Florence to pursue her dream with hard efforts. Mama challenges the racial stereotypes put forth by Mrs. Carter to find a suitable career for Florence as African American woman. Thus, *Florence* reveals the difficulties that black actors in general and black women actresses in particular face to find work in the white-dominated theatrical world. The play also depicts the prejudices that many white people had about African Americans.

Gold through the Trees

Alice Childress's *Gold through the Trees* (1952) is the first play by an African American woman to be professionally produced on the American stage. With the production of the play on Broadway, Childress occupied a profoundly important place in the history of American theater. It is a dramatic revue which explores the history of enslaved Africans from 1619 to the Civil Rights Movement of the 1950s in Africa as well as America in three fragments. The play focuses on the black revolution across the African Diaspora and the struggles of Africans and African Americans against racial slavery. It takes its title from Harriet Tubman's words expressing her newfound freedom as, "The sun come like gold through the trees!" (Childress, *Gold* 34).

In the play, women are the most important players and the stories of cultural tension are told through their lives and interactions. They are the heroes/heroines and the struggling workers. There is not a place here for the antagonist who stays ever outside the frame of the story. These are the intimate conversations after the battle, outside, or before the heat of conflict.

The character simply named Woman is the narrator who narrates the scenes from the beginning of the Atlantic Slave Trade in Africa to Harriet Tubman in the United States and the South African resistance to Apartheid in the 1950s. The woman tells the pathetic story of African Diaspora. This dramatic piece with music is made up of sketches that outline the periods of struggle from the African continent to America and back from the time of the Middle Passage to the contemporary struggles of South Africa. It is emotional, zealous, and revolutionary in which Childress champions the spirit of self-sacrifice for reverence, while mourning the dead and remembering the oppressed people. Her scenarios and characterizations often contrast idealism and realism, or perhaps strength in mission. The fading spirit comes in the long sweep of struggle as a moral universe turns invisibly on its own alliance.

The stage direction of the scene first gives the description of the narrator woman. She is a Sumerian woman dressed as a woman of Ur, a Sumerian City, 2500 years BC ago. The description by the woman symbolically represents the glory and golden age in the history of Africa before European colonization:

> Her headdress is an authentic copy of that of the jewels unearthed in the Ur death pit. The headdress is made of gold ribbons and bands of beads, with leaves and flowers entwined and pendant among them, and on the crown an erect floral spray wrought in gold and lapis lazuli. Gold rings are threaded among her tresses, heavy gold rings hang from her ears, a collar of gold and lapis lazuli encircles her throat, and round her neck she wears many chains of gold and lapis lazuli and carnelian. Her dress is a colourful hand-woven drapery and over drapery. On her arms she wears bracelets of gold and lapis lazuli about seven or eight inches thick. She wears barefoot sandals strung with blue and gold ribbons. (Childress, *Gold* 25)

Moreover, the stage direction about the woman's description indicates the glory of Africa during medieval times. Before the European invasion, Africa was the land of gold. The African people were rich in culture and crafts. The woman narrates the story of Africa's glory in the scene first as,

> I saw Africa [...] green and fruitful. I listened to the stringed music of the Fulani [...]. I remember when the peoples of the Congo were clothed in silk and velvet, and I saw the descendants of Ham in Cush and Egypt [...]. I sat among West Africans as they carved with loving care in ivory, wood and bronzes [...]. I heard the laughter of the youth while the young black hands of the women turned pottery. I come to tell you now [...] not of a happening but an after-happening [...]. I, the eternal woman, take you to a palace somewhere along the West Coast of Africa [...]. The tragedy has happened [...] from the hot, sunny fields a warm breeze carries the wailing lament of wounded warriors [...]. (Childress, *Gold* 26)

This glory of African richness and culture has been lost by the European invasion of Africa. The entire continent suffered by the European, especially American colonialist policy of the slave trade. The Atlantic Slave trade is one of the most shameful episodes in the human history. The slave trade in Africa took place from the fifteenth to the nineteen centuries. It is the largest transportation of slaves in the world history. During these four centuries, millions of African people were violently torn from their homelands and shipped to America. It was an irreparable wound to African civilization. The transportation of African people to America is an agonized incident in their life. The agony and grief in the life of the enslaved Africans are represented through the African queen, when she laments, "Bring forth the ashes—Bring forth that I may cover myself with grief. (*She dips her fingers in the bowl and rubs ashes on her forehead)*" (Childress, *Gold* 26).

The American colonialist policy had wounded the African continent. As a result, many people were killed in the slave trade. The queen is a representative of the African women who suffered due to the slave trade. She continues to lament her grief caused by the slave trade.

> QUEEN. Such grief comes not from dreaming. The sun is shining bright on the fields, and the bodies are lying still and cold in the warm light. What means this day? The living are left broken and groaning. Such a sight! Where are the strong men ... the young men?
> OLD WOMAN. They are gone ... but where are the voices and the laughter of the children? The earth is strewn with broken shields and spears, and the blood of my people covers all. (Childress, *Gold* 27)

The queen fills the grief of suffering of her people who are wounded by the American slave traders. In the hot sun, the bodies of the dead people are lying still and cold in the fields. This is a very melancholic day the queen has seen. On the same fields, some living bodies are left broken and making deep sound of pain. It is a very deplorable situation for the human being. She does not find any strong young man living in the country. The young men are taken away by the Americans as slaves to work on the plantations in America. The old woman cannot believe this inhuman trafficking of human beings. She even does not hear the voices and the laughter of the children because they are also taken by the slave traders. The land of Africa is spotted with scattered weapons such as broken shields and spears. The land is covered with the blood of African people.

The queen cannot bear the pain of wounded people. She calls herself an unhappy queen and wanted to be punished for this destruction of the land. She does not find the king, because the painful sound of the wounded people rings in her ears.

> QUEEN. Their crying rings in my ears, but my heart turns and grieves for the king—O Bay ye! .... His people call for him. The queen calls for him. The maimed things that once were men call his name. (*Calling of the king's name*).
> OLD WOMAN. A king may die as easily as his subjects. Give up all thought of him.
> QUEEN. I walked abroad this morning as the sun rose. In the fields among the broken bodies ... still and quiet ... each face I turned and called by name. Sorieba! (Childress, *Gold* 27)

The people from the strange land have killed the people who were experts in craft and skilled profession. They killed the herdsman, Gbril, who grazes the sheep. Bokari, the goldsmith, was also dead who makes and shines the bracelets. They killed Lahsahnah, the Potter, who made the bowl. Now the bowl holds his mourning ashes. The queen saw the dead bodies of all the people having experts in artifacts, but she could not see the body of the dead king.

> QUEEN. I saw all ... all but the face of my king. Why should they take away the body of a dead king?
> OLD WOMAN. The king is not dead .... With these old eyes I saw him .... I saw our king, head bowed, stripped of kingly ornaments. In chains he walked.

QUEEN. Oh ... wounded and bound in chains.
OLD WOMAN. Not a scar. The strangers from another world touched his body and seemingly admired it. His brother too they bound.
QUEEN. No. You did not see him.
OLD WOMAN. They threw me aside ... and looked with anger upon the one who would take me with them. The king and his brother and many more they took in chains. All the young and beautiful sons of our women. The strong and lovely daughters, torn from their mothers. Only the weak and old are left behind. (Childress, *Gold* 28)

The people from the strange land have not killed the king, but they have taken him to live with them as completely humiliated and uncovered of kingly ornaments. They admired the strong body of the king and put him in chain with his brother. All the young and strong men they have taken with them are in shackle as slaves. They left behind only the little children and the old people because they were useless for traders to work as laborers. The queen feels deep sorrow for the loss of the king and her people. She thinks of herself as unfortunate after hearing the word, slave. The queen mourns:

QUEEN. Let us mourn and beat the earth when we hear it .... Slave! I go back to my grief, my sorrow. Let us raise a cry from our hearts.
OLD WOMAN. Save your tears, my queen. Do not use them all. On seeing a loved one dead we give up all our tears until the sorrow is relieved, because it is an ending. But this awful happening, within my heart I know it is a beginning ... save your tears, queen, for the things that are to come.
QUEEN. What more? An earthen jar fills to the brim and then no more water can be poured.
OLD WOMAN. A flood my queen ... fills the jar until it over flows ... until the water surrounds it ... and the jar floats away. This sorrow is a beginning.
QUEEN. Then death is our only friend.
OLD WOMAN. Dry your eyes. We must lift the wounded and blind them. We must find flood. We must live. Rise up! Take strength ... you are now king and queen. (Childress, *Gold* 28–29)

The queen is horrified by the slavery of African people. She is in deep grief and sorrow that she cannot stand it anymore, but the old woman encourages the queen to wipe out the tears from her eyes. She urges the queen to rise up with the strength gathered in her arms to fight against the impending disaster. The queen dried her tears and led her people.

The second scene deals with exploitation of African Americans in the strange land, American South. The blacks in America were subjected to racism and oppression in the form of enslavement, segregation, and violence. The daily life of the slaves was to labor on the rice, cotton, and tobacco plantations to help the white masters to acquire more wealth. Domestic servants were also a part of this system. They worked with rudimentary housing, less food, inadequate clothing, and the shoes that wore out quickly. The slave owners sought to make their slaves completely dependent on themselves. The white masters created a system of restrictive codes that governed the life of slaves. The slaves were usually prohibited from learning to read and write.

Many masters took sexual liberties with slave women and rewarded them with favorable behavior. But those slaves, whose behavior was found rebellious, were brutally punished by hanging them on the trees or shooting by the guns. These atrocities and exploitations of African Americans are narrated by the woman narrator as, "I remember my grandmother; a little black Bantu woman … that stitched received no reward for their labour" (Childress, *Gold* 30). This narration vividly indicates the hardship in the life of slaves on the plantations. They were starved and sometimes forced to die. They were hunted down by shooting through guns. They were hanged on the branches of the trees. The rebellious slave like Nat Turner and black Gabriel were hanged to death who were leading the slaves to freedom.

Harriet Tubman, a former slave escaped from slavery, is a black abolitionist woman who led the slaves to freedom. She was called Moses because of her courageous efforts to rescue her family and friends from slavery. She was a stranger in a strange land, works odd jobs and saved money to free her family and friends. The narrator woman narrates further,

> I saw the howling indescribable hell-south and I watched as the enslaved bent their path toward freedom with a Moses named Tubman […] in Cape May, New Jersey […] for this Moses was a domestic worker […]. This is the laundry room of a hotel […]. (Childress, *Gold* 30)

The three women characters—Harriet, Lennie, and Celia—are working in the laundry of a hotel to earn money to buy their freedom. They are scrubbing the clothes on old-fashioned washing board. Harriet and Lennie are working vigorously. They are captivated by their task, but Celia is slowing up the washing, because she is tired of washing without dinner. They have to wash five bundles of clothes a day for a dollar and a quarter. Celia hates to wash the dirty clothes of the whites for a little money.

> CELIA. (*Looking at unwashed clothes*) Them white folks loves white clothes and they love to sit in the grass too and I'm sick of scrubbing' grass stains!
> HARRIET. We need money.
> CELIA. (*Snatches up a white dress*) Look at all the money they got. This cost every bit of twelve dollars. (*Mimicking the hotel guests*) Spendin' the summer in a big hotel, ridin' round in carriages. If just one of 'em gave us what she spends in a week we wouldn't have to work eight weeks in no hotel laundry!
> LENNIE. I got a life-size picture of them givin' you that much money. Well, they ain't gonna give you nothin' and you know it. Ain't you glad we got a chance to earn the money? (Childress, *Gold* 31–32)

Here Celia criticizes the white people who wear white clothes and make them dirty by sitting in the grass because it takes more effort to scrub the grass stains. She is also jealous of the white people who waste money living in the hotels. She thinks that the white folks should give her the money which they spend in a week in the big hotel so that her hardships would be reduced for the work of eight weeks. Lennie knows that the white people will not give the money to them, but they are offering the opportunity to earn money by living in the big hotel. Lennie takes positively the luxurious living of white people which contributes to the black people to collect money to buy their freedom.

Lennie and Harriet sacrifice their every happiness to buy freedom. They are willing to work till death to earn money and give it to the Underground. But Celia does not understand it. She thinks that working hard and giving money to the Underground has no sense in getting freedom. She argues that she understands the real sense of freedom and believes in it. But Harriet clarifies the authentic meaning of freedom to her. Harriet says,

> There's no such thing as only "Understanding." Understanding means action. You're responsible for what Celia does and if nobody else does nothing you got to, even if you do it alone. Freedom is a little baby and you its mother. You don't stop loving it and take care of it just because other folks don't care about it. (Childress, *Gold* 32–33)

Celia is frightened to work and give money to the Underground for getting freedom. She is afraid of getting into trouble when she is surrounded by the whites. Harriet is also trembled and afraid of being caught, but she is strongly craving for the freedom. She was also afraid in the dark and the wetland, but she came to the light. So many times, she was afraid of the whites, so she had full hatred for them. She is firmly resolute to get freedom at any cost.

Harriet is furious about the black slavery. She dreams of black family to be free and united in the new land of freedom. In very fearful and horrible conditions, she decided to lead every slave family to the land of freedom. She asks her fellow workers Lennie and Celia to join her hands in the noble work. She wanted every black man and woman to have warm socks and boots to help her to get freedom. She dreams of a new baby of the black woman to be born on the free soil, where the sun comes like the gold through the trees.

In the play, the struggle is the holding on to hope and reaching for the heroism turning into a conflict. The wonderful monologues, songs, and pieces make a deeper connection to the struggle. The play deepens sympathy for the oppressed and often confronts with that the test of pessimism. The conquering of hope is the death knell of the spirit of the black women. Some remarkable passages call for perseverance and heroism, especially in the South Africa piece. In the play, there are no white folks to argue with. Accordingly, the result is an in-house deepening of conflict. Here, the basic struggles of day-to-day persistence appear and it desires for revenge by getting freedom. Thus, the play focuses on the critical need for the heroism of black women.

Trouble in Mind

Trouble in Mind is a protest play which explores the shortage of roles for African American actors in the contemporary theater. The play focuses on an African American actress's struggle for creative self-sufficiency in the predominantly white Broadway theater. The African American actors always play stereotypical roles. Childress has refused to recreate "long-held negative stereotypes of African Americans" (qtd. in Andrews et al. 71). The title of *Trouble in Mind* comes from a blues song of the same name. It is about the troubled production of a fictional, anti-lynching Broadway play, *Chaos in Belleville*, a play within the play. The play is set in Broadway theater in New York City in 1957. In "Foreword" to *Trouble in Mind*, Judith Barlow quotes Alice Childress as, "Broadway was wary of a play whose very subject is the racism of the American commercial theatre." (471)

The play is about racism in American theater and its reality. It presents a group of actors rehearsing for a fictional drama, *Chaos in Belleville*, which distorts the conditions of Southern slavery. It is written by a white dramatist about the black with an anti-lynching significance. Wiletta Mayer refuses to follow the script which wants her to put her own son into the hands of a mob of the white people to lynch him. She insists that the script be changed, because it supports a negative image of the African Americans. *Trouble in Mind* discusses the tension between realistic and racist concepts of blackness. Jochen Achilles quotes a critic as:

> "*Chaos in Bellville*" is a distorted mirror not only of actual events but of the way those events have been interpreted for the stage by African Americans themselves. The metatheatrical structure of *Trouble* thus allows Childress to write a critique of the history of the American stage, where plays by (usually male) White writers purporting to show the Black experience have been embraced while dramas by African American writers are ignored. (Achilles 223)

In *Chaos in Belleville*, Job, an African American slave, loses his life for exercising his right to vote. In fact, he is shot to death when Judge Willis is taking him to jail for voting. After his death, the judge reprimands the entire white community for murdering the fellow and makes them realize that lynching is unlawful. The play asserts an accurate treatment of racial tension in the South. It also supports Wiletta, the humiliating African American stereotype, who has been trying to escape throughout her career in the theater. The play opens with actors and actresses arriving gradually at a Broadway theater for the rehearsal. The heated argument divides the cast into racial lines.

Trouble in Mind has an interracial cast, but features the struggle of Wiletta in the face of systematic racism from white liberals and Wiletta's heroic assertion of black pride. Wiletta Mayer, John Nevins, Millie Davis, and Sheldon Forrester are the African Americans, whereas Judy Sears, Al Manners, Eddie Fenton, and Bill O' Wray are the whites. Wiletta Mayer, a middle-aged, beautiful, and generous actress, is the first one to arrive. She is in a bad mood as Henry, the Irish doorman of the theater, did not open the door immediately upon her arrival. However, her mood changes instantly at the sight of the theater. Further, Henry spoils her ego by recalling that she sang a number in a show called *Brownskin Melody* some twenty years ago. She feels privileged when Henry shows his concern for her and offers to get coffee for her.

John Nevins, a young African American actor, is the next to arrive for the rehearsal. He tries to look self-possessed. Wiletta asks him, "You look bright enough to be a doctor or even a lawyer maybe …. You don't have to take what I've been through … don't have to take it off 'em" (Childress, *Trouble* 486). He replies, "I think the theatre is the grandest place in the world, and I plan to go right to the top …. I know what I want to do, I'm set, decided, and that's that. You're in it, aren't in it, aren't you proud to be a part of it all?" (Childress, *Trouble* 487). He believes himself a little higher because he thinks he knows more about the theater than Wiletta. He is new to the theater and struggling to manage his interest in theater.

Wiletta is an attractive and expert actress in the theater. She is an assertive person whose physical look represents a black matriarch. She has played different roles in her life, consequently she knows the ins and outs of the contemporary theater. Being a matured African American actress with a huge experience of theater with white directors, she takes benefit of her seniority and experience on the stage. Her comments about the theater look to be pessimistic, when she starts instructing John on how to behave with the white director.

> WILETTA. [Theatre] *Show business*, it's just a business. Colored folks ain't in no theatre. You ever do a professional show before?
> JOHN. Yes, some off-Broadway … and I've taken classes.
> WILETTA. Don't let the man know that. They don't like us to go to school …. They want us to naturals … you know, just born with the gift. 'Course they want you to be experienced too. Tell, 'em you was in the last revival of *Porgy and Bess*. …
> JOHN. I need this job but, must I lie?
> WILETTA. Yes. Management hates folks who *need* jobs. They get the least money, the least respect, and most times they don't get the job. (Childress, *Trouble* 487)

John tries to conceal the fact that he does not like her instructions. Wiletta appears to have lots of understanding of the world. She tries to be an advisor and sympathizer of John Nevins, as a new arrival. She instructs him to lie about his professional career in the theater and also advises him not to be overconfident. She most likely knows how to be considerate in front of the white people. She also knows that if she does not act so, she will not stay alive. She says:

> We laugh and dispute him. (*She illustrates.*) "Oh, now, Mr. Manners, it ain't that bad!" […]. White folks can't stand unhappy Negroes […] so laugh, laugh when it ain't funny at all […]. It is Tommish […] but they do it more than we do. They call it bein' a "yes man". You either do it and stay or don't do it and get out. I can let you in on things that school never heard of […] 'cause I know what's out here and they don't. (Childress, *Trouble* 488)

Wiletta appears to be a twofold character. She tries to keep up with John who comes from her native town, but ridicules Millie. Again, she describes theater as a business to John and changes her stand in front of all "Yes, indeed. I don't like to think of theatre as just a business. Oh, it's the art … ain't art a wonderful thing?" (Childress, *Trouble* 491). Immediately, Millie Davis, an African American actress about thirty-five years old, turns up, followed by Judith Sears, a young white actress, and Sheldon Forrester, an elderly man. While moving to the stage, Al Manners, the white director, gives a friendly order of coffee and snack to Eddie Fenton, the white stage manager. Bill O' Wray, a white actor, has not turned up as he happens to be busy with earlier engagements.

Al Manners makes everyone comfortable by ordering coffee and snack for all. However, there is something strange about Manners' behavior. He makes a show open to suggestions made by the cast, but in reality, he does not bear intervention of any kind. His technique of rehearsing is very eccentric that he begins from the middle of the play in segments. He forces Judy when she fails to act as per his directions. He discovers Wiletta's acting inappropriate. He tries to explain her about what kind of acting he wants from her. He scolds her for not acting properly. He irritably says, "Wiletta, if you dare! You will undo us! Are you out of your senses? When you didn't know what you were doing … perfection on the nose. I'll grant you the first interpretation was right, without motivating. All right, I'll settle for that" (Childress, *Trouble* 507). Wiletta indulges in falsehood to win favor of the white management. She pretends closeness with Manners by rebuking him for neglecting his health. She calls the white producer a nice man. However, she gives up this pretense when he humiliates her for the rough acting.

The ambience gets stressed and the rehearsal stops suddenly with Manners going away toward dressing rooms along with Judy. The rehearsing party disperses excluding Wiletta, because she is badly anguished. Just then Henry enters to alleviate Wiletta. She aggressively states to Henry:

> I want to be an actress; I've always wanted to be an actress and they ain't gonna do me the way they did the home rule! I want to be an actress 'cause one day you're nineteen and them forty and so on [...]. I want to be an actress! Henry, they stone us when we try to go to school, the world's crazy [...]. Where the hell do I come in? Every damn body pushin' me off the face of the earth! I want to be an actress [...] hell, I'm gonna be one, you hear me? [...] (Childress, *Trouble* 510)

Bill O' Wray, the last actor to join the cast, is rehearsing the character of Renard, under the direction of Manners. Eddie is giving sound effects on a sign from Manners. The serious rehearsal breaks up when Bill articulates his reservation about a particular use of the word Arab in his dialogue. Manners cannot accept this. He gets irritated. However, he scolds Bill not over the issue of his intervention but over the issue of not mixing with the colored members of the cast during lunch time. He questions Bill, "Will you stop running off at lunch hour? It looks bad …. Unity in *this* company is very important … it looks like you don't want to eat with the colored members of the cast" (Childress, *Trouble* 513). Just then Wiletta arrives and starts offering her neighbor's critique over the play. This cause offences Manners extremely, "Darling, don't think. You're great until you start thinking. I don't expect you to …" (Childress, *Trouble* 514).

Once again rehearsal begins. However, an argument breaks out between Wiletta and Manners over the ending of the play. Wiletta finds the ending very unimpressive. She cannot accept the ending that an African American mother sends her son out to be lynched by a white mob full with hatred because it never happened that way in the history. She wants the ending to be changed which most likely Manners appears to be reluctant to do for several reasons. One reason is that he perhaps wants to communicate a social message through his play. Second, he possibly wants to evoke the audience's sympathy through such an end. However, the fact is that Manners wants the white man to be the hero and the black mother a villain. Then Wiletta puts forth an emotional question, "Would you send your son to be murdered?" (Childress, *Trouble* 537). She gets into an argument with Manners over the ending of the play. She becomes very sensitive about the way in which the play ends. She perhaps does not want to accept that a black mother forces her son to give himself up to be lynched.

With this question, the trickery of Manners, the illusion of being equal, the dishonesty of being supporter of human cause—everything is shattered to pieces. He answers the question without thinking:

> Don't compare yourself to me! What goes for my son doesn't necessarily go for yours! Don't compare him (*Points to* JOHN) […] with three strikes against him, don't compare him with my son, they've got nothing in common […] not a Goddamn thing! (*He realizes what he has said, also that he has lost company's sympathy. He is utterly confused and embarrassed by his own statement.*) I tried to make it clear. (Childress, *Trouble* 537)

The real white self of Manners comes up on the surface. Manners is so angry that he warns Willetta against comparing between his son and her son. He also declares that there is nothing common between his son and hers. Manners' racist attitude, his supremacy, and his pride are exposed. He exits on realizing his mistake but by that time he loses the consideration of the cast. The blacks in the cast are actually in a state of dilemma. They do not appreciate Manners' last remark. However, they are willing to tolerate his racist attitude because of their individual pecuniary restrictions. They convince Wiletta to make an apology for her argument, but she is in no mood to compromise. She says, "No, I didn't. Some live by what they call great truths. Henry, I've always wanted to do somethin' real grand … in the theatre … to stand forth at my best … to stand up here and do anything I want …" (Childress, *Trouble* 541).

Subsequently, they are informed that the rehearsals have been postponed till the next day. Everyone on the stage leaves except for Wiletta and Henry. Wiletta is happy for asserting her self-identity. She weeps over the fact that Manners may express his anger for asserting her black womanhood. It is nothing, but a subsequent monetary slaughter for asserting herself. It looks like her conscious attempt to affirm black womanhood. Even though it is a role, the spirit of a matriarch is encouraged in Wiletta. She asserts her point to such an extent that she is about to be dropped from the play. The talk among the cast intermingled with the rehearsal reveals their racial attitude. They are forced to play stereotyped roles which they themselves are not convinced of.

Discrimination on the basis of race, gender, and class is revealed in a very insignificant way. Childress explores the theme of racism and sexism by using the technique of the play within a play. The play also highlights the fact that there is a scarcity of roles for black actors in contemporary theater. Darwin Turner accurately notes,

> Negro life is regarded as an exotic subject for the American theatre. Therefore, only a limited number of plays on Negro themes are approved. Furthermore, to please his predominantly white audience, the cautious producer wishes to have these themes developed in accordance with his customers' expectations. Too frequently, therefore, he wants the stereotypes of Negro life. (3)

The African American characters are in the state of being victims of discrimination on the basis of race, sex, and class. However, the victimizers keep changing. During the entire play, the African American female actresses appear to be at the receiving end. They become victims of not only the white dominance and superiority but also the black insensitivity too.

Millie Davis is forced to play the role of a nanny, but in reality, she is a very fashionable woman. Wiletta is forced to play a mother who tells her son to give himself up to be lynched. However, these black actresses almost certainly accept performing such roles only to get a job in white dramatic production. These black actresses possibly would turn poor without roles. This certainly proves that the African Americans in America at that time lived only in the restricted space allotted to them. In fact, there was no freedom to disobey the spaces and create new ones. This shows the stereotypical and inflexible construction of the African American society.

Millie is neglected by the whites as well as the blacks. The white director Manners scarcely considers her significance by paying attention to her. Wiletta looks down upon Millie and tries to offend her by making a harsh inquiry about her husband and the roles she has played until now. Wiletta and Millie do not share a friendly relationship. This is attributed to the seniority of Wiletta over Millie on the stage career. It is also due to the difference in their financial status. It is not necessary that Wiletta needs a role out of economic restrictions. But Millie understands and endures discrimination because she needs job. She says "I know what's right but I need this job" (Childress, *Trouble* 540).

This change in Wiletta's attitude does not happen all of a sudden. The action of the play creates a consciousness that Manners is accountable for bringing about this change in Wiletta. Manners declares that he believes in racial equality, but his deeds disagree with his words. He calls the blacks the simple and backward people. His behavior toward the black actors is different from that of the white actors. In the name of being artistic, he insists on using the word "darkies" for the black. He is very rude in directing the black cast. He humiliates Wiletta by asking her to pick up the paper he threw on the floor, when he orders Wiletta,

> (*Notices the paper he threw on the floor*) A trashy stage is most distracting. (Judy *starts to pick up the paper.*) Hold your position! Wiletta, pick up the paper! (John *and* Sheldon *start for the paper.*) I asked Wiletta! (*Catches Wiletta's eye*) Well? (Childress, *Trouble* 497)

Wiletta appears to be impulsive. She has read the play before coming to the rehearsal. She perhaps knows the content of the play very well. She does not object to the ending prior to the rehearsal. She reacts only when her self-esteem is hurt. The humiliation is intensified by the fact that Manners takes Judy to the dressing room when she frequently makes mistakes, but he reproaches Wiletta in front of all for her rough acting. Wiletta is confused by Manners' demand to justify her acting. Sheldon advises her to take low acts as a method of invoking her racial pride.

The character of Wiletta is full of contradictions. Toward the end of the play, she does everything which she prohibits John to do at the beginning. She does not reconcile the white director rather she annoys him to change the end of the play. In the beginning, she advises John to admire the play as something which made them crazy. At the end of the play, she beats the script and certifies the play as "a damn lie" (Childress, *Trouble* 539). Manners wanted Wiletta to speak so that the truth can be seen through her acting. In the end, Wiletta does not speak about the script but the sociopolitical history of the black suffering. Her simple demand to change the script is in fact the struggle for protecting human dignity. Her demand is not the result of temporary instinct. She is in full understanding of its consequences. She makes up her mind to challenge Manners to fire her by showing up in the rehearsal the next day. She says, "Divide and conquer … that's the way they get the upper hand. A telephone call for tomorrow's rehearsal … they won't call me …. But I'm gonna show up any damn way. The next move is his. He'll have to fire me" (Childress, *Trouble* 541).

At the beginning of the play, Wiletta is just one of the black performers rehearsing *Chaos in Belleville*. It looks like Wiletta has had two options: one, to play the role of black mother as instructed by Manners, and two, to protest against the unreasonable clarification of the black mother. The black cast is being humiliated by Manners frequently, but it is Wiletta who stands apart from the cast by asserting her racial identity. It looks like Wiletta always wanted to do something real and splendid.

Through this play, Childress shows the wretched predicament of the blacks by juxtaposing the life of real characters with the roles they play in *Chaos in Belleville*. She shows the futility in the contemporary notion of the black men in general and black women in particular. The white male, Manners, frequently humiliates Wiletta and Millie. Wiletta is isolated from Sheldon and Nevins when she refuses to play a stereotyped black slave mother. She has suffered humiliation at the hands of Manners, Sheldon, and Nevins, in turn look down upon Millie. Insult and humiliation by those who are superior to her in terms of race, gender, and class do not mitigate or moderate her behavior toward the people who are inferior to her.

The beauty of the play lies in the fact that the playwright has delineated the difficulty rooted in one's psychological behavior toward the society in general and the weaker section of the society in particular. Though the play succeeded in evolving an idea, it was criticized for lacking in action. Unfortunately, the performer Wiletta and the playwright Childress shared the same predicament of denial for not submitting to the white norms.

Wedding Band: A Love/Hate Story in Black and White

Alice Childress's *Wedding Band: A Love/Hate Story in Black and White* is about the tragic repercussions of anti-miscegenation laws in the United States. The play explores the explosiveness of interracial love which is caught in the law of Jim Crow in South Carolina. These laws are proved to be anti-woman laws in the south between the period of reconstruction and the first decade of the twentieth century. Childress has seen the suffering of black and white women who were legally isolated and restricted by the inhuman laws. Rosemary Curb wrote, "In essence, the laws which Childress found especially noxious freed the fathers [black and white] of the children of black women from any responsibility for their offspring, and disinherited black women and their children from property rights" (58). According to the laws, sexual mixing of races was strictly prohibited. The birth of the mulatto child was proof of the mother's guilt which justifies her conviction. A woman's testimony about the paternity of her child was not considered valid. Both black and white women suffered differently under these laws.

The play dramatizes the suffering of an interracial love affair between a colored woman named Julia Augustine and her white lover Herman. Julia and Herman would like to escape the south and move to the north where they would be free to marry, but Herman is not free to leave, since he must repay money borrowed from his mother when he purchased his bakery. Faced with the disapproval of her neighbors, Julia has been forced to move several times; it is clear that she is lonely and discouraged. While the law poses the very real threat of arrest and criminal punishment for any interracial couple who marry or live together. The disapproval of Julia's black neighbors is damaging and helps to reveal that racism is directed not only toward blacks but also toward whites. Julia has eighth-grade education and works as a seamstress, a woman who earns her living by sewing. She has violated the anti-miscegenation laws of the state and the common morals of the working class by continuing a monogamous love with Herman. In the play, Julia celebrates the tenth anniversary of her relationship with Herman. He gives her a wedding band to wear on a chain around her neck until they can be legally married in another state. They were never able to get married, for Herman contracts influenza.

The play dramatizes contemporary political and racist attitudes through various characters. It is about racial struggles between the people of different ethnicity. It examines the issue of discriminatory treatment among lower social groups within the black society. It is a strong political statement which protests the denial of black women's rights during a period of American history. Childress in an interview with Rosemary Curb has remarked:

> *Wedding Band* dealt with a black woman and a white man, but it was about black women's rights. I took Herman as an understanding decent human being. But he could not give her [Julia] protection in a society where the law is against them. He couldn't marry her. I didn't give him a last name because if Julia couldn't have it, I felt no need to give it. No one has questioned this. The woman is the one most denigrated in such situations. I wrote the play because the only thing I saw about such things was the wealthy white man and his black mistress.

But most of the interracial couples then and now didn't come from the wealthy but from working class people. So I took a seamstress and a baker, and this made it an unpopular topic for a lot of people who prefer the portrayal of upper strata whites. The play shows society's determination to hold the black woman down through laws framed against her. There are similar laws framed against white women, and of course, unwritten laws. I never run out of subject matter for writing about women's rights–particularly black women, but white women too, which I have included in *Wedding Band*. (59)

The play is set in 1918 in South Carolina. Julia Augustine, a tenant, has recently moved into a working-class ghetto populated by a variety of ethnic groups. Her immediate neighbors are all black women surviving alone. The landlady, Fanny, is a pretentious black woman who is revealed to be superficial and hypocritical. She has absorbed the arrogance and hypocrisy of the white people. Fanny "is landlady and the self-appointed fifty-years-old representative of her [black] race" (Childress, *Wedding Band* 118). Since Julia has paid the rent in advance, Fanny seems to treat her in a special way. Her behavior toward other poor black tenants seems to be intolerable. This is where Fanny's double standards become evident. She is an excellent example of wealthy black people in the role of victimizer. She maligns the reputation of other tenants.

She is delighted with her new tenant, Julia, because she is the only one who has paid the rent in advance. She relays gossip about the other renters. She introduces Mattie to Julia by saying she works "in a white-cat-house …. Sporting house, house of … a whore house … washing joy towels for one cent apiece" (Childress, *Wedding Band* 120–21). As if that is not enough, she charges ten cents to read out to Mattie her husband's letter. Thus, she exploits Mattie's illiteracy. When Julia refuses to listen to Fanny's trash, she tries to invoke a sense of sisterhood in Julia on the ground of color. Fanny is conscious of the fact that both she and Julia are light-skinned women, so she states, "We high-class, quality people oughta stick together" (Childress, *Wedding Band* 122).

Fanny seems to be an elitist. All her goodness and humanity seem to be melting away when Herman falls ill and takes to bed in Julia's house. On the one hand, she asks Herman graciously about his health. On the other hand, she wants Herman to be out of her yard. She is simply worried about her reputation in the society. The racial hypocrisy of Fanny can be seen from the fact that she decides to get Julia out of the yard for all the mess. The worst part is that she does all in the name of race, "Only reason I'm sleepin' in a double bed myself is 'cause I got to bear the standard for the race. I oughta run her outta here for the sake—the race too" (Childress, *Wedding Band* 149).

Fanny appears to have a dictatorial attitude. It appears that she imposes her preferences and decisions on others. She likes "men of African descent" (Childress, *Wedding Band* 149) and so, she does not approve of Julia's relation with Herman. As a matter of fact, she tries to separate them not once but twice. Knowing the fact that Julia is with Herman, she calls her for the prayer service with the concealed motive of separating them. The second time she gets into the steering role when Herman falls ill on her premises. She does not allow Julia to call a doctor to treat Herman. Instead, she sends Lula to bring in Herman's sister to take Herman's charge and she separates Herman and Julia.

The backyard of the house of Fanny opens to three houses; one is rented to Mattie who lives with her eight-year-old daughter Teeta, and the other is rented to Lula who lives with her young son Nelson. These women have been victimized by their brutal husbands and have experienced personal tragedy. These women have struggled against economic oppression and social injustice. Mattie is a poor black woman who is not legally married to October, the man with whom she shared most of her adult life. She was married to a fellow named Delroy. This fellow abused her, attempted to tread her, and beat her before running away. She tells Julia that her first husband left her after years of habitual battering and verbal abuse. She and October were married in a religious ceremony on Edisto Island eleven years ago. Thus, the state of South Carolina only recognizes her first marriage. October serves in Merchant Marine and has been out on the ocean since long. She sustains herself by making candies and looking after a white girl. Julia reads the letter of Mattie which is written by October:

> I try not to hear 'couse I do want to get back to your side. Two things a man can give the woman he loves [...] his name, and his protection [...]. The first you have, the last is yet to someday come. The war is here, the road is rocky. I am ever your lovin' husband, October. (Childress, *Wedding Band* 131)

While reading the letter, Julia realizes that Herman can provide her neither his name nor his protection as long as they live in the south.

She turns penniless when Teeta loses the last quarter she has. She tries to knock down the post in order to retrieve her quarter from the hole. At that time, Julia helps her with a quarter, so that she can buy sugar to make candy. Mattie suffers at the hands of the system. The Merchant Marine does not give Mattie the allotment money because she does not have legal documents of her wedding with October and divorce from Delroy. It would be interesting to note that South Carolina Constitution prohibited divorces. Mattie turns pauper and is forced to borrow money from Julia for the second time. However, the same Mattie fails to understand Julia's circumstances. She acknowledges the concept of marriage, and the name and protection it gives to a woman before Julia in order to look down upon her. When Julia tries to explain the circumstances that prevent Julia and Herman from getting married, Mattie walks away. She does not show the respect that Julia deserves as Julia is in a relationship with a white man without marriage. Her struggle for survival has hardened her stance against the white.

Lula is another black woman neighbor of Julia. She supports herself and her adopted son by making paper flowers. She has suffered abuse from her husband so she seeks consolation from a friend. She tells Julia,

> My husband, Gawd rest dead, used to run "round with other women; it made me kinda careless with my life. One day, many long years ago, I was sittin" in a neighbor's house tellin' my troubles; my only child, my little boy, wandered out on the railroad track and got killed. (Childress, *Wedding Band* 125)

Then, she has adopted Nelson from the orphanage to free herself from the guilt of being responsible for her son's death. Her adopted son, Nelson, is now full grown and is at home on leave from the army. Fanny tells the suffering of Lula to Julia:

> I'll tell you somethin' […] that sweet-face Lula killed her only child […]. In a way-a speakin'. And then Gawd snatched up her triflin' husband. One nothin' piece-a man. Biggest thing the ever done for her was to lay down and die. Poor woman. Yes indeed, then she went and adopted this fella [Nelson] from the colored orphan home. Boy grew too big for a lone woman to keep in the house. He's big, strappi, overgrown man now. I wouldn't feel safe livin' with a man that's not blood kin, 'doption or no 'doption. It's 'gainst nature. Oughta see the muscles on him. (Childress, *Wedding Band* 121–22)

Fanny considers it unnatural for Lula to live alone with such a handsome muscular boy, who is not her blood kin. She cannot recognize and acknowledge her own attraction for him. Even with that she probably has not been able to absolve herself of the guilt. She appears to be a motherly woman who loves her adopted son extremely. One can feel her motherly instinct on an occasion when she goes down on her knees in the courthouse full of white people to save Nelson. Even though she knows that the way in which Nelson flirts with Julia is wrong, she feels hurt when Julia does not respond to Nelson's advances:

> Nelson, go see your friends. *(He waves good bye to Julia and exits through the back entry.)* He's got already friend, her name is Merilee Jones. And he was just tryin' to be neighborly. That's how me and Nelson do. But you go on and stay to yourself. (Childress, *Wedding* 124)

Lula seems to know that Nelson is a fighter and will not take any nonsense from the whites. So, she always discourages him from fighting with the whites. She does not get angry over the fact that the white threw a bucket of water on Nelson. On the contrary, she reprimands Nelson for wearing uniform while on leave. Her earnest desire is to see her son Nelson safely and nicely settled. Yet, she sends Nelson back to the army for his better future, fully conscious of the fact that it might be the last time she sees him. She suggests Julia to be good to Nelson:

> LULA. Tell him how life's gon' be better when he comes back. Make up what should be true. A man can't fight a war on nothin' … would you send a man off-to die on nothin'?
> JULIA. That's sin, Miss Lula, leavin' on a lie.
> LULA. That's all right—some truth has no nourishment in it. Let him feel good. (Childress, *Wedding Band* 169)

Lula seems to be a very submissive kind of woman who never appears to trouble about her fate. She probably can never hate any white for she appears to believe that only the goodness of the black will help them survive. However, Lula's goodness does not stop her from being bitter toward the whites. She cannot accept any kind of intimacy with the white. She does not seem to approve of Julia's relation with

Herman. So, she excuses herself when Julia tries to explain her relation with Herman. As a matter of fact, her interfering attitude makes Julia feel guilty about her relationship with Herman. She can never trust the whites. Therefore, she does not allow Mattie to touch the packages thrown by Herman as she suspects it to contain dynamite.

Julia, a colored seamstress, has just moved in as a new tenant in the third house. She cannot marry the man she has been keeping company with for ten years because he is a white. Mattie flatly states by the shocking revelation of Julia's love affair, "Man that won't marry you thinks nothin' of you. Just usin' you" (Childress, *Wedding Band* 132). Julia's neighbors avoid her when they come to know about her relationship with a poor white man. It reveals the attitudes of various characters toward Julia when they come to know about Julia's legally prohibited interracial relationship. Due to the pervasive racism, black women are suspicious of white cordiality with them. It is a significant truth of American social history that black women have so long been used as commodities by the white men. The relationship between the black woman and the white man is only one of the exploitations.

Lula and Mattie are so petty and narrow-minded in their racist assumption about their need for social status. Thus, Mattie concludes that Julia is carrying on the affair with white man for money.

> MATTIE. Oh, darlin', we all do things we don't want sometimes, you grit your teeth and take all he's got; if you don't somebody else will …. Rob him blind. Take it all; Let him froth at the mouth. Let him die in the poorhouse—bitter, bitter to the bone!
> LULA. A white man is somethin' else. Everybody knows how that lowdown slave master sent for a different black woman every night … for his pleasure. That's why none of us is the same color. (Childress, *Wedding Band* 133)

This assumption has testimony when the poor white bell man, who sells linens to black women, proposes Julia and offers to pay her for sexual favors with stockings. Julia furiously throws money at his feet and drives him out: "Get out of my house! Beneath contempt, that's what you are …. Get out! Out, before I take a stick to you …. I wish you was dead, you just oughta be dead, stepped on and dead" (Childress, *Wedding Band* 127–28).

Herman comes to Julia's home to celebrate the tenth anniversary of their relationship. He brings Julia an elaborately decorated wedding cake and a wedding band to wear on a chain around her neck until they can be legally married in another state. This witnesses the tension festering between Herman and Julia due to their inability to get married under the prevalence of anti-miscegenation law. Herman has collapsed at Julia's home after being inflicted by influenza. When he lies on Julia's bed, she wants to call the doctor so that Herman can be treated. However, Fanny does not allow her to do so because of the enforcement of the anti-miscegenation law and the law which demands that influenza victims be kept under quarantine. She refuses to call a doctor for fear of legal action directed against her for sheltering this couple. She also fears that social disgrace will be aimed against everyone present, especially herself. Fanny sends for Herman's mother and his sister so that Herman is shifted out of her property.

But Herman's mother does not move him until she has the protection of the darkness. Like the landlady, Herman's mother is more interested in keeping up appearances than in saving Herman's life. Years of racial hatred explode in the room as Julia and Herman's mother shout racial insults at each other.

> HERMAN'S MOTHER. And you, you oughta be locked up ... workhouse ... jail! Who you think you are!?
> JULIA. I'm your damn daughter-in-law, you old bitch! The Battleship Bitch! The bitch who destroys with her filthy mouth. They could win the war with your killin' mouth. The son-killer, man-killer-bitch .... She's killing him 'cause he loved me more than anybody in the world ....
> HERMAN'S MOTHER. Better off .... He's better off dead in his coffin than live with the likes-a you ... black thing! ....
> JULIA. The black thing who bought a hot water bottle to put on your sick, white self when rheumatism threw you flat on your back ... who bought flannel gowns to warm your pale, mean body. He never ran up and down King shoppin' for you .... I bought what he took home to you ....
> HERMAN'S MOTHER. Lies ... tear outcha lyin' tongue.
> JULIA. ... the lace curtains in your parlor ... the shirt-waist you wearin' – I made them ....
> HERMAN'S MOTHER. Black, sassy nigger!
> JULIA. Kraut, knuckle-eater, red-neck ....
> HERMAN'S MOTHER. Nigger whore ... he used you for a garbage pail....
> JULIA. White trash! Sharecropper! Let him die ... let 'em all die .... Kill him with your murderin' mouth—sharecropper bitch!
> HERMAN'S MOTHER. Dirty black nigger .... Dirty black bitch.
> JULIA. Daughter of a bitch! ....
> HERMAN'S MOTHER. I'm as high over you as Mount Everest over the sea. White reigns supreme .... I'm white, you can't change that. (Childress, *Wedding Band* 161–62)

Finally, Herman is taken away amid many accusations and much rancor. Racial hatred is coupled with bitterness. Julia furiously asks Herman's mother to get out of her house:

> JULIA. Out! Out! Out! And take the last ten years—a my life with you and ... when he gets better ... keep him home. Killers, murderers .... Kinsmen! Klansmen! Keep him home. (*To Mattie*) Name and protection ... he can't gimme either one. (*To Lula*) I'm gon' get down on my knees and scrub where they walked ... what they touched ... (*To Mattie*) ... with brown soap ... hot ye water ... scaldin' hot ... (*She dashes into the house and collects an armful of bedding* ...) Clean! .... Clean the whiteness outta my house ... clean everything ... even the memory ... no more love .... Free ... free to hate-cha for the rest-a my life. (*Back to the porch with her arms full.*) When I die I'm gonna keep on hatin'. I don't want any whiteness in my house. Stay out ... out ... (*Dumps the things in the yard*) ... out ... out ... out ... and leave me to my black self! (Childress, *Wedding Band* 162–63)

Julia dressed in her wedding costume. She seems artificially excited. She has been drinking wine. Julia is surrounded by her neighbors, and it is revealed that her neighbor Mattie is not legally married, since South Carolina does not permit divorce. Although her first husband had beaten and deserted her, Mattie cannot be free of him so that she can marry the father of her child and the man with whom she has lived for eleven years. At this moment, Herman arrives with two tickets to New York. Julia is unable to forget the confrontation of the previous day or a lifetime of racial hatred, so she gives the tickets and her wedding band to Mattie and her child. Julia in fact does not like his coming back. Both of them start arguing on racial lines, only to realize that they both love each other. The following dialogue reveals the truth:

> HERMAN. I was just glad to close the door 'gainst what's out there. You did all the givin' …. I failed you in every way.
> JULIA. You nursed me when I was sick … paid my debts …
> HERMAN. I didn't give my name.
> JULIA. You couldn't … was the law …
> HERMAN. I never did a damn thing for you. After ten years look at it—I never did a damn thing for you.
> JULIA. Don't low-rate yourself … leave me something. (Childress, *Wedding Band* 174–75)

As Herman and Julia dialogue, they remember the years of love and intimacy, and they finally resolve the tensions that separated them. Herman is ill, however, dying. Julia locks Herman's mother out of her house, and the play ends with Herman dying in his lover's arms. It looks that Herman might die. Julia takes Herman in her house. This time she does not allow Herman's mother and his sister to take him back to their house. The play ends with Julia comforting Herman who is struggling with his breath.

Wedding Band explores the historical period when interracial marriages were prohibited in the state of South Carolina to prevent miscegenation. It traverses time and embodies the historical continuation of racial discrimination. The play details the difficulties and dangers of continuing with an interracial relationship. Childress has probably unfolded the predicament of black women through an interracial love story in *Wedding Band*. This play is predominantly peopled by black women belonging to different socio-financial groups. All these women—Julia, Mattie, and Lula—have their own lot of sufferings. The difference in their socio-financial status leads them to ill-treat each other. The same condition compels them to live together in ghetto-like rooms.

Julia, like a typical black woman, is subjected to racist, sexist, and classist discrimination. However, her suffering intensifies one more count. She is forced to keep her relationship secret because South Carolina constitution restricts interracial relationship. She has to keep changing her residence in order to avoid getting penalized as per the existing South Carolina legal system:

> Oh, the things I can tell you 'bout bein' lonesome and shut-out. Always movin', one place to another, lookin' for some peace of mind. I moved out in the country […].

Pretty but quiet as the graveyard; so lonesome. One year I was in such a lovely colored neighborhood but they couldn't be bothered with me, you know? I've lived near sportin' people [...] they were very kindly but I'm not a sporty type person. Then I found this place hid way in the backyard so quiet, didn't see another soul [...]. And that's why I thought yall wanted to tear my house down this mornin' [...] 'cause you might-a heard 'bout me and Herman [...] and some people are [...] well, they judge, they can't help judgin' you. (Childress, *Wedding Band* 132–33)

Such a situation seems to have made Julia vulnerable. Her relationship with Herman appears to have isolated her from her black community. A woman's relationship with a man is a matter of privacy; but in the case of Julia, it becomes a matter of public accusation because she has entered into the so-called legally illicit relationship with Herman. It shall be unlawful for any white man to intermarry with any woman of either the black race or any mulatto. Any such marriage shall be utterly null and void and of no effect.

Mattie and Lula walk away when Julia reveals to them about her relationship with a white man. Julia is an independent woman and not a burden to anyone. Yet, she has to not only bear the brunt of Nelson's hatred but also explain him as to why she fell in love with Herman: "In that place where I worked, he was the only one who cared … who really cared …. Most folks don't have to account for why they love" (Childress, *Wedding Band* 153).

The racist attitude of Herman's family does not accept their relationship, but simply adds to Julia's woes. Annabelle, Herman's sister, finds that the love of Julia with Herman is disagreeable and the behavior of Julia with her mother is revolting. Herman's mother wants Julia to be locked up in jail for having relation with Herman. She is so angry with her son that she wants him to die of influenza instead of living a disgraced life after having relation with Julia, a black woman. The helplessness of Julia can be measured from the fact that she cannot call a doctor when Herman contracts influenza because it is against the law for him to be lying up in a black woman's bed. Her suffering intensifies when Herman's mother refuses to call the doctor immediately for treating Herman. His mother establishes her supremacy over Julia on the basis of her white color.

Julia's relationship with Herman has not just brought about displacement and isolation for Julia but it has also maligned Julia's reputation. Her character has been taken for granted. She has to keep changing her residence in order to keep relationship with Herman secret due to the prevalence of miscegenation law. So, the poor white hawker Bell Man assumes that Julia is available. He slips into Julia's room and makes indecent advances toward her. Lula's son Nelson also tries to flirt with Julia when he comes to know that Julia lives alone.

In short, she is accepted by neither the blacks nor the whites for having a relationship with a poor white man. This is her plight, her tragedy that seems to be an embodiment of powerlessness which every black woman experiences at one or the other stage of their existence on the American soil. It can be said easily from their ten long years of relationship that Julia is unwilling to leave Herman despite their inability to get married;

but, she is not even happy in this relationship: "Miss Lula, please don't …. You know it's against the law for black and white to get married, so Gawd nor the tea leaves can help us. My friend is white and that's why I try to stay to myself" (Childress, *Wedding Band* 132).

It seems that the collective effect of whatever Julia has experienced has not only alienated her from the society, but has also made her pessimistic. She fights with the person whom she loves the most. Somewhere Julia feels that Herman's attitude toward racism has never been clear. She alleges that Herman never allowed her to discuss how the white lynched the black: "Every time I open my mouth 'bout what they do … you say …. 'Kerist, there it is again ….' Whenever somebody was lynched … you 'n me would eat a very silent supper. It hurt me not to talk … what you don't say you swallow down" (Childress, *Wedding Band* 174).

Julia is caught between her love for Herman and her hatred for the whites. Her love for Herman starts retreating when he recites hate speech at the call of his mother. By the time Herman realizes how he has hurt Julia all these years by failing her in every way, he is on the verge of death. The moment Herman accepts his failure Julia feels intense love for him:

> JULIA. When you first came in this yard I almost died-a shame … so many times you was nothin' to me but white … times we were angry … damn white man … times I was tired … damn white man … but most times you were my husband, my friend, my lover ….
>
> HERMAN. Whatever is wrong, Julia … not the law … me; what I didn't do, with all-a my faults, spite-a all that …. You gotta believe I love you …. 'cause I do …. That's the one thing I know …. I love you …. I love you. (Childress, *Wedding Band* 175)

Julia senses deep love of Herman for her. She decides to reject Herman's mother, his sister, Fanny, Lula, and Mattie by asserting her right to be by Herman's bedside.

The play looks to be operating at two levels: one, it shows the kind of relationship the blacks and the colored share among themselves, and two, the way the whites treat the blacks. The issue of racism, the white against the black, the colored against the blacks, and the most important is the man–woman relationship and their financial status all together operate to create what we call as the black experience. Apart from Julia, even Lula and Mattie have been suffering due to the social environment in which they are placed. Lula and Mattie have suffered from marital violence. Lula seems to be living with the burden of killing her son due to her carelessness. Mattie cannot divorce the man who attempts to kill her because of the tyrannical divorce law of South Carolina. The unreliability of their existence does not seem to make them understand the pain and sufferings of Julia. Instead, they exclude and torment Julia for keeping illegal relationship with a white baker.

It appears that the emotional support they seek in their life is directly or indirectly instrumental in enhancing their sufferings: one, Lula is forced to send her adopted son back to the army in order to save him from getting lynched; two, Mattie's marriage with October is not recognized by Merchant Marine. They cease to torment Julia only when they realize the pain of their own circumstances. Julia appears to be emerging strong when she is subjected to social orchestration by her neighbors. She probably wages the battle at a number of levels due to her relationship with a poor, white baker. At personal level, she loves Herman whose mother hates her and is eager to get him married to a white woman. She bids defiance to the law as well as the social norms of South Carolina. This is the predicament of Julia.

Apart from Julia's predicament, the play definitely delineates all those things that contribute to black suffering and their predicament in the hostile white world. The play becomes appealing and realistic because it brings out vividly the discrepancy evident in the attitude of the black society in general. The play confronts racism, but Childress reveals that racism is not only intended for blacks, it is also exhibited by blacks. In the play, whites, Asians, and Jews are also victims of racism. Childress exposes the reality of life for black and white Americans as she explores the weakness of humanity so rooted in maintaining rules and social lines that it forgets that there are lives at stake.

Wine in the Wilderness

Wine in the Wilderness portrays hostilities and prejudices prevailing within the black community. The unique feature of this play is that all the characters in the play are blacks who are separated by class, education, political, and cultural conditions. Childress takes a very firm stand toward the social, economic, and political rights of the blacks in the play. *Wine in the Wilderness* is woven around a poor young black woman, Tommy. It opens amidst heavy riots between blacks and whites which transform into a conflict between the blacks among them. Vinia Jennings rightly observed that:

> The discrepancies between the underclass, undereducated heroine of *Wine in the Wilderness* as the true Africentric, proud of blacks and her blackness, and bourgeois, intellectual blacks whose white assimilationist and classist values expose their racial disingenuousness. (65)

Childress focuses on the status of African American women. Her characters include domestic workers, laundry workers, the unemployed, dancers, artists, and teachers. She visualizes the emotionally oppressed heroines who struggle to gain their freedom. She uses humor to highlight her core thematic concerns such as male–female relationships, class divisions within the African American community, and the nature of political and social action. In this play, she exposes the false declarations of the African American brotherhood. She criticizes the brutality of a racist society that does not recognize the other. It deals with the cultivated black artist's vision about the black woman throughout history and a lot about a common black woman at the outset of a Harlem riot during the summer of 1964.

The play demonstrates the utter street violence and looting which is going on outside of the apartment of Bill Jameson. Lots of noise and screaming can be heard in the distance. Oldtimer, a man in his sixties, enters Bill's apartment, carrying a bundle of loot he has taken during the chaos of the riot. The police are looking around the building, and Oldtimer is afraid of being arrested for theft. One of the things he has taken is a bottle of whisky which he shares with Bill who helps him to hide his bundle of loot by attaching it to a rope and dangling it outside of the window. As a result of the race riot outside, Oldtimer carries in a haul of loot consisting of liquor, foods, and clothes with price tags still attached. Bill Jameson cautions him, "Stealin' ain't worth a bullet through your brain, is it? You wanna get shot down and drown in yor own blood … for what? A suit, a bottle of whiskey? Gonna throw your life away for a damn ham?" (Childress, *Wine* 183). He instructs Oldtimer that, "A revolution should not be looting and stealing. Revolutions are for liberation" (Childress, *Wine* 184).

But Oldtimer is not a shoplifter in real sense, because he has not stolen anything. Whatever he has brought is the scattered leftover in the street. He only picked up the things rioters dropped in the street and crushed the underfoot. He replies angrily to Bill, "My days we didn't have all these grants and scholarship like now" (Childress, *Wine* 184). Bill has reasonable living standards based on a superior education with the help of grants and scholarships. Thus, Oldtimer utterly reminds him that looting may be a form of liberation for those who are so poor that any material development is welcome. The central conflict of the play is a conflict of attitude toward the African American identity. This conflict between different attitudes in the black community is seen by the real situation of poor blacks represented by Oldtimer and Tommy.

The conflict of the perception toward the poor blacks is evident in the image of black women projected by Bill's painting. Bill Jameson, as a black painter, is engaged in drawing a sketch of triptych in his one room apartment. A triptych is a collection of "three paintings that make one work … three paintings that make one subject" (Childress, *Wine* 185). Through this triptych, Bill seems to show how a black woman is and how she ought to be. He has finished two parts of the triptych. In one he painted an innocent, charming, young black girl in the Sunday dress and hair ribbons and in another his ideal of a stunning African beauty. She wears colorful African clothes and a golden headdress. He calls her, "Mother Africa, regal, black womanhood in her noblest form" (Childress, *Wine* 185). As a subject of the third part, he requires a messed up black woman. He imagines the third image of his triptych as a defamation of black womanhood from innocence and perfection to total downfall. He describes the third woman as:

> She's gonna be the kinda chick that is grass roots […] no, not grass roots […]. I mean she's underneath the grass roots. The lost woman […] what the society has made out of our women. She's as far from my African queen as a woman can get and still be female; she's as close to the bottom as you can get without crackin' up […] she's ignorant, unfeminine, coarse, rude […] vulgar […] a poor, dumb chick that's had her behind kicked until it's numb […] and the sad part is […] she ain't together, you know […] there's no hope for her. (Childress, *Wine* 186)

The lost woman in his triptych is the creation of a chauvinistic and elitist imagination. He finds her vulgarity and poverty the source of her hopelessness. Normally artists are considered to be thoughtful, kindhearted, and perceptive. However, Bill seems to be missing these qualities that an artist possesses. He is painting a triptych with a view to win a prize. He wants his triptych to decorate some public place. He has painted his ideal black woman who is beautiful. The series of three paintings is meant to express his statement about black womanhood. He says,

> "Wine in the Wilderness" will go up against the wall to improve the view of some post office [...] or some library [...] or maybe a bank [...] and I'll win a prize [...] and the queen, my black queen will look down from the wall so the messed up chicks in the neighborhood can see what a woman oughta be [...] and the innocent child on one side of her and the messed up chick on the other side of her [...] MY STATEMENT. (Childress, *Wine* 187)

Bill wants the black women to be beautiful and feminine. He wants the matriarchal system within the black community to be removed. He states, "The matriarchy gotta go. Yall throw them suppers together, keep your husband happy, raise the kids" (Childress, *Wine* 203). He receives a phone call from Sonny-man informing him that they are bringing Tommy, an ugly and ignorant black woman as a model for the third part of his triptych. They have found her stranded in the bar due to the riot. Sonny-man and Cynthia arrive at Bill's apartment along with Tommy who does not know their hidden motive of bringing her there. Bill's friends introduce him to Tommy which, they think, represents the hopeless type of woman he has in mind for his third painting.

Tommy, however, realizes Bill's true intention to paint her as a representative of a woman who is ignorant, unfeminine, coarse, rude, vulgar, poor, and dumb. She angrily criticizes Bill and his friends for thinking that they are better than she is and for looking down on the masses of the African American community who are less educated and less privileged than they are. Bill extends shelter to Tommy not because she is affected by riots but he wants to paint her as "the real thing from underneath them grass roots. A black country chick right outta the wilds of Mississippi" (Childress, *Wine* 186). Tommy appears to be an object for Bill whom he can paint for earning name, fame, and money. He is insensitive to Tommy's suffering. He insists, "And so I must paint you tonight .... Tommy in her moment of tragedy" (Childress, *Wine* 193).

Bill cannot accept black women as they are living and breathing around him. He finds the neighboring women second-rate chicks. He is an educated black fellow who keeps reading the history of the black struggle in the United States and celebrates all those people who struggled very hard to see that the black community in the US gets equal rights. Yet, he fails to realize that the black community in the United States has survived only due to the efforts of the black women. He never likes the black women leading and to be on the front side of the war. In fact, there appears to be a contradiction in his attitude toward black women. He expects Tommy to know about all those people who helped in the liberation of the black people. When Tommy shows her eagerness to learn about the black history, he ignores her, saying, "Aw, baby, why torment yourself? Trouble with our women ... they all wanta be great brains. Leave somethin' for a man to do" (Childress, *Wine* 202).

Childress artistically unfolds the problem of class discrimination, the problem of the educated blacks who adopt the white middle-class values. Consequently, they give maltreatment to poor black woman through an incident in Tommy's life. Tommy, in her thirties, is a factory worker who wears mismatched clothes and a cheap wig, and flees from the moments of the race riot. "She is dressed in a mismatched shirt and sweater, wearing a wig that is not comical, but is wiggy …. She wears sneakers and bobby sox, carries a brown paper sack" (Childress, *Wine* 188). Her language is not polished and her behavior is not refined. She says, "All right, and I got one for you …. Like my grampaw used-ta say …. Here's to the men's collars and the women's skirts … may they never meet" (Childress, *Wine* 190).

Tommy's house has been burnt down in the riots. She has been brought to Bill's house by Sonny-man and Cynthia. Tommy is a good-humored person whose spirit is not affected in spite of losing her house. She makes other people laugh through her brief comments. Again, she is fully aware of her limitations. She takes wine. She is somebody without pretenses. She accuses black people of burning her house. As a matter of fact, her plight presents another aspect of the black life—the blacks have looted the black. The blacks have tortured the black. She says, "the Afro-Americans burnt down my house" (Childress, *Wine* 191). Tommy is neither innocent nor stupid. She cannot be easily convinced to get painted. She is conscious of her ugliness and untidiness. When Bill studies her for his portrait possibilities, she is pleased by the thought but she cannot understand it. She says:

> Paint me? For what? If he was gonna paint somebody seems to me it'd be one of the pretty girls they show in the beer ads. They even got colored on television now […] brushin' their teeth and smokin' cigarettes […] some of the prettiest girls in the world. He could get them […] couldn't you? (Childress, *Wine* 192)

It is interesting to note that Tommy appears to misjudge the intentions of all three—Sonny-man, Cynthia, and Bill. She has been brought to Bill's house under the pretext of introducing her to their friend Bill. Therefore, she assumes it to be some kind of match-making activity. When Bill agrees to get her Chinese food, she is led to believe that Bill might fall in love with her. Tommy proposes Bill to be her friend and he accepts her proposal. Bill accepts Tommy's every demand as he is eager to paint Tommy in all her mess. Tommy might be mistaken in her judgment but she seems to be clear about her intention. She speaks her mind when she is left alone with Cynthia. She reveals her intention of trapping Bill into marriage. However, she declares that she does not want to push him fast. She wants to play her cards carefully. In fact, she makes an attempt to know about Bill and his work when both of them get isolated. At the same time, she is not willing to take any nonsense from Bill. She is ready to react the moment she is hurt. Bill forcefully makes Tommy sit for painting and in doing so he spills the orange juice over Tommy. Hence, she refuses to sit for painting in wet condition. When Bill addresses her as "Bitch," she retorts, "You must be talkin' about your mama!" (Childress, *Wine* 205). This incident shows that Tommy knows when to assert herself.

Tommy's outward appearance suffers an alteration when she overhears Bill's telephonic conversation praising his painting celebrating African womanhood. Tommy, who cannot see this painting, assumes that Bill is praising her womanhood. As a result, she is inspired with new strength and passion. She is suddenly awakened to the feeling of being loved and admired. She removes her wig and adopts her natural African look. Her changed look confuses Bill. She finally succeeds in catching Bill's attention. Her relationship with Bill assumes a new dimension when Tommy and Bill are in each other's arms. Tommy is no longer a model posing for Bill and he is no longer a painter. Bill is protective at first, but, when Tommy speaks that she loves him, he is moved by this exposure to gain new insight into his art and his vision of African American womanhood. He realizes that he has been misguided in his approach to the art and his attitude toward the African American community. Bill finally understands that Tommy herself represents his ideal vision of the African American woman, *Wine in the Wilderness*. He convinces her to stay and pose for a painting to represent her in this new light.

Tommy gets dissatisfied with Bill when Oldtimer reveals to her that she is "The worst gal in town. A messed up chick …" (Childress, *Wine* 212) She is in the last painting of Bill's intended triptych. The hypocrisy of Bill and his friends gets exposed when Tommy comes to know through Oldtimer that she has been brought to represent the messed-up black woman. Tommy seems to feel humiliated, deceived, and misused. Now Tommy realizes why Sonny-man and Cynthia brought her to Bill's apartment and why Bill wanted to paint her. She exposes the egotism of Sonny-man and Cynthia. Tommy discovers Bill's true intentions and becomes infuriated. She realizes that Bill looks down on her for being less educated and less privileged than he and accuses him of looking down upon the masses of the African American community, although he claims to represent the community through his art.

Tommy does not want her to be used by Bill. So, she decides to leave his apartment. She is terribly annoyed. She declares that she does not want any polite treatment from anybody and that it has been her mistake to assume that writers and painters know more than she knows. She contends that people like Bill and his friends celebrate the black heroes from history but hate black women like Tommy:

> If a black somebody is in a history book, or printed on a pitcher, or drawed on a paintin', […] or if they're a statue, […] dead, and outta the way, and can't talk back, then you dig 'em and full—a so much–a damn admiration and talk 'bout "our" history. But when you run into us livin' and breathin' ones, with the life's blood still pumpin' through us, […] then you comin' on 'bout how we ain' never together. You hate us, that's what! You hate black me! (Childress, *Wine* 214)

Tommy declares that she addresses Bill as nigger fondly. It seems that anyone who belongs to her race and anyone who is a dark-skinned person is a nigger for Tommy. It seems that she takes the insensitivity of the so-called educated black people to heart. Tommy teaches them the meaning of nigger "When they [white] say 'nigger', just dry-long-so, they mean educated you and uneducated me. They hate you and call you 'nigger'. I called you 'nigger' but I love you" (Childress, *Wine* 216). She also teaches them what is to be a black woman. She asserts her individuality as,

> Bill, I don't have to wait for anybody's by-your-leave to be a "Wine in the Wilderness" woman. I can be it if I wanta […] and I am […]. I'm not the one you made up and painted, the very pretty lady who can't talk back […] but I'm "Wine in the Wilderness" […] alive

and kickin', me [...]. Tomorrow-Marie, cussin' and fightin' and lookin' out for my damn self 'cause ain't nobody else 'round to do it, dontcha know. And Cynthia, if my hair is straight, or if it's natural, or if I wear a wig, or take it off [...] that's all right; because wigs [...] shoes [...] hats [...] bags [...] and even this [...] [*She picks up the African throw she wore a few moments before [...] fingers it.*] They're just what [...] what you call [...] access [*fishing for the word*] [...]. Accessories. Somethin' you add on or take off. The real thing is takin' place on the inside [...] that's where the action is. That's "Wine in the Wilderness" [...] a woman that's a real one and a good one. And y' all just better believe I'm it. (Childress, *Wine* 217)

She confesses her love for Bill, but she values her individuality more than her love for him. A new understanding of black experience dawns on him and he decides to give Tommy the center place in his triptych titled *Wine in the Wilderness*. Tommy slowly returns and takes her seat on the model stand. Bill, realizing the fakeness in his perception of black womanhood, ultimately decides to give Tommy the place she deserves in the triptych—the center position.

In this play, Childress seems to have very vividly brought out the scholarly agitation within the black community which in general was socially, economically, politically, and psychologically exploited. However, the oppressors were different on each case in point. The conflict between the oppressor and the oppressed is not always necessarily the conflict between the black and the white. There is a conflict within the black community too. The oppressed blacks suppress the weaker ones within the black community. The literate blacks exploit the illiterate blacks and the black males exploit the black females. This is the brutal cycle of black oppression. In fact, this is the nature of human beings. Bill, Sonny-man, and Cynthia belong to the educated class among the blacks. However, they are suffering from an identity crisis. They have uplifted themselves through their education, but their vision of life seems to be indistinct. They oppress the weak within the community not with the intention of upsetting them but perhaps out of their failure to understand what it is to be a black.

Sonny-man is a professional writer whereas his wife, Cynthia, is a social worker, but they seem to be completely arrogant. They possibly know that their friend Bill is looking for a woman who is ugly and ignorant for his model. They meet Tommy amidst riots in the bar. Her untidy appearance, mismatched clothes, and impetuous personality lead them to believe that she is the kind of woman that Bill is looking for. Therefore, they pull Tommy to come to Bill's apartment in the name of protecting her. This gesture of Sonny-man and Cynthia leads Tommy to believe that they are her good friends.

Cynthia is a twenty-five-year-old, sophisticated, and polished black woman, but she seems to suffer from conceptual confusion regarding black identity. She seems to be uncertain about what it is to be a black woman in the society where slavery, racial discrimination, and inequality are prevalent. So, she ridicules the matriarchal system predominant among the blacks. Her attitude toward Tommy seems to be equally negative. She is a middle-class, educated, African American woman, whose attitude toward Tommy is arrogant and demeaning. She finds Tommy rude, rough, and impatient. Thus, although she and Tommy are both the African American women,

Cynthia exhibits a lack of respect for Tommy, allowing her to be used by a man whose attitude toward her is insulting.

Cynthia and Tommy have a discussion that demonstrates Cynthia's ideas about how African American women should behave in their relationships with men. She tells Tommy that she is too coarse and unfeminine. She should allow men to have the upper hand in her relationships with them. Cynthia also criticizes Tommy for wearing a wig, instead of showing her natural hair. But, as Tommy later points out, the reason she wears a wig is that women like Cynthia make her feel ashamed of being her natural self. She says to Tommy, "You're too brash. You're too used to looking out for yourself. It makes us lose our femininity .... It makes us hard ... it makes us seem very hard. We do for ourselves too much" (Childress, *Wine* 197). She wants Tommy to annihilate her personality and be feminine. She wants black women to assume the role of white women and thus allow the black men to get their manhood back. She states: "You have to let the black man have his manhood again. You have to give it back, Tommy" (Childress, *Wine* 197).

Cynthia seems to have an air of superiority due to her education and upbringing. So, she does not approve Tommy's attempts to trap Bill into a permanent relationship. For Cynthia, this appears to be an arrangement which cannot be smooth into a relationship. The pretense of Sonny-man and Cynthia being compassionate to the depressed blacks is exposed. The hollowness in their characters is distinctly brought out by Tommy. Sonny-man addresses Tommy as a sister. Tommy is anguished by this address that she rebukes him:

> SONNY-MAN. The sister is upset.
> TOMMY. And you stop callin' me "the" sister ... if you feelin' so brotherly why don't you say "my" sister? Ain't no we-ness in your talk. "The" Afro-American, "the" black man, there's no we-ness in you. Who you think you are?
> SONNY-MAN. I was talkin' in general er ... my sister, 'bout the masses.
> TOMMY. There he go again. "The" masses. Tryin' to make out like we pitiful and you got it made. You the masses your damn self and don't even know it. *(Another angry look at Bill)* Nigger. (Childress, *Wine* 215)

Tommy proves to be decent ethically. She refuses to be painted bad or ugly. Despite her sufferings and agony, her sense of decency does not seem to flop. When she comes to know that Bill wants to paint her as a messed-up chick, she refuses to pose as a model. She in anger says,

> Better not. I'll kill him! The "black people" this and the "Afro-American" [...] that [...]. You ain't got no use for none-a us [...]. 'Til I got here they didn't even know your damn name. There's something inside- a me that says I ain't suppose to let nobody play me cheap. Don't care how much they know! (Childress, *Wine* 213)

Tommy is influential in enlightening Bill about the black experience. Toward the end of the play, an archetypal shift is seen in Bill's attitude. He finds Tommy beautiful. He realizes how hostile and prejudiced his feelings about the black matriarchal stereotype have been. Bill realizes that Tommy herself is his true African queen, a woman like many in her community. He understands that Tommy, the black matriarch, should be his *Wine in the Wilderness*, because of the splendor of her strength. He has learned to see beauty in the stereotype. His realization of the beauty of the black matriarch is a historical outstanding of deserved admiration. He convinces Tommy to stay so he can paint her portrait as his new vision of African American womanhood. He decides to change the subject of his triptych and declares to paint Oldtimer, Sonny-man, and Cynthia along with Tommy decorating the center.

Tommy is not a defiled, broken, and delicate woman who crawls off into some corner to suffer from an anxious breakdown and spend the rest of her life accusing men for her emotional and physical spoil. James V. Hatch says of Tommy, as "Alice Childress has created a powerful new black heroine who emerges from the depths of the black community, offering a sharp contrast to the typically strong 'Mama' figure that dominates such plays as *Raisin in the Sun*" (737). She marked against Bill Jameson and his middle-class black friends because they look down on their culture. They displace themselves and criticize grassroot blacks. Hatch precisely observes the play and its heroine:

> The beauty of *Wine in the Wilderness* is in part due to the author's sensitive treatment of Tommy, 'a poor, dumb chick that's had her behind kicked until it's numb, but whose warmth, compassion, inner dignity, and pride makes her more of a woman than Cynthia will ever be. (737)

Childress has presented the plight of the black community in general. However, she probably showed that the difference can be made by the community itself. She attempts to present the black woman in a new light. Her heroine is morally upright, proud of being black, and equally assertive about her status. Tommy stands against the society and ultimately wins her long-deserved appreciation. She asserts her individuality by not letting Bill paint her as a messed-up chick.

In the play, Childress addresses the theme of perceptions of African American women within the African American community. Bill and his friends feel that African American women have dominated the African American men in the past and should learn to be more subservient to the men in their lives. Tommy, on the other hand, argues that women like herself—tough, vigorous, yet helpless—should not be criticized but should be embraced and celebrated by the African American men and the community as a whole. Cynthia represents Childress's vision of the attitude of some educated, middle-class African American women toward African American women who are less educated and less privileged than them.

The play is the celebration of collective black self-determination in which Tommy determines to preserve her black female identity in an intraracially elitist and sexist atmosphere. Her self-determination inspires Bill Jameson, an artist to see himself, and a new purpose for his art through her eyes. Tommy educates Bill and his friends that art is the reality which is useful, because it tells history and culture. His triptych on black womanhood is initially a symbol of an unconcerned attitude toward ordinary black people.

The play ends with Bill Jameson's reform that confesses his mistake and reviews his drive to model for a triptych on the history of the struggle of black people. He requires all his friends, especially Tommy, whose liberation lies exclusively in their interdependence and in love and respect for each other. Tommy gives Bill thorough knowledge of history and a genuine understanding of the black community. She shapes an image of black people that gives Bill a new perspective for their expression in his triptych.

To conclude with the plays of Alice Childress, it is detected that these plays highlight the triple jeopardy and subjugation of African American women due to racism, classism, and also by the white and African American patriarchal social order. Her plays depict the racial, gender, and class inequalities and social injustices and often delineate the uncompromising African American women protagonists whose difficulties convey the restrictions faced by them.

Works Cited

Achilles, Jochen. "Allegory and Iconography in African American Drama of the Sixties: Imamu Amiri Baraka's Dutchman and Alice Childress's Wine in the Wilderness." *American Studies: A Quarterly* 45. 2 (2000).

Andrews, William et al. *The Concise Oxford Companion to African American Literature.* New York: Oxford University Press, 2001. Print.

Barlow, Judith E. "Foreword to Trouble in Mind." *Plays by American Women: 1930–1960.* Ed. Judith E. Barlow. New York, London: Applause Theatre Book Publishers, 2001. Print.

Brown-Guillory, Elizabeth. "Black Women Playwrights: Exorcising Myth." *Phylon* 48. 3 (1987).

Burke, Sally. *American Feminist Playwrights: A Critical History.* New York: Twayne Publishers, 1996. Print.

Burrell, Julie M. "Review: Childress Alice Selected Plays." *Theatre Journal* 65. 2 (2013).

Childress, Alice. "Florence." *Wine in the Wilderness: Plays by African American Women from the Harlem Renaissance to the Present.* Ed. Elizabeth Brown-Guillory. New York: PRAGER, 1990. Print.

———. "Gold through the Trees." *Selected Plays: Alice Childress.* Ed. Kathy A. Perkins. Evanston, IL: Northwestern University Press, 2011. Print.

———. "Knowing the Human Condition." *Black American Literature and Humanism.* Ed. R. Baxter Miller. Lexington: University Press of Kentucky, 1981. Print.

———. "Trouble in Mind." *Plays by American Women: 1930–1960.* Ed. Judith E. Barlow. New York, London: Applause, 1994. Print.

———. "Wedding Band: A Love/Hate Story in Black and White." *Selected Plays: Alice Childress.* Ed. Kathy A. Perkins. Evanston, IL: Northwestern University Press, 2011. Print.

———. "Wine in the Wilderness." *Selected Plays: Alice Childress.* Ed. Kathy A. Perkins. Evanston, IL: Northwestern University Press, 2011. Print.

Curb, Rosemary. "An Unfashionable Tragedy of American Racism: Alice Childress's Wedding Band." *MELUS* 7. 4. *Ethnic Women Writers of II of Dwelling Places* (winter 1980).

Hatch, James V., and Ted Shine. "Modern Black Women." *Black Theatre USA: Forty-Five Plays by Black Americans, 1847–1974.* Eds. James V. Hatch and Ted Shine. New York: The Free Press, 1974. Print.

Jennings, La Vinia Delois. "Alice Childress." *Twayne's United States Authors Series, 652.* New York: Twayne Publishers, 1995. Print.

Turner, Darwin T. "Introduction." *Black Drama: An Anthology.* Eds. William Brasmer and Dominick Consolo. Columbus, OH: Charles E. Merrill Publishing Company, 1970. Print.

Wilkerson, Margaret B. "From Harlem to Broadway: African American Women Playwrights at Mid-Century." *The Cambridge Companion to American Women playwrights.* Ed. Murphy Brenda. Cambridge: Cambridge University Press, 1999. Print.

Chapter Three

LORRAINE HANSBERRY

Life Sketch and Works

Lorraine Hansberry was born in Chicago, Illinois, on May 19, 1930, to Nannie Perry Hansberry and Carl A. Hansberry. Her home was a center of African American social, economic, political, and cultural life. She grew up in an upper-middle-class family. Her father was a powerful realtor who has built his fortune on the sale and rental of kitchenettes to relieve the crowded housing conditions of the African Americans. He won a Supreme Court case against housing discrimination. Her mother was a ward committee woman who helped to manage the buildings and tenants. The parents taught their four children pride in themselves and in their race. In African American Writers Conference in 1959, Hansberry said, "I was born black and a female" (qtd. in Burke 125). She, thus, acknowledged her identity of being black and female. This double consciousness marks her dramatic writing.

In 1938, Carl Hansberry moved his family into a "restricted" (Carter 40) area near the University of Chicago to test real estate agreements excluding African Americans. Mobs threw bricks and concrete stabs through the family's window toward them. Hansberry recalls her "desperate and courageous mother, patrolling our house all night with a loaded German luger, doggedly guarding her four children, while my father fought the respectable part of the battle in [The U. S. Supreme Court]" (qtd. in Burke 125). This incident forms one of the themes of *A Raisin in the Sun* in which an African American family tries to move from a ghetto into the suburbs.

In 1944, Lorraine graduated from Betsy Ross Elementary School. During 1948 and 1950, she attended University of Wisconsin studying art, literature, and drama and stage design. In the early 1950s, she worked as a journalist and associate editor for *Freedom*, an African American progressive newspaper in New York City founded by Paul Robeson. During this time, undercurrents of social protests were mounting and these protests filled the pages of *Freedom*. In 1953, she married Robert Nemiroff and they moved to Greenwich Village where she began writing. Their settlement in Greenwich Village forms the setting for her play, *The Sign in Sidney Brustein's Window*. In 1964, her marriage to Nemiroff ends in divorce, but their creative collaboration continues. And she dies of cancer on January 12, 1965, at the age of thirty-four. Her published work consists of five plays, numerous speeches, poems, essays, and newspaper articles. Unpublished are several film and play scripts, portions of a novel, and adaptations.

A Raisin in the Sun (1959) was translated into thirty languages across the globe. The play became a popular film in 1961. *The Sign in Sidney Brustein's Window* (1964), the second play to be produced during her lifetime, offers Hansberry's objectivity toward her subject to be dealt with. Her book, *The Movement: Documentary of a Struggle for Equality* (1964), a photographic essay on the civil rights movement, appeared in Britain under the title *A Matter of Color: Documentary of the Struggles for Racial Equality in the U. S. A.* (1965). This book was not read by people practically, because she was a creative artist of the theater and not a political theorist. She had little talent for politics than as she had for drawing or painting.

Hansberry has answered Genet's *Les Negress* (1960) by writing *Les Blancs* (1972). In 1970, Nemiroff edited the script and produced it to very mixed reviews. Nemiroff described it as "the first major work by a black American playwright to focus on Africa and the struggle for black liberation" (qtd. in Ashley 156). It is an unfinished work which is later completed by Robert Nemiroff by saying:

> Synthesizing the scenes already completed throughout the play with those in progress, drawing upon relevant fragments from earlier drafts and creating, as indeed, dialogue of my own to bridge gaps, deepen relationships or lighten the drama along the lines we had explored together. (Shafee 85)

The Drinking Gourd (1972), the next play completed by Hansberry, was never produced. It was put on the shelf with notations commending its excellence and was later published posthumously by Robert Nemiroff. *The Drinking Gourd* is an incisive analysis of American slavery as "a self-perpetuating system based on the exploitation of cheap labor" (Wilkerson 11). *What Use Are Flowers?* (1972) was conceived as a fantasy for television. It is a response to contemporary debates about the destruction or survival of the human race. Hansberry first described *What Use Are Flowers?* as "a bit of a fantasy thing about war and peace" (Gunton 192).

To Be Young, Gifted and Black (1969) is a patch work play pieced together by Nemiroff from the produced and unproduced works, letters, speeches, and articles of Lorraine Hansberry. It has fragments of more than ten separate fractions. It contains:

> portions of the now-published plays, A Raisin in the Sun, The Sign in Sidney Brustein's Window, Les Blancs, The Drinking Gourd, and What Use Are Flowers?; excerpts from the unpublished fragments of her Autobiographical novel, All the Dark and Beautiful Warriors; passages from an unfinished play, Toussaint; paraphrases from Sean O' Casey; segments of Hansberry's Letters; Journals, essays, poetry and interviews; and a few comments by Nemiroff himself. (Cheney 134)

The play is subtitled as *The World of Larraine Hansberry*. It is an attempt to "Present Miss Hansberry, the writer, and the background which produced her and provided the material for her work …" (Gunton 187). In his foreword to the book, Nemiroff calls it as "The portrait of an individual, the workbook of an artist, and the chronicle of a rebel who celebrated the human spirit" (Cheney 133). The play presents many facets and shades of African American life, such as "black nationalism, cocktail parties, slavery, financial problems, family squabbles, humour, and universal concerns of man's hope and dreams" (Cheney 133). It is her autobiographical play toured the country after her death, became the off Broadway hit of 1969 and later toured more than 200 college campuses.

Among Hansberry's files is a manila folder titled *Toussaint: A Musical Drama in 7 Scenes*, dated May 1958. *Toussaint*, an unfinished play about the Haitian Liberator Toussaint L' Overtures, is a very different work. It is a historical drama. All Haitian history from the birth of Toussaint to his death has been represented. An impressive view of Toussaint's life and his crucial role in the Haitian revolution would have been staged. Hansberry considers *Toussaint* as her epic and writes, "I intend to depart from the traditional canonization of historical heroes, and try ... to write a man—and yet, at the same time, not to lose the wonder of his magnitude" (Cheney 146). Hansberry sought to portray *Toussaint* as a master of diplomacy and politics as an uneducated but a brilliant rival who frightened Napoleon.

A Raisin in the Sun

A Raisin in the Sun is set against a backdrop of explicit racism and unavoidable segregated housing and discriminated race relations in America in the 1950s. Hansberry's inheritance continues the struggle for racial justice and decency in America. Clive Barnes describes it as "a quiet black cry in a white wilderness" (qtd. in Hansberry, *A Raisin in the Sun* 221) It is an authentic portrait of the aspirations, anxieties, ambitions, and contradictory pressures affecting humble African American people in Chicago. Hansberry addresses the sensitive question of liberating them from the burden of racial discrimination. The characters in the play upraise a universal representation of black people's hopes and dreams. It is concerned with the problems of the Younger family which belongs to the black race. The family is struggling to advance against terrific odds but never loses hope. It takes conviction and commitment to "bring hope out of hopelessness, courage out of fear, and idealism out of fatalism" (Cooper 59).

The Younger family lives in an overcrowded building that they have to share the bathroom with another family. The survival of the family depends on their ability to accommodate themselves in the white world. The African Americans have to live in the social situations which are thoroughly controlled by the whites. Brooks Atkinson identifies the racial minority people as "human beings who want, on the one hand, to preserve their family pride and, on the other hand, to break out of the poverty that seems to be their fate" (qtd. in Ashley 151).

The title and the theme are taken from "Harlem," a poem of Langston Hughes, which asks:

What happens to a dream deferred?
Does it dry up
Like a raisin in the sun?
Or Fester like a sore
And then run?

Does it stink like rotten meat?
Or crust and sugar over
Like a syrupy sweet?
May be it just sags?
Like a heavy load.
Or does it explode? (qtd. in Ashley 224)

The poem expresses the sense of kinetic energy and tension which underlies the frustrations of the African Americans. The energy can be turned into violence, self-destruction, and despair or genuine realization. Hughes bunches the ambiguities and tensions in his poem around the experience of a dream deferred. A dream deferred may simply end in the drying up of hope like a raisin in the sun. The adversities of frustration may motivate the syrupy sweet realization of human potential.

The dreams of the Youngers have gone unfulfilled too long. Their hopes of enjoying the fruits of freedom and equality have been postponed as they struggle merely to survive economically. Frank Rich described that the play "changed American theatre forever" by forcing "both blacks and whites to re-examine the deferred dreams of black America" and by posing "all her concerns in a work that portrayed a black family with a greater realism and complexity than had ever been previously seen on an American stage" (qtd. in Steven 19). The play celebrates both black culture and black resistance to white oppression through many generations. As Hansberry says, "The thing I tried to show was the many gradations even in one Negro family, the clash of the old and new, but most of all the unbelievable courage of the Negro people" (qtd. in Steven 22). The three generations of Younger family depicted in the play differ in dreams yet the family is unified in their heroic defiance of white hostility and threats.

In the play, Hansberry dwells on the deferred dreams of the poor African Americans. The play dramatizes the efforts and frustrations of a family in pursuit of the American dream. The Younger family is industrious working-class black people in Chicago. Mrs. Younger—Mama, the sixty-year-old matriarch of the family, comes North with her husband a few years before the play begins in order to fulfill the American dream for her children. The dreams of pleasure and prosperity have almost dried up when the play begins, because the family has survived except for Mr. Younger. Walter Lee Younger, Mrs. Younger's thirty-five-year-old son, has been working for years as a chauffeur. He is disgusted with his demeaning labor and his inability to go into business for himself. Ruth, his wife, is tired of her work as a domestic servant. She is deeply troubled by her sagging marriage, which she bears like a heavy load. Beneatha, Walter's twenty-year-old sister, is a medical student who has developed her own tough intellectual crust. She is too engrossed in her own plans and fantasies to understand or tend to the sore festering in her family.

For Lena Younger, Walter Lee's mother, a new house, the stability, and the happiness of her children are her principal dreams. And this is the completion of a dream she and her late husband—who has been worked to death like slaves—conceived together. When Youngers received ten thousand dollars as insurance money paid upon the death of Walter Younger Sr., Lena Younger (Mama) and her adult son Walter Lee clash over the money's use. Mama wants to save some money for her daughter Beneatha's college education and to make a down payment on a new house in order to get the family out of the cramped quarters and shared bathroom of their tiny apartment. Her dreams are uncovered:

> RUTH. Well-what are you going to do with it [Insurance money] then?
> MAMA. ... some of it gets to be put away for Beneatha and her schoolin'—and ... been thinking that we may be could meet the notes on a little old two-story somewhere. With a Yard where Travis [her grandson] could play in the summer time, if we use part of the insurance for a down payment .... (Hansberry, *A Raisin in the Sun* 223)

This indicates that Youngers—Big Walter and Lena—have dreams of lifting themselves from lower-class to middle-class status. They seek better education for their children and entrance into professional occupations.

Mama possesses the absolute devotion to her family. The most important things in her life are her children. When Ruth suggests that she [Mama] should use the insurance money to take a trip, Mama explains that she could never spend the money on herself, but must spend it on the family. Mama decides that the best way to safeguard her family is to move them to a house where they can escape the tensions that plague them. Therefore, she makes a down payment on a house which is "the nicest place for the cheapest amount of money" (Anderson 93).

Mama's dream is her family and her reasons for its existence. She quotes her late husband to Ruth, "seems like God, didn't see fit to give the black man nothing but dreams—but he did give us children to make them dreams seem worthwhile" (Hansberry, *A Raisin in the Sun* 234). Mama is willing to sacrifice anything for her family. She learns that Ruth is planning to have an abortion, because she is so distressed about her and Walter's existence and relationship. Being a woman, Mama can understand Ruth's emotions and explains to Walter, "When the world gets ugly enough, a woman will do anything for her family ..." (Hansberry, *A Raisin in the Sun* 244). Her belief is her version of the American dream.

Mama wants her son, Walter, to be the head of the family; therefore, she gives him the insurance money to look after the family and encourages him. She believes that her dismissal of her son Walter Lee's plans for the insurance money may have been demeaning and destructive. Then Walter is so bitter that he cannot buy his liquor store. So, he gets drunk and quits his job. Mama's hatred of liquor is typical of many Southern women—especially blacks. Mama has seen alcohol destroying a man and ultimately his family. Walter says to Mama "You the head of this family. You run our lives like you want to" (Hansberry, *A Raisin in the Sun* 87). But mama reconsiders, turning over the remaining 6,500 dollars to Walter: "I am telling you to be the head of this family from now on like you supposed to be" (Hansberry, *A Raisin in the Sun* 94). She puts the remaining money in his hands and grants him his independence coupled with a large responsibility. She is then forced to stand by him after he loses the money. She has understood the necessity of independence to growth. Hence, she should join with her children in struggling against an outside threat to independence.

Mama tends and nurtures her children. She envisions that her house will be the place where the family can grow and flourish in better conditions. It is fitting that her family would give her gardening tools and gardening hat. This symbolizes that she needs to nurture them and help their dreams grow. Mama dreams the family to advance materially without becoming materialistic. According to Claudia Tate, Mama's posture reflects not only racial but gender conditioning:

> The black heroine seldom elects to play the role of the all-enacted outsider or the lone adventure in her quest for self-affirmation. This does not mean that she is unconcerned about her self-esteem […] but rather than her quest […] has different priorities and takes place in a different landscape […]. She is usually literally tied down to her children. (qtd. in Matuz 243–44)

Mama acts only for what she considers the good of her well-loved family. She does not wish to control her children and her grandson for the sake of maintaining power. She wishes only to continue to provide growth and opportunity for them. She, along with her husband, had done so in the past. The evidence is there when she points out to Walter Lee, "You ain't satisfied or proud of nothing we done. I mean that you had a home; that we kept you out of trouble till you was grown; that you don't have to ride to work on the back of nobody's streetcar" (Hansberry, *A Raisin in the Sun* 244).

Mama is not blind to Walter's needs. She makes him trustee of the remaining insurance money. Even when he loses the money to his partner, she continues to love him. She thinks that "the time to love somebody the most … [is] when he's at his lowest and can't believe in his self 'cause the world done whipped him so!" (Hansberry, *A Raisin in the Sun* 135–36). She wants to buy freedom for her children. She wants to save her family from the dissolution threatened by the internalized social and economic pressures. She believes in the family needs, a home that will provide Travis with a room of his own.

Ruth's dream, as mother and wife, is somewhat similar to her mother-in-law. She dreams of a room with an inside toilet for her son. She dreams as one of those triply oppressed by the white society—as African American, as a woman, and as a worker. Her dream conflicts with Walter Lee's. She sides often with Mama and shares Mama's basic suspicion of Walter's plans and doubts his judgment. She makes Walter ineffective and keeps him from asserting himself as a protector of the family. Ruth occupies a midpoint between mama and Beneatha. She works as a domestic and suffers indignity at the hands of employers. She is a loyal wife to Walter. Like her mother-in-law, she sees marriage as a woman's destiny. She does not share Walter Lee's passion for money, business, and social position. She would be satisfied with a peaceful home life and an adequate income. But as she begins to understand the compulsion of Walter Lee's dream, their relationship becomes closer. They restore the sweetness to their marriage, when they begin to talk. They go to the movies and dance in the living room. When they begin to talk softly again, there is the rebirth of their marriage. They begin to fulfill their dreams of a happy family in spite of the financial crisis.

Her life is the most traditional—a life of sacrificing and being sacrificed. She encourages Mama to use the insurance money to take a trip to Europe. She reveals her own longing for such a release for Lena. Ruth's outlet is pleasure in Beneatha's ability to break through many barriers that box Ruth in. This is why she is willing to make financial sacrifices to help her sister-in-law. Her last hope is to regain the affection between her and Walter. She wants ideal home. She is tired of contemplated relations. She wants the commitment between the members of the house. For that she sacrifices her life. This dream is revealed when Walter approaches her tenderly after a fight and she tells, "Honey, life doesn't have to be like this. I mean sometimes people can do things so that things are better … you remember how we used to talk when Travis was born … about the way we were going to live …. The kind of house …" (Hansberry, *A Raisin in the Sun* 80–81).

When Ruth is pregnant, she has not shared this knowledge with the family, because she does not intend to keep the baby. She does not want to bring another child into overcrowded Younger apartment. She without consulting anyone makes a downpayment on an abortion. She knows that she has the right to control her body. She takes the decision of abortion to save her family from additional economic hardship. It does not seem to her that there is the time to bring a child into the world. When Lena buys the house, Ruth expresses her joy at being able to continue her pregnancy by shouting "Praise God! Please, honey—let me be glad …. [To Walter] you be glad too" (Hansberry, *A Raisin in the Sun* 83). Thus, she cannot hide her delight. This house offers a reason to continue her pregnancy. When Lena breaks the news about her purchase of the house, Ruth becomes "aware for the first time perhaps that the life therein pulses with happiness and not despair" (Hansberry, *A Raisin in the Sun* 86). She had been driven to the thoughts of abortion. She would like the child to be born in a house filled with love and purpose.

When Walter loses the money, Ruth promises to Mama, "I will work twenty hours a day in all the kitchens in Chicago …. I'll strap my baby on my back if I have to and scrub all the floors in America and wash all the sheets in America if I have to—but we got to move …" (Hansberry, *A Raisin in the Sun* 129). Thus, she expresses both her own agency and the urgency of the family's need to leave the ghetto, because she does not want to live farther in the overcrowded ghetto. She wants her children to be grown up in an American colony, not the black dirty ghetto. She wants, like Lena, to turn out the dream of Big Walter to be true. She has this American dream in which she wants to be free from the black ways of life. She decides to rescue her children from the historical clutches of lynching [born and unborn].

Beneatha dreams of a medical school. She wants to develop her intellect and be of service to humanity by practicing medicine. She is already socially mobile, finding a place among other petty bourgeois aspirants on the rungs of education. She is, on the one hand, secure in the collegiate world of ideas and elitism and, on the other hand, she is undeceived about the symbols of class and status. She wants to have an identity beyond self and family in the liberation struggles of her people. She is very much the new woman who is committed to the blacks, improving them and society through education, professions, social and political action, and a proud awareness of their African heritage. She is determined to become a doctor because she believes that doctors, preachers, and teachers make the world a better place. She describes an incident from her childhood which suggests a serious and long-lasting motivation for a career as a doctor. She appears a more generous and tolerant human being. She tells Joseph Asagai about her friend Rufus's accident which inspires her to become a doctor. When Rufus was badly hurt but returned from the hospital almost as good as new:

> And I remember [...] the ambulance came and they took him to the hospital and they fixed the broken bones and they sewed it all up [...] and the next time I saw Rufus he just had a little line down the middle of his face [...]. That was the most marvelous things in the world [...]. I wanted to do that—I always thought it was the one concrete thing in the world that a human being could do—fix up the sick, you know—and make then whole again. (Hansberry, *A Raisin in the Sun* 122–23)

Beneatha is impressed by the need for compassion and passionate belief in the probability of change. She had always pinned her personal aspirations and hopes for a more equitable and compassionate society on the prospect of becoming a doctor. She reflects Hansberry's belief that social idealism—the commitment to a better society—is intimately tied to individual moral obligation. The social justice is the collective expression of idealism deeply felt by individuals. Beneatha has a strong sense of racial pride compounded with humanistic commitment. She is intensely aware of her racial background and steeps herself in the culture of her forbears. In Beneatha, Hansberry opens the door slightly on the midpoint of the black intellectual in America. She says, "Beneatha Younger is the only character in the play who stems from Miss Hansberry's home" (Gill 227). She is Lorraine Hansberry's personality.

Beneatha would like to be an African and a revolutionary, because all Africans are revolutionary for that she, at the end of the play, apparently entertains Asagai's proposal. Her decision to go to live with him in Africa suggests a symbolic as well as a personal link between blacks of America and those of Africa. She takes more seriously Asagai's teasing remark that her straightened hair reflects the "assimilationism" (Hansberry, *A Raisin in the Sun* 240) of African Americans. This remark leads her to change to African heritage. She wears the African dress that Asagai has given her. She plays African music on the record player and attempts an African dance. Thus, she introduces the beauty of all these vital aspects of African tradition. Her willingness to be an African indicates that she is searching for her identity. She dreams of her original identity by accepting African tradition. She is drawn to the cultural style and exotic politics of Africa. It seems to have restored national pride and identity through her rebellion. She does not want to be an assimilationist by accepting the American dream. Hence, she does not see the American dream.

Walter Lee, a black chauffeur, wants to tear down the social and economic walls built around him and his family by a white racist society. He wants to provide greater freedom for his son than he himself has had. He also desires to give his family a chance to experience a fresher, more tolerable, and more human environment. The white supremacist structure of the society placed economic pressures upon him. These economic pressures lead him to display hostility toward his wife for increasing his financial burden by becoming pregnant, toward his mother for not giving him the insurance money, and toward his sister for wanting some of the insurance money to continue the study to become a doctor. When mama gives him the remaining money, he sees the chance of changing his life. He behaves more gently and responsively to all the three women in the home. He takes his wife, Ruth, to the movie for the first time in ages. He presents a gift to his mother warmly and affectionately teases his sister about the ambition and idealism for which he had previously prohibited her. His ability to change his behavior after gaining the money clearly shows that he has been influenced by financial pressures. His new sweetness and concerns last until he loses the money.

Walter dreams of owning all and doing all the things he sees Mr. Arnold, a white man, doing and owning. On one level, he is merely aspiring to full and acknowledged humanity and on another level, he yearns to strut his manhood. Hansberry shows us that Walter has the "realizable dream of the black petty bourgeoisie" (Matuz 240). The primary meaning of the play is the tragedy of Walter's reaching for the American dream. Walter seems to possess an excessive degree of self-respect and expect too much out of life for himself and his family. He manages to escape the inferiority which destroys many blacks. He manages to acquire the strength to dream. His thinking is his acceptance of American values, rather than stereotypes, myths, and untruths about the blacks. His belief in American values holds that anyone can become anything he wants to be in the hands of opportunity. His strength lies in his belief in himself and in his ability to do what other successful Americans have done. He is influenced by his own black family and the values they believed in and lived by. These values prepared Walter to accept mainstream American values and to strive to reach his goal.

These family influences are of two kinds and produce two significant results. First is the love of his parents Walter received during his childhood led to the development of his strong sense of self-esteem. This love enables him fully to accept American values and gives him the confidence to pursue his dream. Second is the courage and dignity invested in his parents' courageous struggle to overcome adversity. This teaches him to be better than ordinary which resulted in love for his race and pride in his heritage. Walter accepts the American value which holds that owning one's own business is the primary path to economic success and prosperity because he is high-minded and wants to be something.

Walter's dream of success was nurtured by the young white men whom he saw in town and sought to imitate. The young white men of his age personify for him the true American dream, a dream he knows he is worthy of. He says to Lena:

> Mama—sometimes when I'm downtown and I pass them [White young men] cool, quiet-looking restaurants where them white boys are sitting back and talking 'bout things [...] sitting there turning deals worth millions of dollars ... sometimes I see guys don't look much older than me—. (Hansberry, *A Raisin in the Sun* 244)

He gets the encouragement from downtown scene of the young white men. The action of the young white men stimulates him to hope, dream, think, and even scheme. He believes he can do what they do and that he deserves to have what they have. Walter reaches for the complete American dream by imitating strong, ambitious, and even ruthless men. What Walter dreams of is the power that money brings. Power is the essence of the only kind of manhood he is willing to accept. Some degree of self-exaggeration is attached to the American dream. Those who attain it become great American heroes. Walter's dream, however, is balanced by the primary purpose that is a radical change in his family's living conditions. It means a wholly different and improved standard of living. Walter, thus, dreams of a substantial move up to the socioeconomic ladder, the complete abandonment of poverty, and the chance to live the kind of life most Americans dream of living. The selflessness and nobility of this dream give Walter its dignity and spiritual dimension.

Walter's goal rests on a morally sound foundation. He dreams of a lovely home with a gardener, two expensive cars, and the choice of the best schools for his son's education. He dreams of a status of middle-class Americans. He would be making his father's dream come true. In short, possessing wealth is not inherently wrong or immoral. The poor does not have a monopoly on morality. As Walter knows, money is not the root of evil; it is what evil people do with it that leads to immorality.

Walter realizes that it requires a great deal of money to live the kind of life his family deserves. The conflicting world views between Lena and Walter are about the meaning of freedom and their efforts to attain it. The freedom that Lena seeks is freedom from racism and discrimination or the unfinished business of slavery. Walter seeks a much more important kind of freedom, that is, economic freedom. Walter recognizes the power of money as the source of both social and political freedom in America. He knows that money is the best remedy for the evils of racism, discrimination, and poverty. And with this kind of freedom, only one can realize the American dream. Walter's dream remains not only because of defects in the American system but also because of the lack of recognition of his responsibility. The defect in his character that affects his dream is his flaw in judgment. A greater flaw would be his lack of knowledge of how a business is run. At the same time, Walter fails to see the potential value of education. Therefore, he fails to attain his goals.

Walter Lee's desire for money and position revolves around wanting to give Travis a strong image of his father. Walter dreams of multiplying 10,000 dollars into a sum that will buy a home complete with a gardener and education at one of the great schools in America for his son. He does not want money just for its own sake, but as a means of acquiring education, decent housing, and human dignity. He also wants money and social position so that he can give Ruth the leisure time, peace, clothes, and jewelry that she has never had. The insurance money represents to Walter a piece of the materialistic American dream. Racism leads whites to attempt to buy the blacks' freedom. Walter seeks enough material resources to improve his family's economic situation and to improve his son with a future. He embraces materialism and power. He seeks merely a transfer of power and not a change in the systems of power. His dream is somehow unique to black people rather than the archetypal American dream.

The real achievement is a part of the American dream—a house in the suburbs. But the more important part of the dream is freedom for the individual, and for the family. The Youngers are indeed a young family. They are beginning to grow spiritually and socially. Each of the Youngers changes during the course of the play. One day someone may hurl a brick through their window, but the Youngers will withstand the attack together. As they begin to take pride in being young, gifted, and black, their neighbors may relent and accord them due respect to all men and women.

At the play's end, Walter and his family are as poor and powerless as they were before. The family members, as the play ends, pack their worn furniture and deferred dreams and prepare to face the threats, fears, and possible violence waiting for them in their new home. The new house provides a "pinch of dignity" (Washington 123) for them. It allows them a bit more breathing and living space, but their lives are essentially unchanged. The personal and familial crises are finally resolved by the open challenge offered by the white world. Karl Lindner is the representative of the white community into which the family had planned to move. He offers to buy the house from them at a profit. The spiritual regeneration of the Younger family is ultimately on a 10,000 dollar check. It is only the money which makes it possible for them to challenge the system under which they have suffered. Money is the necessary prerequisite for their return to dignity and pride. Younger family is struggling to retain human values and integrity. The family is forcing to the change in a society where human worth is measured by the dollar.

Walter's family stands united against the offer on the house made by a white group. Walter tells Karl Lindner that he has decided to move his family into a new home, both for the sake of his son who "makes the sixth generation of our family in this country" and for his father who "earned it" (Hansberry, *A Raisin in the Sun* 138). In making this decision, Walter acknowledges his links not only to his family but also to his race through past, present, and future generations. He identifies with their mutual struggle against racist restrictions. He is moved not by a yearning to live near whites, but by a refusal to let whites spit on his family's face. It reveals both the diversity of the family members and their unity and bravery in standing up to the insult, threats, and violence.

Younger family reaches down for the courage to integrate into a white neighborhood. They represent courage and moral creativity. For white liberals, the Youngers' decision to move becomes the essence of what liberalism stood for during that time. Racial integration was the empowerment of black Americans and the salvation of white America. Robert Nemiroff comments on the play to the higher level of socio-moral analysis:

> For the deepest level it is not a specific situation but the human condition, human aspiration and human relationship—the persistence of dreams, of the bonds and conflicts between men and women, parents and children, old ways and new, and the endless struggle against human oppression, whatever the forms it may take, and for individual fulfillment, recognition, and liberation—that are at the heart of such plays. (qtd. in Cooper 59)

The Youngers are the stuff of life itself. It is a problem play and the problem is blackness in white society. The underlying humanity of the characters and decency of their struggles and in spite of their blackness will prevent them from their dream drying up. Walter and Ruth present the black male and black female conflict in all its painful rawness. As Gerald Weales observes:

> The conflict within the play is between the dreams of the son, Walter Lee, who wants to make a killing in the big world, and the hopes of his mother and his wife, who want to save their small world by transplanting it to an environment in which it might conceivably flourish. (qtd. in Gunton 18)

The play is first and foremost a celebration of black life and black strength through generations of survival and struggle. Walter gains our sympathy by his struggle against the social and economic pressures in a racist society. He sees that the three women in his life have always helped him to bear the burdens of living in a racist white society. They are prepared to be powerful allies to struggle against the latest attempt of restriction.

Hansberry's themes are concerned with unfulfilled faith and the drying up of dreams. Hence, the irony of the title and of the themes is based on an acceptance of the dream: spiritual and material fulfillment in America, and at the same time on a realistic recognition of dreams or hopes that have dried up. African nostalgia has been nurtured by the Youngers' dreams which remain realistically compensated by the facts of their American identity of the dream. The play is mingled with two themes—the ambiguity of the American dream and the integration as the African American's means of realizing the dream. The Younger's deprivations due to poverty expose the gap between the American dream and the African American reality. The dream is defined not only in moral terms—freedom, equality, justice, and self-realization, but also in material and socioeconomic terms.

The Sign in Sidney Brustein's Window

The Sign in Sidney Brustein's Window (1964) is the second and the last of Hansberry plays to be produced during her lifetime. Hansberry dedicates the play to "the committed everywhere" (Bigsby 162). And in doing so, she expresses not only her own personal philosophy of life but also her conception of the purpose of art and the idea of commitment:

> The commitment of which she speaks is one to life rather than death, hope rather than despair and to human potential rather than human failure. Her enemy is thus neither the rich industrialist nor the racial bigot but rather the indifferent and self-deceived. (qtd. in Kanakaraj 45)

At the center of the play is Sidney Brustein—a man who is torn between the torture of not caring and the weight of commitment. The play is more than a philosophical treatise which deals with the solipsism of the intellectual, the need for commitment, the oppression of women, existentialism, patriarchy, political opportunism, betrayal, and the sexual double standard. Hansberry makes a point repeatedly that people must commit themselves to a goal. He, who is committed whether to art, social causes, or another person, is truly a valuable member of society and a person whose deed will help to bring a more humane society in which all may prosper.

The play focuses on Sidney Brustein, a Greenwich Village intellectual who, through his new and struggling newspaper, supports a local politician's campaign. He is so central to the play in fact that he never leaves the stage. Similarly, Sidney is the cultural center of the play. The play sets in a homogeneous culture, but many cultures collide in Greenwich Village. The people who enter Sidney's apartment represent a surprisingly wide variety of backgrounds. The range of ethnic backgrounds is unusual. Sidney himself is Jewish; his wife, Iris, is Greco-Gallic-Indian; his friends and acquaintances include Alton Scales—a cream-colored black; Wally O' Hara—an Irish-American reform politician who needs to be reformed; and Sal Peretti—an Italian-American juvenile Junkie who works for Sidney and who dies of an overdose of American oppression. The range of social background is similarly striking: Iris's sister, Mavis, is a middle class; her another sister, Gloria, is a call girl; Sidney's brother Mammy is a successful businessman; his upstairs neighbor is a struggling, parasitical, homosexual, carefree playwright—David Ragin—and their friend Max is an abstract but rather primitive painter who is not quite sure whether he prefers food or sex.

The range of the characters' cultural attitudes varies as widely as that of their backgrounds. Max insists on art for art's sake. Alton, an ex-communist, retains his belief in the ideals of Marxism. He insists on art exclusively as an instrument of class struggle. Mavis believes that there is too much pain in real life and wants art to offer a peaceful escape. She believes in middle-class values. David strives for an art that presents only the agonizing part of life. He believes in the futility of all activity although he remains actively committed to his writing. David is convinced that prostitutes are the heirs to the wisdom of the ages. Wally urges the need for activist reforms. Gloria, the prostitute, is sacrificed on the altar of business and knows the folly of both views but has no wisdom to offer in their place. Alton loudly proclaims his identification with all the oppressed and his overwhelming sympathy for them. He is filled with a hate for homosexuals and unable to forgive the woman he loves for having allowed herself to be victimized as a prostitute. Iris, vocally tolerant of everybody, offers all sexual abnormalities.

The play deals with the strained conjugal relationship of Sidney with his wife Iris, because he refuses to recognize the reality of the world, but chooses rather to remold it, and her to suit his own personal vision. Sidney has been having a bad time with his wife: "a feather weight who wants to be an actress but is willing to leave him to do television commercials" (Gunton 184). Sidney tends to lapse into a romantic dream of man as an innocent and free spirit suitably removed from the conventional corruption of the city. In this mood, he takes Huck Finn as an archetype of noble dissociation and sees Iris as a mountain nymph. There is a bitter anxiety in Iris's demand to know which role she would play—Margaret Mead or Barbara Allen. Her life is lived as a counterpart to her husband and his sudden and impractical enthusiasms throw an increasing strain on their relationship. The crisis between Sidney and his wife is ultimately a crisis of Sydney's liberalism. Iris rebels against the sterility of life which gravitates around idealistic dreams and simplistic struggles.

Sidney has closed his failed nightclub and has purchased a newspaper. But he is more an intellectual than a businessman. His wife quarrels with him for his failure in business and for "an undefined sexual problem" (Kanakaraj 46). Sidney cares deeply about the sufferings of others and strongly opposes all forms of social and political oppression. He displays concern to the point of meddling daily in the lives of those around him. Sidney compels his wife to distort her character by living up to his fantasy image of her. He is transported by reverie to his imaginary world of the mountains in which he dreams, "the Iris of his mind appears barefooted with flowing hair and mountain dress, and mounts the steps. She embraces him and then … dances in the shadows before him … gives him a final kiss and flees" (Hansberry, *The Sign* 71–72).

Sidney has evolved a fantasy of the pure air of the mountains with only a spiritedly barefooted mountain girl beside him. And he has pressured his wife, Iris, to be that girl. This fantasy is not a full-time refuge for him but a flight for those moments when social and personal strife become too painful. Due to her attraction to Sidney, Iris had originally been contented to play this role for him. When Sidney becomes free with the clear brooks, pines, and mist, Iris quietly tells him that she hates her long hair. Having come from a different environment and considering it boring, she has gradually become dissatisfied with his fantasy about her and strives to make him aware of the true urbane-loving personality. The strain between his fantasy and her reality finally drives her to leave him. Sydney's chauvinistic fantasies drive Iris away from him, because she increasingly feels the need to live in accordance with her recognition of her inner realities and drives. Only at the play's end, when Sidney seems more able to face reality in general and the reality of women in particular, Iris is willing to return to him.

Iris is the primary woman in Sydney's life. Despite his progressive outlook on society, Sidney's views on women are nearly degraded. He demeans Iris's attempts at intellectual discourse and reinforces a girl-child image, complete with flowing hair and idyllic ignorance. When Iris begins to rebel against this image by cutting off her long hair, Sidney is shocked. In an attempt to gain some independent status and to compensate for her failures as an actress, she settles for television commercials whose products make unjustifiable claims. However, Iris's desire for the banner of stardom does not blind her to the truth about the progressive politician whom Sidney is supporting. She realizes that Sidney is a stooge of the political bosses who have always fostered drug traffic and other criminal activities in the area. She notices that Sidney, with all his erudite intellectuality, has not seen through a cheap politician.

When Iris tells Sidney that she is going to a party, his high spirits are quickly grounded. He forces her to tell him that the theater acquaintance Ben Asch will also be a guest. Sidney suspects that Ben is her lover. Iris concedes that she is "the world's lousiest actress," but says, "I just want something to happen in my life" (Hansberry, *The Sign* 72). When Iris leaves, Sidney is depressed and calls upstairs for David to come up. Sidney asks David to write Iris a part in his next play. Sidney is offering to write David a good review in payment for creating a part for Iris. In Sidney, Iris indeed found a thinker. But he lacks the empathy and compassion to understand her desire to become an actress, to escape her rural background, "to know that when I die more than ten or a hundred people will know the difference. I want to make it, Sid" (Hansberry, *The Sign* 78). Until the end of the play, Sidney sees Iris as an unspoiled mountain girl, an adolescent beauty. He realizes that he has caused immeasurable damage by upholding a false concept of woman. He also realizes that he must free himself from all such concepts and see his wife as an individual if their marriage is to be preserved. And he finds that his wife wishes to be an ally in this struggle.

For Iris Parodous, creativity and sexuality mingle in a state of arrested development. Her acting is obviously in an embryonic form. She is attractive, dense, and graceful, but she has not studied her craft seriously. David describes one of her performances as horrible. The play implies that Iris will pass through the stages of Golden Girl and mountain lass and mature as both an actress and a woman.

Gloria Parodous could only metaphorically be considered an artist. She has sensitivity and compassion associated with the artist. She loves and is loved by Alton. Her sexuality is distorted, almost schizophrenic. She endures sex, sometimes sadistic sex, for money. So, she longs for the warmth of Alton's love. She has made her fortune as the model of the bright American girl. Despite his intermittent emotional torture, David is a committed and fulfilled being who gives more than he takes. Gloria's name has vague religious overtones which may suggest her essential innocence. At the same time, she may have been named for Gloria Morous, Gloria Swanson. She appears sexual with medium-length blonde hair. She is the high-priced prostitute who wants rich men. She takes this shortcut to success by becoming a prostitute. At the age of nineteen, she had come to the city from the country and had become a high-fashion whore. Iris says. "I happen to have a sister who is a fancy call girl, a big-time, high-fashion whore …. She's racking up thousands of tax-free dollars a year and it's her life so—" (Hansberry, *The Sign* 50–51). She has accepted the need for a compromise that "if you want to survive you've got to swing the way the world swings" (Hansberry, *The Sign* 138).

Gloria had the fantasy that she could leave her milk-lined, sordid profession, by marrying Alton, a young black man. After seven years and three attempted suicides, she sees a chance to save herself. Alton proposes her and she decides to accept it. When Alton discovers that she is a call girl, however, his own racial past combines with physical disgust. Gloria becomes for him a commodity which has been used by white men. In revulsion against this past, he sacrifices compassion to pride, "I don't want white man's leavings, Sidney. I couldn't marry her" (Hansberry, *The Sign* 102). Sidney underlines the racial nature of Alton's failure. His concession is equally an admission of the futility of an intellectual commitment unsupported by emotional engagement.

Gloria's guilt causes her to try suicide four times. She has accepted her father's deathbed proclamation. She chooses Alton as the groom, who is attractive, intelligent, and compassionate. She perhaps could have prevented Alton's rejection of her, if she had told him the truth before he learned it from someone else. She had given up her business and planned to lead a new life. But she felt she could not escape her past. As a call girl recruited for her innocence, Gloria has been paid to let men make her part of their distorted sexual fantasies. She has suffered such mental and physical abuse that she begins taking drugs to escape. After being severely beaten by one of her clients, she decides to break free from the life by marrying Alton. When Alton has been told about her profession, he is so disgusted by the destruction of his idealized conception of her that he is unwilling even to talk to her.

Turning with shock from this, she is approached by another of Sidney's friends—David. He wants her to aid him in a perverted sexual fantasy. She deliberately takes an overdose of drugs. After learning from a note that Alton will not marry her, Gloria begins drinking and taking pills. After much drinking and singing, she plants a long-wet kiss on David's mouth. As Sidney lies drunk and self-absorbed on the couch, she goes into the bathroom and kills herself. Gloria's suicide is a form of non-commitment to herself. She is the most tragic victim of the oppression of women. For her, there is no new beginning at least not in this life. She had become trapped in a role that her world made attractive, a role that she continued to accept and to which she became addicted. Her end is inevitable self-destruction. Hansberry places in the hands of Gloria the true education of Sidney and reveals the varied permutations of women's victimization.

Gloria is failed not only by Alton but equally by Sidney, Iris, and Mavis as well. When Mavis hears of the proposed marriage she is horrified. While aware of the therapeutic value to her sister, the idea of miscegenation seems worse to her than prostitution. Even though she has quit prostitution, she feels branded for life. David tells her, "Trying to live with your father's values can kill you ..." to which Gloria replies, "No, sweetie, living without your father's values can kill you" (Hansberry, *The Sign* 132). David is convinced that prostitutes are the heirs to the wisdom of the ages. Gloria knows the folly of both views but has no wisdom to offer in their place. Though Alton proclaimed his identification with all the oppressed and his overwhelming sympathy for them, he is unable to forgive the woman he loves for having allowed herself to be victimized as a prostitute.

The racial issue is a minor theme of the play, because 1964 is certainly a time of racial turmoil. The play basically reflects harmony and acceptance between blacks and whites, Jews and Christians, and people of varied backgrounds. Representative of the middle class, Mavis is not a hopeless racist. Iris and Sidney tell her of Gloria's engagement to Alton in a taunting insensitive manner. Then she becomes more accepting of Sidney's Jewish heritage. She will eventually understand Alton's blackness and David's sexuality. Being set in Greenwich Village, the forerunner of social and artistic growth, the play signals a society conscious of rich ethnic backgrounds but free of racial strife.

Alton Scales epitomizes black identity and pride. When Iris playfully accuses him of being a "white boy playing black boy," he replies, "I am black boy. I didn't make up the game, and as long as a lot of people think there is something wrong with the fact that I am a Negro. I am going to make a point out of being one" (Hansberry, *The Sign* 41). For this reason, he has no choice but to reject Gloria after he learns of her tawdry past. Alton declares that he would have forgiven Gloria, if she were a black. Hansberry illuminates, "Alton ... could not consciously have known the day before that he would have made such an assessment of the woman he loved" (Cheney 82). The hour for the plain dignity of the black man had arrived and prevented his taking white man's leftovers. He could not transplant his decision. He himself is guilty of racism when he admits that he could accept and forgive a past of prostitution if the woman he loved were black. Likewise, Gloria bitterly condemns Alton when she declares that other prostitutes deliberately sleep with black men, because these men cannot look down on them. She is, however, speaking of the man, she loved and who rejected her only minutes before. Their love was a causality of the white man's oppression of the black—a history which Alton could not forgive.

Alton has many admirable and sympathetic traits. As a black, he could pass light for white but he chooses to remain true to his heritage no matter what the cost. He is also a compassionate person who becomes deeply moved by the death of a junkie—a former communist who left the party because he considers the Russian suppression of the Hungarian freedom fighters a barbarity. Where Alton differs from Sidney is in the degree to which right and wrong, the sympathetic and unsympathetic, are entangled in his most important act and his rejection of Gloria for having been a prostitute. His father's pride would hurt by having to accept the white man's leavings to survive. The racial pride makes him want to identify fully with his fellow blacks and their struggles. However, his view of Gloria as another piece of the white man's leaving must be rejected for the sake of racial pride. It not only displays a racial attitude, but is also an unsympathetic and narrow-minded act. He loses sight of Gloria as the individual; he loves and regards her only as a fallen woman. He is being no less insensitive toward Gloria.

The case of Alton involves an even more complex intertwining of virtues and vices than Sidney, because he demonstrates that it is possible for a member of an ethnic minority simultaneously to be a victim of racism and to act as racist. Alton explains to Sidney why he cannot marry Gloria now that he knows that she has been a prostitute. Alton recalls his father's humiliation at being forced to accept all the thrown away. His mother brought home stolen things from the house of the white family for whom she worked as a maid. He tells his friend and near brother-in-law that he cannot accept white man's leavings.

Sidney can understand the pain inflicted on Alton and his father by a racist and oppressive society. He also knows the pain that Alton is about to inflict on Gloria. When Sidney asks what Alton would do "if she was a black woman" and Alton makes no reply, Sidney asserts that "that's racism, Alt" (Hansberry, *The Sign* 102). Alton acknowledges the truth of the statement. It is clear that Alton behaves much less justly and humanely than he himself would wish. He might not have been able to bring himself to marry a black woman who had been a prostitute. At least he would have talked to her, not dismissed her without a hearing. Even though he is aware of this failure, he cannot or will not alter his behavior. Alton represents the agony of the time, the depth of the world that racism has inflicted.

Sidney knows that forced relationships between ethnic groups can be vicious and humiliating, as in the case of white plantation owners and black slaves. As Alton laments bitterly "I got this color from my grandmother being used as commodity, man. The buying and the selling in this country began with me" (Hansberry, *The Sign* 101). However, Sidney also knows that voluntary contact between members of different groups may be highly fruitful. Hansberry's involvement with the plight of the black is incorporated in a more general concern here. The human failure is evidenced in the hardening of prejudice in racial matters. It becomes for her indicative of a more fundamental failure which underlies the unpredictable enthusiasm of Sidney and the disaffiliation of Iris. The commitment which Hansberry urges is a devotion to the humanity which goes beyond a desire for political and moral freedom. All the characters in the play fail in this commitment.

All the three Parodous sisters are in psychic problem. Gloria continues to accept clients who are sometimes cruel and violent. When she arrives at the Brustein apartment, she is badly injured. The analyst helps her make the break from prostitution, but he does not steel her against the world. Mavis began analysis five years before, when Iris married Sidney and Fred began his affair. The analyst no doubt helped her cope, but her life is depressingly asexual, segmented, and hollow. Iris talks more about her doctor than her sisters but comments about treatment become a satire on psychiatrists.

Iris exchanges the terms such as love–hate obsession, mother complex, and unconscious versus subconscious motivation. Sidney never opposes the fact that the terms have no real meaning to her. They are only jargon, a substitute for facing real problems.

The Parodous sisters enjoy a close relationship. They are also close to each other in age: Gloria is twenty-six, Iris is twenty-nine, and Mavis is in her early thirties. Hansberry delineates each character in terms of names and physical appearance. Iris's name suggests a flower of delicacy, beauty, and femininity. Mavis's name lacks imagination. Mavis was the name of a very sweet popular chocolate soft drink of the time. It was also the brand name of a cheap scented talcum powder. Gloria's name has vague religious overtones which may suggest her essential innocence. Iris, with her lonely flowing dark hair, may be considered the most sexual. Hair is an ageless symbol of fertility. Gloria with medium-length blonde hair appears sexual, but hers is cold often twisted sexuality. Mavis's short sculptured red hair denies sexuality. She is the only sister with children. Iris's blue jeans style suggests a free spirit. Mavis's simple elegant clothes reflect the control she imposes on her life.

Iris resents the dresses Mavis buys for her, but she wears one to a party where she hopes to make contacts for an acting job. Iris pretends a tolerant attitude about Gloria's misadventure. She begs Sidney not to tell Alton the truth so that Gloria may start a new life. Mavis genuinely tries to understand the ideas of Iris and her village friends. Perhaps Gloria had lived to marry Alton; Mavis could have accepted his blackness. At first, seeing Fred who has a touch of the poet, Mavis was happy before they were married. Fred drove forty miles to see her and then drove forty miles back home in a battered car.

After their marriage, Fred became steady and ordinary. Their sexual appeal for each other faded and Fred took a mistress. Mavis is still grateful that he married her: "there was no rush at home to marry Mavis Parodous" (Hansberry, *The Sign* 109). So, Mavis is trapped. "I take care of my boys. I shop and I worry about my sisters, it's a life" (Hansberry, *The Sign* 111). She lacks a sense of self-worth. Mavis is portrayed as a bourgeois matron. She is the stereotype of the uptight gentile whose racial prejudice and provincialism come through in the simplest of conversations. Sidney and his friends enjoy many laughs at her expense. Yet it is Mavis who teaches him about courage. She has lived with the secret that her husband has supported a young mistress and illegitimate son for years.

Thus, the play is a life study of modern man and woman caught up in the conflict between not caring and caring too much. Family relationship, racism, conflict between individuals, and between man and society are the themes of the drama. To these themes, Hansberry added many contemporary issues like marriage, homosexuality, prostitution, politics, psychoanalysis, abstract art, and absurdist plays which have increased the complexity of the play.

Les Blancs

Hansberry's play, *Les Blancs*, explores the African quest for freedom from European colonialists. It deals with the apathetic struggle of black protagonist, Tshembe Matoseh, against the colonial powers exploiting his country, Zatembe. He craves to end the injustices in Africa, not to destroy the black race. The play makes a strong statement about race by highlighting the intersectional connection of colonialism, racism, sexism, and patriarchy. Hansberry attacks colonialism by portraying the colonial powers that seized control over African lands and people. Joy L. Abell writes,

> Hansberry studied African history and read about uprisings in Kenya and other African nations before beginning *Les Blancs* to create a work that is obviously a well-informed examination of events in Africa. However, despite the play's inherent Africanness, readers must remember that it was written by an African American for an American audience. In this context, it is possible to view the play both as a condemnation of colonialism in Africa and, on another level, as a commentary on race relations in early 1960s America. (459)

The play is set in the fictitious African nation Zatembe, resembling Kenya of the mid-1950s, when the natives of the land took up arms against the white settlers. It investigates the bloody Mau Mau Revolution in Kenya during the 1940s led by Kikuyus with Jomo Kenyatta against the British and other European nations. Kenyatta was a powerful leader dedicated to peace and reconciliation. It is the first major work by an African American playwright to focus on Africa and the struggle for African liberation. Philip Uko Effiong says:

> In recreating an African colonial scene in *Les Blancs*, Hansberry advances the need for dialogue between the oppressed and the oppressor, yet she insists on action and commitment, supports the procurement of sovereignty at any cost, and visualizes the genesis of a new black world. The play does not resolve any problem but raises thought-provoking questions about history, Africa, America, anger, and confrontation; it shows that people are largely a fusion of evil and good, valor and fear, conviction and confusion, indifference and involvement. Hansberry argues for humanism even as she directs her themes through a predominantly African historical and socio-artistic experience. (273)

The action of the play takes place in two places: home of Tshembe's father where his half-brother Eric lives and the Mission compound, a hospital. The black and white characters delineate the features of colonial rule. Madame Neilson, the white blind wife of the Reverend Neilson, is a missionary woman who, along with her husband, has spent forty years in Zatembe. She believes in the intended unification of Africa and Europe. Charles Morris, in his late forties, is a white liberal who is more concerned with European interests. He has come to write the story of Reverend Neilson, who founded the Mission forty years earlier to provide the Africans with spiritual and medical aid.

Major Rice, in his fifties, is a white colonial officer who fights the black rebellions. He blusters against the rebellious blacks because the whites were being butchered in their beds. He represents the European military breaking in Africa. The medical doctors Marta Gotterling and Willy Dekoven are missionaries who restore to health no more than they exploit. Among the blacks, Tshembe's brother Abioseh is a Roman Catholic priest who has sold out to European principles. Eric, his mixed-race half-brother, externalizes the clash between Europe and Africa. Peter, a servant in the day and warrior at night, portrays the rebellious trickster.

Tshembe Matoseh is a handsome young African who has returned to his homeland to attend his father's funeral from abroad, leaving behind his European wife and son. His father was a leading nationalist who called for African participation in the local government of Zatembe. Tshembe is confronted with a black woman's spirit which is a symbol of African freedom. She demands him to liberate his country from grave injustices by the white rulers. He has no doubt about the truth of what the spirit of a woman tells him about his country. He is not sure whether his great duty is to this woman warrior or to his white wife and their son that he left in England. With her urgent prompting, he recalls not only the seizure of his people's land but also the ruthless cutting away of the legitimate power of his father, Abioseh Matoseh. The position of his father was so weakened that he could not openly seek remedy for the rape of his wife by white colonialist, major George Rice. Tshembe is outraged by a sexual act involving his mother. But he knows that she bore no guilt of it, because she has been forced by Major Rice. As a result of this, she loses her life while giving birth to Eric. He equates her rape with the rape of his country both at the hands of European invaders.

The woman spirit then insists upon the duty Tshembe shares with his brothers, Abioseh and Eric, and furthers the underground resistance movement that their father began. He encounters the ongoing rebellion but refuses to take a part in it. He is caught up in his country's struggle to overthrow the white colonialists after many years of peaceful efforts to obtain freedom. His people appeal to him to lead the violent struggle. Throughout the play, he is in dilemma whether to join in the native efforts or to take sides with the colonialists. He is torn between two conflicting desires. Steven Carter says:

> Tshembe is a black Hamlet torn between staying with the Ophelia like European wife who offers him security, love, children, comfortable nights in front of the telly and a way of living within society as it is presently constituted, or heeding the spirit of a black woman warrior who reminds him of the injustices inflicted on his father and his people and who challenges him to be his "father's son" and pick-up the spear of purifying change. (85–86)

Tshembe is in two minds throughout the play. He finally resolves the crisis of his mind when he is no longer to withhold himself from the strong urge of his heritage. He immediately identifies himself with the struggle of the people of his race. His journey is from confusion to clarity, because he has taken the decision after due consideration and reason. Tshembe strongly advocates the cause of freedom of Africa, at the same time he passionately wants to go back to Europe to be with his family. He dreams of feeding the pigeons in Hyde Park, of watching the television with his wife, and playing with his infant son. Having traveled more than a thousand miles to see his dying father, he has no desire to become involved in Africa's problems. This confusion in the mind of Tshembe is evident in his discussion with Charlie, a white American Journalist. He says,

> I should not have come. [Smiling with his own thoughts] My wife is European, Mr. Morris […] a marvelous girl. We have a son now. I've named him Abioseh after my father and John after hers. And all this time I have, mainly, been thinking of all I longed to be in a dim little flat off Langley Square, watching the telly with my family […]. (Hansberry, *Les Blancs* 79)

Hansberry provides a metaphor from African lore, Modingo, the wise hyena, who lived between the lands of the elephants and the hyenas. Modingo was asked by the hyenas, the earliest inhabitants of the Jungle, to settle their territorial quarrel with the elephants who demand more space because of their size. Modingo means "One Who Thinks Carefully Before He Acts" (Hansberry *Les Blancs* 95). Modingo understands the arguments offered by both and refuses to join either side until he has thought over the matter. While he thinks, the hyenas wait too long. Meanwhile, the elephants move in and drive the hyenas from the jungle altogether. It was such a bitter joke that was played upon them while they reasoned. Peter in a speech urges Tshembe to dedicate himself to his country:

> Men have forgotten the tale of Modingo, the wise hyena who lived between the lands of the elephants and the hyenas [...]. A friend of both, Modingo understood each side of their quarrel. The elephants said they needed more space because of their size, and the hyenas because they had been first in that part of the jungle and were accustomed to running free. When the hyenas called on Modingo, he thought and thought, seeing justice on each side. The hyenas sat and waited while Modingo continued to think. Knowing of the hyenas' stillness, the elephants gathered their herds, moved at once—and drove the hyenas from the jungle. Now the hyena laughs his terrible laugh at this bitter joke—the product of reason and caution. (Hansberry, *Les Blancs* 95)

Peter equates the elephant with the white man occupying the land. The hyena is associated with the noble black man. And of course, Tshembe becomes Modingo, the wise hyena. The hyenas symbolize the black man and the elephant with its usurping strength the white man. The hyena urges Tshembe to forego his own desires, to dedicate himself to African cause. Ntali [Peter], one of the African insurgents, explains matters to Tshembe in an effort to engage him in their struggle. The story of Modingo is retold in vain by Ntali to Tshembe to persuade him to join the tribal council as one of its leaders. Tshembe expresses his unwillingness to kill men, especially harmless missionaries and their wives. Still, Peter goes with hope in Tshembe as he says, "Tshembe Matoseh, the Wanderer—who has come home with the white man's tongue … [Searching his eyes] I hope you do not have his heart …" (Hansberry, *Les Blancs* 97). Tshembe has the white man's tongue but his heart is still African.

Modingo wishes to settle the dispute by reason. Tshembe hopes to solve the problems of his people with petitions, delegations, and discussions. But that time for the peaceful discussions has passed. Like the hyena, the black man was first on the land and was used to running free. When the white man, like the elephant, gathers his herds or armies, the hyenas must revolt or be destroyed. Robert Nemiroff rightly observes:

> It is unclear whether Hansberry knew the mythic origins and significance in African folklore of the elephant and hyena [...]. But whether she did or not, her use of these animals to create, as a metaphor for the conflicts in Les Blancs, a myth of her own about a Hamlet-like hyena and how the species got its "laugh," is an interesting example of how intimately and imaginatively the playwright entered into the culture and psychology of her tribal characters. (Cheney 79)

There is the original sin of the whites who raped, pillaged, and colonized the country. There are years of torture, indignities, and enslavement suffered by the oppressed people of Zatembe. They try to justify their suffering by their acts of brutal murder of white settlers including innocent women and children. Tshembe ruthlessly struggles with the complexity of truth. He delineates the role that race has played in colonialism. He lists the major colonizing powers to demonstrate their acts of oppression in Africa. When Charlie tries to slender down Tshembe's views by accusing him of hating all white men, Tshembe laughs:

> Oh dear God. Why? […]. Why do you all need it so? This absolute longing for ray hatred! I shall be honest with you, Mr. Morris. I do not "hate" all white men—but I desperately wish that I did. It would make everything infinitely easier. But I am afraid that, among other things, I have seen the slums of Liverpool and Dublin and the caves above Naples. I have seen Dachau and Anne Frank's attic in Amsterdam. I have seen too many raw-knuckled Frenchmen coming out of the Metro at dawn and too many hungry Italian children to believe that those who raided Africa for three centuries ever "loved" the white race either. (Hansberry, *Les Blancs* 78)

Charlie is a white liberal reporter. But he does not want to recognize his share in the collective responsibility for a radically defined society. He insists that he is not all white man, but simply Charlie Morris. He wants to have a relationship with Tshembe, but he is unaware that the relationship between a black and a white cannot be simple. Though Charlie is a person, an individual, Tshembe knows that he is all white men. For him, race is unimportant because all men are alike under the skin. Tshembe patiently destroys his generalization of the race. He calls

> Race—racism—is a device. No more. No less. It explains nothing at all […]. It is simply a means. An invention to justify the rule of some men over others […]. I am simply saying that a device is a device, but that it also has consequences: once invented it takes on a life, a reality of its own. So, in one century, men invoke the device of religion to cloak their conquests. In another, race. Now, in both cases you and I may recognize the fraudulence of the device, but the fact remains that a man who has a sword run through him because he refuses to become a Moslem or a Christian—or who is shot in Zatembe or Mississippi because he is black—is suffering the utter reality of the device. And it is pointless to pretend that it doesn't exist—merely because it is a lie. (Hansberry, *Les Blancs* 92)

To lower Morris's sense of superiority, Tshembe compares the experience of natives' in Zatembe with the black experience in America. He demonstrates that the device of racism which is so useful in the subjugation of blacks in a white power structure is hardly unique to Africa. Tshembe swings between the part of him rooted in Africa and the part of him which has set down personal and cultural roots in Europe. The European culture has created more than colonialism. Much of what Europe has done remains immensely valuable to the whole world, including Africa. This appreciation is stated in the play by Tshembe: "Europe—in spite of all her crimes—has been a great and glorious star in the night. Other stars shone before it—and will again with it" (Hansberry, *Les Blancs* 125).

As an intellectual, he hates his history which is enforced itself on him. He demands that his life should be judged in terms of the African liberation movement. But he knows that he cannot stand outside history without harming himself. He exists in the gulf between despair and joy. He refuses leadership in the rebellion, saying quite simply, "there are men in this world ... who see too much to take sides" (Hansberry, *Les Blancs* 95). But he has no choice but to take sides.

The revolutionaries are those who know what must be done. Charlie Morris tries to understand the essence of the earnest white liberal. He sympathizes with the black Africa, but he feels no personal responsibility. He tells Tshembe, as the African smiles ironically at the British helicopters overhead: "I didn't put those things up there! I'm me—Charlie Morris—not the White Man!" (Hansberry, *Les Blancs* 123). Racism blinds Charlie to the real causes of revolution as well as to his own responsibility. From one encounter with Tshembe to the next, he stumbles through the chaos of his ignorance. He means well, but it is too late for goodwill. The wheels of violent revolution have already been set in motion by the very first contact between colonizer and native. Charlie is the white man who shares the collective white guilt of oppressing the black people. Further, he truthfully hopes that change can occur without bloodshed. For all his good intentions, Charlie remains merely a liberal, not a revolutionary. For Hansberry, a revolutionary is someone willing to die for the cause of total African self-rule and freedom. Yet she was a perceptive judge of human behavior and did not limit greatness to blacks.

Dr. Willy DeKoven is a striking example of the white sympathizer. He tells Charlie that Africa saved his life, but he became an alcoholic largely because of the injustice he has seen the white man meted out to the black man. He tells Charlie of Reverend Neilson's patronizing his black African children, and of the European's passive refusal to bring modern health care and education to the African mission. When Dr. DeKoven says, "They will murder us here one day—isn't that so, Tshembe?" (Hansberry, *Les Blancs* 116). He is not speaking in an accusing tone. He is calmly accepting his lot. He is prepared to die so that others will live in freedom.

Madame Neilsen is a European woman who embraces African tradition. She has spent the better part of her life in Zatambe. She has developed affection for both the land and its native people. She is a maternal figure to Tshembe. She was a friend of his mother, Aquah, from whom she learned the pattern of the tribal drums. She considers Zatembe her home and understands that revolution is inevitable. She urges Tshembe to do his part despite the fact that, as a symbol of colonialism in Zatembe, she will be most likely a victim of the revolutionary forces. She is a white sympathizer who loves her husband but sees the destruction he has wreaked on the black African. Her husband believed the white race superior to the black. He allowed Tshembe's mother, Aquah, to die. He called the black Africans his children. To atone for her husband's ignorance, Madame Neilsen consciously risks her life. She urges Tshembe to become committed, to fight for freedom in the land she has come to love: "Our country needs warriors, Tshembe Matoseh, Africa needs warriors" (Hansberry, *Les Blancs* 126).

During this emotionally packed exchange of thoughts with Madame Neilson, Tshembe realizes his duty. He spontaneously says, "I am one man, Madame. Whether

I go or stay. I cannot break open the prison doors for Kumalo. I cannot bring Peter back. I cannot .... [He breaks off] I am lying, Madame. To myself. And to you. I know what I must do ..." (Hansberry, *Les Blancs* 126). Young Abioseh does not die the death of a hero. He is perhaps less aware of the real price of freedom than Charlie Morris. The tragedy of Abioseh's death lies in fratricide: the nation has triumphed over family. Having taken the oath early, Peter dies the death of a martyr. Tshembe becomes a black Hamlet, torn between thought and action. He chose the painful path of action and freedom.

Major Rice considers Zatembe his home, but his connection to the land has not developed through balanced relations with its people. He says, "This is my country, you see. I came here when I was a boy .... Men like myself had the ambition, the energy, and the ability to come here and make this country into something. They had it for centuries and did nothing with it" (Hansberry, *Les Blancs* 71). He claims that Zatembe is his spiritual home, but he enjoys a privileged position. By virtue of the status of a white man, he may claim home anywhere he chooses. Being a European, he believes himself superior to those he rules. This superiority allows him to make a home in the midst of a community filled with people he neither respects nor understands.

Tshembe's youngest brother, Eric, is the product of an unholy European and African union. He is born out of his mother's rape by the white colonizer, Major Rice. His status as a person of mixed European and African heritage creates uncertainty and uneasiness in the play. He identifies with his African heritage due to the rejection in the hands of Europeans. His mother was left to die in childbirth by the man who established the mission, Reverend Neilson. Madame Neilson explains to Tshembe that Eric was the product of an evil act which naturally separates the races. At the same time, Eric finds kindness with DeKoven. But this relationship is destructive one, because DeKoven supplies him alcohol. Eric is the physical embodiment of Tshembe's struggle. Eric must decide which part of himself—the European or the African—he will fight for. Finally, Eric announces that he is joining the revolution.

Lorraine Hansberry and her characters reveal that a sense of history is vital for an understanding of the present and the future. Until forced into the violence of the Mau Mau Revolt, the Kikuyu people were basically peaceful and democratic. Aware of their rich and varied old African myths, folktales, and religious ceremonies, even the sophisticated Tshembe Matoseh dresses himself in traditional clothes for his father's funeral. When Tshembe asks Eric to tell him of their father in his last hours, Eric says, "He was just an old savage who went to his death rubbing lizard powder on his breast ..." (Hansberry, *Les Blancs* 57).

In African religions, the lizard symbolizes the messenger who brings news from God that men should die. Generally, the lizard was overtaken by another messenger— usually the slow chameleon—who brought news of resurrection and immortality. Having traveled more than a thousand miles to see his dying father, Tshembe has no desire to become involved in Africa's problems. The woman appears reminding him of his heritage and urges him to fight for his people.

In the African myth, the hyena represents God's means of showing his intentions. In the play, the hyena urges Tshembe to give up his own desires and to dedicate himself to the African cause. When the woman appears a second time, Tshembe is stricken by her power, beauty, and sensuality. She circles in symbolic movements of life, the slaughter and enslavement. She becomes the "sleeping lioness" (Hansberry, *Les Blancs* 81). In African myth, the lion symbolizes the punishment and protection of God in his most terrifying form. As the woman joins the lion, they become archetypes of the initiation rite of man's coming into maturity. The sensuous woman signifies sexual initiation. The lion represents either the blessing or condemnation of God. For Tshembe, initiation and capture of God (the lion) are modernized.

Hansberry not only uses African myths to suggest the idea of rites of passage, but she employs old folktales to heighten the drama of the revolution. Tshembe must commit himself to the Kiwis, to Africa, to freedom. He must decide to lead the revolutionary forces. He is initially reluctant to embrace violence for change. He informs the spirit that haunts him, "I HAVE RENOUNCED ALL SPEARS" (Hansberry, *Les Blancs* 81). He places his hopes for peace on his former guide, Amos Kumalo. Kumalo's attempt to negotiate with the Europeans ends in his arrest and imprisonment. Tshembe quits himself to the fact that violence is the only means of communication their oppressors have left open to the revolutionaries of Zatembe.

In *Les Blancs*, Hansberry suggests the strong bond between the Kiwi and nature— the basis of African religions. Preparing for his father's funeral, Tshembe dresses in traditional clothing and paints his face with yellow orange, rituals. He is willing to enact these rituals out of respect for the traditions of his father and condemns Abioseh for abandoning them. Abioseh rejects the religion of his father to work his way into the power structure he believes will ultimately rule the country. He assumes the European involvement in Zatembe is inevitable as the inclusion of native Africans in the government. He says to Tshembe, "The West will compromise because they must …. And then, my brother [Tshembe], it will be our time! Black men will sit beside the settlers. Black magistrates, black ministers, black officers!" (Hansberry, *Les Blancs* 110). Tshembe is doubtful of what he sees as his brother's simplicity. He accuses Abioseh of selling his soul to the enemy, becoming a member of a "cult … which kept watch fires of our oppressors for three centuries" (Hansberry, *Les Blancs* 61–62).

Tshembe is a well-educated man; old Abioseh was courageous in presenting the petition to Reverend Neilson; Peter plays the role of submissive servant, but he is actually Ntali; Ngago wears a modern khaki dress. But none of these men have forgotten African myth and religion: the source from which they extract their strength to fight for their lives and their country. Even young Abioseh believed that he must get rid himself of his past to embrace Christianity. He says to Madame Neilson just before his death: "What a marvelous light. How beautiful this day has been. How I wish you could have seen the sunset …. Do you remember the stories you used to tell us to explain the sunset? … that the sun was eaten by a giant who rose out of the ocean" (Hansberry, *Les Blancs* 127–28).

In the play, Dr. Amos Kumalo who resembles Jomo Kenyatta is a crucial touchstone to the black and white Africans. Kumalo, mentioned at many critical stages in the play, has a different meaning for each character. Charlie Morris worships him as the "The man of peace" (Hansberry, *Les Blancs* 90). While Major Rice dismisses him as a savage who is a "half-demented darky prophet" (Hansberry, *Les Blancs* 101). To Peter (Ntali), Kumalo is a British puppet, who will merely trade with white overseers for black. Madame Neilsen criticizes his arrest, but Willy Dekoven implies that Kumalo is no longer "the Great White Hope" (Hansberry, *Les Blancs* 112). Tshembe alternately sees Kumalo as a "scholar, a patriot, a dreamer and a crazy old man" (Hansberry, *Les Blancs* 75).

In short, there are two Kenyattas in the play: Kumalo, the returned expatriate, and Tshembe Matoseh, who seeks a peaceful resolution to the conflict. So, he convinces a resistance leader, Ntali, to halt his attack on a respected nonviolent African leader, Amos Kumalo. He asks Ntali to talk to the colonial government about a peaceful solution. But he finally recognizes and welcomes revolution as Africa's only hope. He finally determines that armed resistance is only the way to end the exploitation and degradation of the black people. He finds that the first person he must kill is his own treacherous brother, Abioseh, who betrays Ntali to Major Rice. His brother, Abioseh, has converted to the Catholic priesthood. He disapproves the native effort and betrays one of the leaders to the local police.

Tshembe realizes that he must kill his brother for his own safety and for the success of the movement. Tshembe's decision of killing his brother illustrates the level of sacrifice which was needed for the change. It demonstrates his profound commitment to the idea of liberation of Zatembe. However, he shoots a bullet into Abioseh that attracts the attention of government forces. Toward the end of the play, Tshembe acts for which he is ordained. The stage direction describes:

> As ABIOSEH turns back to him, TSHEMBE takes out the pistol he has been concealing in his robe and considers it, not so much seeking courage as thoughtfully, then levels it. For a moment the two brothers stand facing each other, aware of all the universal implications of the act, the one pulls the trigger, the other fails, and with a last effort at control TSHEMBE crosses to the body, kneels and gently closes ABIOSEH's eyes. (Hansberry, *Les Blancs* 128)

Reverend Neilsen has been killed by the resistance fighters. Tshembe is leading the revolution. He becomes one of Hansberry's celebrated revolutionaries. He believes that the true authority in a country belongs to the people of that country. He takes part in the efforts to oust the European invaders. The successful effort will settle the central issue of the rightful ownership of the land in Zatembe for him and his people. Thus, colonialism and racism are linked together by suffering and humiliation of centuries, and this experience unifies all black sensibilities.

The moment comes when Tshembe must embrace his destiny and fight the historical intruders. The decision is loaded with pain because he must begin by murdering his own brother who has turned conspirator. So, he sets off the attack which kills the gentle white woman, his surrogate mother, who has nurtured him from his birth. As the play ends, a hyena-like crying laughter breaks forth from Tshembe. Throughout the play, Tshembe understands the complexities of his ability to see both sides and to love genuinely across color lines is at war with his native history. His mind is tied to the spirit of Africa. A woman dancer constantly calls him to action, back to the struggle of his people. Just as Modingo wishes to settle the dispute by reason, Tshembe very much hopes to solve the problems of his people with petitions, delegations, and discussion.

The Drinking Gourd

The Drinking Gourd is a three-act play about American plantation slavery. Edward Farrison says, "It is a compact yet comprehensive, authentic, and vivid portrayal of the 'peculiar institution,' correctly called the sum of all villainies, as it was especially in the cotton kingdom on the eve of the Civil War" (qtd. in Gunton 191). The institution of slavery was at its height in the southern states of the United States, while northern states abolished slavery during the latter half of the nineteenth century. The African Americans were living the life of servitude under the control of white masters due to the racial slavery. They were working either in the houses as maidservants or on the plantations. The white masters committed innumerable atrocities on them. They were not allowed to obtain education and to accumulate any property. The way to freedom for them was to march to the northern states by paying money to the white masters. Being incapable of purchasing their freedom, the only ray of hope for their freedom was to escape by running away secretly to the north. Margaret Wilkerson exactly observed that:

> *The Drinking Gourd* is an incisive analysis and indictment of American slavery as a self-perpetuating system based on the exploitation of cheap labor. More than an historical piece, this provocative work identifies the slave system as the basis for the country's economic philosophy and later capitalistic development; it dramatizes the devastating psychological and physical impact of the slave institution on both master and slave. (11)

The Drinking Gourd of the title is the Big Dipper. For a slave in the south, it pointed to the north, the way to freedom. Bertie Powell writes that:

> *The Drinking Gourd* portrays American plantation slavery which [...] characterizes a phase of the black experience. The title was taken from a spiritual, "Follow the Drinking Gourd," linked with the Underground Railroad and derived from the slave metaphor for the Big Dipper which points to North Star. (Gunton 193)

This North Star was considered the beacon to freedom for the many enslaved blacks attempting to escape to the north in the night. *The Drinking Gourd*, set in the 1850s, is about the racial slavery in America. Through the play, Hansberry puts on her views on the cultivation of cotton and tobacco, the hours that slaves spent on the plantations, and erosion of the fertile southern land. The play exhibits the conflicting sections of South America—planters, slaves, and poor whites. Robert Nemiroff, in his "A Critical Background to *The Collected Last Plays*," puts forth:

> What interested her [Lorraine Hansberry] in "The Drinking Gourd" was the dissection of personality in interaction with society. Not personality viewed in the abstract, as some universal, unchanging human nature; but as human nature manifesting itself under the impact of a particular society, set of conditions, and way of life. Her object was not to pose black against white, to create black heroes and white villains; but to locate the sources of human behavior, of both heroism and villainy, within the slave society. (151–52).

Hannibal, the main character, is a slave about nineteen years old who is thinking about running away to the north. At the opening of the play, he is playing the banjo. Tommy, the ten-year-old son of Hiram Sweet, his master, is forcefully keeping time by clapping his hands to the beat of the music. At the long coastline, the stark figure of a thoughtful American having side whiskers, longish hair, and a military uniform emerges. He is the narrator who turns to the sea and speaks:

> This is the Atlantic Ocean [...]. Over there, somewhere is Europe. And over there, down that way, I guess, is Africa [...]. And all of this, for thousands and thousands of miles in all directions, is the New World [...]. And this, this is soil. Southern Soil [...]. And that is Cotton seed. Europe, Africa, the New World and Cotton. They have all gotten mixed up together to make the trouble [...]. You see, this seed and earth—[...] only have meaning—Potency—if you add a third force. That third force is labor. (Hansberry, *The Drinking Gourd* 714)

At the beginning of the play, the narrator explains that the cotton seed and the earth only have power with force of labor—slaves. The labor is so economical that a white master could work a black man to death and buy another more cheaply that treats the first one humanely. He adds, "Labor so plentiful that, for a while, it might be cheaper to work a man to death and by another one than to work the first one less harshly" (Hansberry, *The Drinking Gourd* 715). In white Manor house, slaves agonizingly sing the song: "Steal away to Jesus, steal away, steal away home, —I ain't got long to stay here" (Hansberry, *The Drinking Gourd* 715).

Rissa, the slave cook, is busy serving small portion of food onto the plates of the waiting slave. Sarah, a slave girl of nineteen, holds out her plate while she stoops to play with Joshua, a slave child of seven or eight. He, clutching his grandmother (Rissa), is tired of Sarah's romantic interest in his uncle Hannibal. When Sarah informs Rissa that Hannibal was away from the fields that afternoon, she softly asks if the driver Coffin who is also a slave but corrupted by the tool of slavery system knows it. Sarah replies: "Coffin knows everything. Say he going to tell Master Sweet first thing in the morning" (Hansberry, *The Drinking Gourd* 716).

Hannibal is a representative of a large number of slaves willing to pay any price to obtain freedom. He attempts to satisfy his aspiration by obtaining education and by preparing to escape to the north like his brother Isaiah. He knows that the labor demanded from him on the plantation is not for his benefit but for the benefit of his white master. Rissa tells him that she planned for him a position as a servant in the Big House where he can get decent food, nice things to wear, and learn nice manners. He views that being a servant in the Big House is no less degrading than working on the plantation. He absolutely denied bending to the will of the white master. He does not want to accept the position in his master's house as a servant. He tells his mother, "And ever since I could talk I done told you I ain't never gon' be no house servant, no matter what! To no master. I ain't, Mama, I ain't" (Hansberry, *The Drinking Gourd* 728). He copes with the worst kind of indecency and violation of human rights in the house of white master. He refuses to accept the enslavement in the house of his white master. He screamingly says, "I don't want Master Everett's red jacket and don't want Master Sweet's scraps. I don't want nothin' in this whole world but to get off this plantation!" (Hansberry, *The Drinking Gourd* 728).

Hannibal is a black man who is internally wounded by the black slavery system. He insists to be treated as a human being by the white master. On the plantations, he works only to make the Sweets feel bitter. He refuses to accept slavery and tells his mother:

> And I tell you like I tell Coffin—I am the only kind of slave I could stand to be—a bad one! Every day that come and hour that pass that I got sense to make a half step do for a whole; every day that I can pretend sickness 'stead of health: to be stupid, 'stead of smart, lazy' Stead of quick—I aims [sic] to do it. And the more pain it give your Master and the more it cost him—the more Hannibal be a man! (Hansberry, *The Drinking Gourd* 728)

He wishes to struggle against his exploitation and advance his knowledge of the world. He resists the brutal restrictions placed on his ambitions by the slavery. He confronts Everett Sweet, his master's elder son. Consequently, Everett put out his eyes. After having been blinded, his readiness to run away from the plantation clearly shows the potency of his determination and continuing desire for freedom. He has carefully analyzed every aspect of slavery. He has taken education which is a pathway from slavery to freedom. His mother initially blessed God that her son can read the words of the scripture. He tells his mother that the ability to read "ain't no miracle …. It took me a long time and hard work, but I learned" (Hansberry, *The Drinking Gourd* 729). This statement implies that he does not allow his mind to be enslaved to religious thinking.

He knows that his labor is being stolen from him for his master's benefit, not for him. Moreover, he has deliberately adopted a strategy of sabotaging his master's stealing by laziness, tool breakage, and disobedience. His strength is seen when he firmly asserts that slavery system is an inhumane institution which treats black slaves as movable property. In planning his escape, he finds himself "savoring the notion" that "Whatever you hear Marster say 'bout slavery—you believe the opposite. There ain't nothin' hurt slave Marster so much … as when his property walk away from him. Guess that's the worst blow of all. Way I look at it, every slave ought to run off 'fore he die" (Hansberry, *The Drinking Gourd* 718). He is extremely aware of every step he takes and its risks. He knows well what could happen if he is found studying with Tommy. He feels that literacy (education) is worth any price. After being blinded, he still feels that it is worth attempting to escape.

Hannibal's thoughtfulness and imagination extend beyond his analysis of slavery. The composition he writes for Tommy about drinking gourd is perhaps the best example of his poetic, probing approach to life:

> When I was a boy I first come to notice […] the Drinking Gourd. I thought […] it was the most beautiful thing in the heavens. I do not know why—but when a man lie on his back and see the stars there is something that can happen to a man inside that be […] bigger than whatever a man is […]. Something that makes every man feel like king Jesus on his milk white horse racing through the world telling me to stand up in the glory which is called—freedom. (Hansberry, *The Drinking Gourd* 731)

This composition is clearly the work of a thoughtful person. His concept of something happening inside a man is bigger than whatever a man is. This commencement represents a remarkable attempt to enlarge his understanding by expressing a difficult thought almost beyond his grasp. The image of King Jesus on the horse racing through the world is the personification of freedom. Hannibal's learning of reading is a means of gaining an enlarged view of the world. It signifies that he is the best-educated character after the narrator in the play.

Hiram Sweet, a white master of a plantation, is not certainly an evil man, but the system of slavery has given him the illusion of splendor. The Sweet plantation is a tiny kingdom complete with slaves. He has conformed to the highest standards and ideals of slave ownership. He has built up a comfortable life for himself on the basis of forced labor. He sends his elder son to the finest schools in the United States and Europe. On the contrary, his slaves are forbidden to learn to read and write. His family is clothed in fine garments in the latest fashion. But his field slaves wear coarse clothing and house slaves get cast off. For Hiram, his plantation is sweet. He continually recalls everyone how he started the kingdom thirty-five years earlier, "with four slaves and fifty dollars … I planted the first seed myself and supervised my own baling …. I made this one of the finest … not one of the biggest, plantations in this district" (Hansberry, *The Drinking Gourd* 720). He is proud that his hard work and ambition made him the highest in his society.

Rissa clarifies to Hannibal that Hiram is indeed a kind master. He did not trouble much his slaves and hardly put the whip on the slave. However, she also pointed out that Hiram only forces the slaves to work for nine and half hours in the field instead of twelve to fourteen hours. Some planters force their slaves to work for eighteen to twenty hours during harvest time. He loses money, because he applies relatively human policies that do not produce enough to compete with larger, less liberal plantation owners. He takes care of the slaves when they are too old to work. Some masters set old slaves free when they are useless on the plantation. Unlike other masters, he does not force black slave women to have sex with him. Moreover, Rissa seems more comfortable with Hiram. She helped him to start his plantation thirty-five years ago. In addition to this, Hiram knows all of his slaves personally and shows genuine concern about their welfare.

Another aspect of human nature is seen in Hiram's idea of manhood that involves violence, power, and family tradition. His most treasured possession, gun as an old weapon, he kept in perfect condition. He tells Rissa, "My father gave me this gun and I remember feeling, I was fourteen, I remember feeling, I'm a man now. A true man. I shall go into the wilderness and not seek my fortune—but make it!" (Hansberry, *The Drinking Gourd* 723). Hiram has confirmed the highest standards and ideals of slave ownership. He has built a comfortable life for himself on the basis of forced labor. He demands immense respect from everyone. His slaves receive respect from no one including him. His ego has been so inflated by all the power at his command that he can say and believe. In an angry tone justifying a special favor, he is granting Rissa's son Hannibal, he says to his wife:

> I am master of this plantation and every soul on it. I am master of those fields out there and I am master of this house as well […]. There are some men born into this world who make their own destiny. Men who do not tolerate the rules of other men or other forces […]. I have asked no man's permission for the life. I have lived […]. (Hansberry, *The Drinking Gourd* 723)

Slavery was a business in the United States in which human beings were bought and sold like cattle. Hannibal's brother Isaiah ran off because his master, Hiram, sold his wife, the mother of his son Joshua. Sarah says to Hannibal that you "seem like your brother just went out his head when Marster sold Joshua's mother" (Hansberry, *The Drinking Gourd* 717). Hiram is indirectly involved in Hannibal's blinding and torturing. He supports the prohibition of education for slaves. He knows the dangers of learning among slaves. The enlightened slaves could get information about the outer world. They could become conscious of the abolition movement, the conflict between North and South, the slave agitations and revolts, and the means of keeping slaves under control. The learned slaves can pass messages to conspire for escape, rebel, or massacre their masters. Therefore, the slaves must be prevented at any cost from gaining education. Hannibal's acquisition to read and write certainly offends master Hiram. He had convinced Hiram's younger son Tommy to teach him reading and writing in exchange for lessons on how to play the banjo.

Hiram's elder son, Everett, becomes very angry by knowing Hannibal's ability to read and write. Education for slave is a crime which is committed by Hannibal. He outrages and says:

> You have used your Master's own son to commit a crime against your master [...]. There is only one thing I have ever heard of that was proper for "educated" slave [...]. When a part is corrupted by disease—one cuts out the disease. The ability to read in a slave is a disease—. (Hansberry, *The Drinking Gourd* 732)

Therefore, he ordered Zeb, the poor white overseer, to blind Hannibal by putting out his eyes, because as long as he can see, he can read. Hannibal's eyes are gouged out by Everett because he discovered that Hannibal has learned to read and write. He fears that Hannibal will use his literacy to set other slaves free. Though the body of Hannibal is wounded, his spirit is not still broken. With the help of his mother, he plans to escape with Sarah and his nephew. He does not lose his positive sense of his purpose to be free. He walks out wounded to his community to set them free. He takes life's wound and keeps walking toward freedom. The character of Hannibal embodies the black sprit in America which walks for survival with freedom.

Rissa is an old slave woman and mother of Hannibal who has restricted and shortened her ambitions. She has no hope of gaining freedom or a tolerable life for herself. Her sole aspiration is to get her son Hannibal out of the fields where he has a dangerous clash with the driver Coffin. She aspires to see her son as a servant in the house, because in the house, he would be safe, better fed, and better clothed. To do this, she takes advantage of every opportunity to remind Hiram that she was one of the slaves who helped him to establish the plantations. She is a strong woman who helped Hiram to make the plantation a success. She is a patient, long-suffering, devoted, heroic, and loving black mother.

Rissa epitomizes the evolving black woman who moves from mammy to militant. She is subservient and protective of her master Hiram, until he allows her son to be physically maimed. She ignores the needs of her family and caters faithfully to her master. She possesses these virtues, but she is not forgiving. When Hiram's son, Everett, blinds and tortures her son, she neither pardons him for not preventing this cruelty nor places his welfare above that of Hannibal's. When dying, Hiram goes to Rissa's cabin in the slave quarter where she is caring for her blind son. She courageously reprimands her master, when he comes to console her. He tells her that he did not order to gouge the eyes of her son. He tries to defend himself by saying that "I—I wanted to tell you, Rissa—I wanted to tell you and ask believe me, that I had nothing to do with this. I—some things do seem to be out of the power of my hands after all …. Other men's rules are a part of my life …" (Hansberry, *The Drinking Gourd* 734). Rissa is angered and embittered with Hiram. She sweeps away his defense by asserting, "Why, ain't you Marsters? How can a man be marster of some men and not at all of others—…" (Hansberry, *The Drinking Gourd* 734).

She turns away from him and continues tending to her son. Hiram leaves the cabin as a defeated master. Being weak from his illness, he falls into the dirt outside Rissa's cabin. When he lies dying outside her cabin, she does not go for his support. Ignoring his cries for help, Rissa closes the door on him as he dies near her doorstep. She evolves into an extremely independent and assertive woman when her family is threatened. As stage directions state:

> He cries out for help and one by one the lights of the cabins go out and doors close. He moves crawls a little on the grass, trying to get back to Rissa's cabin. Inside, we see her at the table again, preparing another cloth for Hannibal. She lifts her eyes and looks out of the window to see the figure of the man she can distinctly hear crying for help. She lowers her lids without expression and wrings the cloth and returns to Hannibal's bedside and places it over his eyes and sits back in her chair with her hands folded in her lap. She starts to rock back and forth as Hiram's cries completely cease. (Hansberry, *The Drinking Gourd* 734)

Hiram's death symbolizes the sad demise of the institution of slavery. The end of the play represents that the insidious effects of slavery would be far-reaching. Hansberry argues that America will continue to pay a high price for the adoption of a slave economy. In the final lines of the play, the Soldier says:

> Slavery is beginning to cost this nation a lot. It has become a drag on the great industrial nation we are determined to become. It lags a full century behind the great American notion of one strong federal union which our eighteenth-century founders knew was the only way we could eventually become one of the powerful nations of this world. And, now, in the nineteenth century, we are determined to hold on to that dream […]. And so—we must fight. There is no alternative. It is possible that slavery might destroy itself—but it is more possible that it would destroy these United States first. That it would cost us our political and economic future […]. It has already cost us, as a nation, too much of our soul. (Hansberry, *The Drinking Gourd* 309–10)

Thus, Rissa seems to take revenge on him. By the end of the play, she removes Hiram's cherished gun from the cupboard and goes out through the kitchen. She takes Joshua by the hand and together they go to Hannibal's clearing where Sarah and the blind Hannibal stand patiently ready to travel. She gives Sarah the gun, embraces her, and watches the three young people disappear into the woods.

The most vigorous strength in the life of Rissa is her love for her children and grandchildren. In the beginning of the play, she fears about Hannibal's security for which she pushes him into accepting the position of a house servant, because this job will protect him from being killed on the plantation while escaping. She is convinced that her elder son Isaiah has been killed while escaping. Consequently, she is terrified that similar fate waits for Hannibal. But by the end, she learns that in slavery system, there is no security for the slave either on plantation or in the house of white master. However, she plans the escape of her son Hannibal and grandson, Joshua, in accompany of Sarah. She stays back to avoid the realization of whites about the escape of her children. She is a perfect black mother who tries to save and protect her children from being killed in the hands of white masters and overseers.

Maria Sweet is a powerless white woman like so many women in American society. She also aspires to be equal to her husband Hiram and son Everett. But she can only fulfill her drive for power through a man, because she is unable to exercise power directly. Indirectly she directs her husband into doing what she wants. She is a patient wife who always tries to maintain peace in the discussion between husband and son. She helps Hiram to maintain his self-image as a man of strength. She warns her son, Everett, so many times, not to be rude to his father. But in a severe heart attack of Hiram, due to his inability to control his plantation, she advises her son to take over the control of the plantation. She says to Everett:

> You must take over the running of the plantation—no [...] listen to me, and you must make him believe you have done no such thing. Every night, if necessary, you must sit with pencil and pad and let him tell you everything he wishes. And then—well, do as you please. You will be master then. But he will think that he is still, which is terribly important. (Hansberry, *The Drinking Gourd* 724).

Sarah, the young black girl, seems very simple but recognizes the evils of slavery. At the play's beginning, she is afraid of what might happen to Hannibal as a result of his inattentiveness on the plantation, constantly challenging the authority of the driver Coffin, and leaving the plantation without permission as well as beholding running off. When Hannibal says her, "That's the Big Dipper, Sarah, The Drinking Gourd pointin' straight to the North star!" She replies, "Everybody knows that's the Big Dipper and you better hush your mouth for sure now, boy. Trees on this plantation got more ears than leaves" (Hansberry, *The Drinking Gourd* 717).

Sarah, as a slave, is remarkable for her growth from a timid girl to a fearless woman. She was terrified at the thought of escaping, even of making the slightest gesture of disobedience in front of whites. At the end of the play, she holds a gun in hand and leads the blind Hannibal and Joshua to freedom. The reason for this change is her strong love and affection for Hannibal. When Everett puts out Hannibal's eyes, she is horrified. This horror changes her to help Hannibal to get away. The small boy, Joshua, will add more difficulties to an impossible task of escaping with blind Hannibal. But her love for Hannibal makes her heroic. They together show a collective strength for survival.

Thus, there are three distinct classes of people in the maintenance of slavery: the white master, the poor whites, and the black slaves. The play focuses on the painful and troublesome journey of African Americans from slavery to freedom. The play deals with the problems and concerns of the lives of the black slaves and their question of liberation.

What Use Are Flowers?

Hansberry has been alarmed and outraged during her youth by World War II and the dropping of the atom bomb on Hiroshima. She, however, became committed to the cause of world peace. Once, when an interviewer inquired about her dreams for future, Hansberry responded, "I would like very much to live in a world where some of the more monumental problems could at least be solved. I'm thinking, of course, of peace. That's part of my dream that we don't fight. Nobody fights. We get rid of all the little bombs—and the big bombs" (Carter 49).

In spite of her considerable effort on behalf of world peace through the post-atomic war play, Hansberry was not totally opposed to violence. She believed firmly in the justice of some wars such as in the right and necessity of revolution in history, the wars of national liberation, self-defense of the people against their oppressors, and the armed struggle against fascism. She asserts:

> Blacks must concern themselves with every single means of struggle: legal, illegal, passive, active, violent and non-violent […]. They must harass, debate, petition, give money to court struggles, sit-in, lie-down, strike, boycott, sing hymns, pray on steps—and shoot from their windows when the racists come cruising through their communities. (qtd. in Carter 49)

She believed most of all in humanism because she contended that one should not equalize the oppressed with the oppressor. She was convinced that the oppressed were reacting to intolerable conditions. Such conditions were imposed by the oppressor and therefore the primary guilt or injustice lay with the oppressor. She warned white racists not to rely on the supposed passivity, endurance, and infinite forbearing of black people. She knew that her fellow blacks could act inhumanly too. They could respond to ferocity with viciousness. Then the whites would have to blame themselves for their own suffering and that of their children.

In the play, all the characters are children except one. The children are rescued once by a woman teacher. They are redeemed five years later by an elderly, moral, and ethical man, the Hermit, a former college professor, who elects to spend his final days with a group of rowdy children for no clearly visible reason. For that, teaching may have driven him into solitude. He does not seem fully convincing as a leader who, virtually overnight, can transform wild children from eaters of raw flesh to singers of Beethoven. The Hermit strips bare the children's savage defenses to find innate goodness, beauty, and love. After twenty years of seclusion, the Hermit has discovered perfect sweetness in the midst of the crowd of children. He instills the children with humanity and independence. The play is basically about the atomic holocaust and the Hermit's restoration of humanity to the wild children who are not able to laugh or speak. The Hermit decides to civilize the children and chooses those aspects of civilization worthy of repeating and necessary to their spiritual and intellectual growth.

The play, set on a vast rocky plain of a great forest, begins with mystery. The Hermit, an old bearded man dressed in tattered clothes and animal skins, walks with a stick and carries his possession in a bundle. He encounters several savage children who puzzle him because he expects them to act like civilized children. The children are no more than ten years old, all naked with long hair. They are totally silent as they follow a small animal. When their rock falls on the animal, they rush crying to tear into the raw flesh. The Hermit awakes to this melee and is confused especially by the savage young girl. He screams that they are animals. They are astonished by this voice and sudden appearance. One boy picks up a rock, while the other children make efforts to fight. The Hermit scolds them for their lack of manners. He then asks for directions to the city—unaware of the atomic holocaust.

The mystery is eventually clarified that a nuclear war has destroyed all human life except for the Hermit and this small body of children who have been left alone for quite some time. The Hermit turned his back on humanity twenty years earlier because of his disgust at its folly and violence. He is shocked to find himself the sole representative of this detested civilization. Therefore, he is the only person who can teach its values to the children. Subsequently, he decides to become their teacher. He is achingly aware of both the irony of his situation and the probable futility of the effort. In spite of his teachings and the apparent progress of his pupils, every time a child reverts to violence. The Hermit attempts to ensure the continuance not merely of the human race itself, but also of some basic traits of culture.

The Hermit gives the children vocational training in ceramics and pottery. Of all the children, Charlie is the first to grasp more abstract concepts—work and use. All the children are clothed in leaves or animal skins, but only Lily still wears long hair. The children's clothes and groomed hair signify their return to civilized society. A strict but loving teacher, the Hermit, threatens to beat them if they do not speed up their lessons. Now, as pupils of the humanities, the children try to understand the concept of beauty. The Hermit responds to their questions: "*What Use Are Flowers?* ... Ah, but the uses of flowers are infinite! One may smell them—one may touch their petals and feel heaven—or one may write quite charming verses about them" (Hansberry, *What Use Are Flowers?* 106–7).

The Hermit sings a verse of Greensleeves which makes the children laugh. Charlie comes to his aid with a primitive flute, which he has made to surprise the other children. Surprise is another concept the Hermit has taught them. The children sit in silence and refuse to join in. But the music itself, not the pleading of the Hermit, finally induces them to sing along. In the darkness, Charlie's flute haltingly plays the first notes of Beethoven's Ninth, the ennobling choral. Lily beats a great clay drum, as the Hermit conducts Charlie and the singers:

> Joy, thou source of light immortal! ...
> Daughter of Elysium! ...
> Touched with fire, to the portal

Of thy radiant shrine we come.
Thy pure magic frees all others
Held in custom's rigid rings;
Men thought the world are brothers
In the haven of thy wing. ...
(Hansberry, *What Use Are Flowers?* 119–20)

The Hermit's most intense despair comes when his prize Pupil, Charlie, has a fit of jealousy. Another boy, Thomas, is praised for rediscovering the wheel shortly before his death. He even complains of being tormented in his last hours by the children, whom he regards as unteachable. In the last action of the play, Charlie leaves the dead Hermit and joins the crowd of children surrounding Thomas, who is patiently reconstructing the wheel that Charlie had broken. This act simultaneously implies that Charlie has gained some understanding and self-control as a result of the Hermit's lessons and affection.

Hansberry develops both plot and characterization on a somewhat more basic level than in her other plays. In a letter quoted by Nemiroff in *A Critical Background*, Hansberry described how her plot centers on the efforts of the Hermit to teach the last remaining children "his knowledge of the remnants of civilization which once ... he had renounced." And she concludes: "He does not entirely succeed and we are left at the end, hopefully, with one appreciation of the fact of the cumulative processes which created modern man and his greatness and how we ought not to go around blowing it up" (Carter 147).

Here the key phrase is the cumulative process which applies to the creation of both characters and cultures. When the Hermit finds the children, they are neither blank slates nor noble savages. They were prelingual creatures whose only survival skills are their physical strength and capacity for violence. The Hermit teaches them language, vocational skills, and the humanities. He is demonstrating the agonizingly slow and difficult process of developing the most fundamental tools of civilization. The frequent interruption of his humanizing lessons by jealousy and violence reveals how delicate these tools have been throughout history. These fragile tools still are there, especially considering humanity's greatly increased potential for destruction through nuclear warfare.

Another significant aspect of the drama is Hansberry's views on reason, beauty, and truth. Hansberry defends all of these qualities because she knew that unless their value was asserted, they might indeed become inadequate or illusory. Hansberry assumes that there was "no prior arrangement of life on this planet" and "the reason for survival does not exist in nature" (qtd. in Carter 148). She further affirms:

> I wish to live because life has within it that which is good, that which is beautiful and that which is love. Therefore, since I have known all of these things, I have found them to be reason enough and—I wish others to live. Moreover, because this is so, I wish others to live for generations, and generations and generations. (qtd. in Carter 148)

To this, she might have appended reason and truth because she also defended them in the play.

Her defense of beauty is the most explicit, although she also defended the other qualities strongly. After the Hermit has given the children a base of practical skills, he announces that they "are ready to graduate to an area of knowledge which, sadly enough, used to be known as the humanities" (Hansberry, *What Use Are Flowers?* 116), and begins this decision with a presentation about beauty. By doing so, he clearly places beauty on a higher level than the practical. While introducing them to music as an example of beauty, he tells them that "it will be perhaps the most satisfying thing I shall ever be able to teach you" (Hansberry, *What Use Are Flowers?* 117). At the Hermit's prompting, Charlie plays "Greensleeves" on a "crude but competent flute …. The children's faces reflect the miracle" (Hansberry, *What Use Are Flowers?* 118).

The Hermit is unable to supply an answer when asked what is music. Perhaps he might be considering the answer self-evident or finding it too difficult to explain to the children. It is clear that he regards music as an important source of joy and consolation that provides a large part of life's value and helps to sustain human beings. It confirms the link between joy and beauty. It also implies that an appreciation of beauty may provide humans with the best foundation for constructing a sense of community. The other examples of beauty that the Hermit cites are those of the girl, Lily. She is more beautiful than the flower for which she is named, the flowers whose petals one may touch and feel heaven. And when the children will become proficient in language, no power on earth will be able to stop them from composing charming verses.

Goodness is less easily defined than beauty. But it appears in the play, especially in the form of willingness to sacrifice for the continuance of human race and the ability to control one's capacity for violence. Toward the end, the Hermit admits to his prize pupil, Charlie: "I've not tried to weigh you down with a lot of moral teachings; for one thing there hasn't been time. And so much of what I would have tried to tell you about all of that would have been absurd and obstructive and you will get into your own habits in time about that" (Hansberry, *What Use Are Flowers?* 129).

However, he goes on to praise the woman who brought the children to this remote area to try to ensure the survival of the human race. She then returned to the area of danger to get others but was doubtless caught in the next atomic blast and did not return. Her example leads the Hermit to proclaim that: "The notion … that this particular unpremeditated, experiment of the cosmos which was the human race—well that it ought to go on. It was defiant notion, and only something as fine, as arrogant as man could have dreamed of triumph over this reckless universe" (Hansberry, *What Use Are Flowers?* 128).

The Hermit has given the facts of the annihilation of humanity. His words praising the virtue of aiding the survival of humankind seem appropriate and wise. However, he cautions about the need to be flexible about morality. He urges Charlie to make sure that Lily, the only female among the children, always gets enough to eat. It does not matter how great a shortage might confront them and how much damage might be done to the other male children by this decision. He admits, "Yes, I know, I taught you to share; but you can't have permanent rules about things. The only rules that count are those which will let the race … continue" (Hansberry, *What Use Are Flowers?* 126).

The other form of goodness is holding back one's impulses toward violent aggression. Violence among adults brings humanity to the brink of destruction. Violence among children could finish the joy. The impulse to violence is overwhelmingly powerful within everyone, including the Hermit. As he confesses to Charlie:

> I am nothing more and nothing less than a bundle of mortality, an old package of passions and prejudices, of frightful fears and evasions and reasonings and a conscience. And deep in my heart, I long for immortality as much as you do already without even understanding it. We all did—and cursed one another for it! And renounced one another for it! That is why I went into the woods, you see. I was outraged with mankind because it was as imperfect, as garrulous, as cruel as I. (Hansberry, *What Use Are Flowers?* 126–27)

The Hermit's speech points toward one of the primary sources of violence. The longing for personal immortality even at the expense of everyone else especially is coupled with anger at the sight of one's own imperfections mirrored in others. These imperfections imply the folly of expecting personal immortality. In renouncing humanity, therefore, he really renounces himself, the self which is formed in relation to others. The Hermit values the continuation of the human race enough to devote his last remaining time and effort to tutor the only children left. He places a higher value on himself when he storms off into the wood years earlier. His scratchy awareness of his failings in knowledge and character is balanced by his realization of how much he has to offer the savage and ignorant children.

Hansberry's defense of love at times seems more equivocal than her defense of beauty and goodness. This may be partly the result of the Hermit's inability to deal honestly with any topic related to sex. He wants to warn Charlie about the problems almost certain to arise in having only one female among so many males. He also warns Charlie about the need to protect her to make sure that the human race continues. The Hermit cannot explain this in detail because of his deep inhibitions about discussing sex with young people. He seems almost as inhibited about expressing feelings of affection. However, the Hermit acknowledges the example of the great, self-sacrificing love of the woman who brought the children to the remote area. He knows that sexual love will be necessary to enable humanity to survive. He also feels love for the children, especially Charlie, but finds it hard to speak of. Moreover, the Hermit knows and appreciates the love that Charlie and others have for him. As he approaches death, he tells Charlie:

> The truth of it is that you really are going to miss me [...]. All of you. You will discover an abstraction that we never got to because there wasn't time, affection. And, for some of you, something worse than that even [...] some of you—you for instance, because we have been closest—will feel it; it will make you feel as if you are being wrenched apart. It is caused "grief" and it is born of love. (Hansberry, *What Use Are Flowers?* 125)

Thus, even in the Hermit's eyes, love is one of the things that give life value. It may not always be pleasant or practical. The Hermit demonstrates his love that came for children and stayed with them, even though the times when they disappointed him and he disappointed himself. The play's ending suggests that the potential for total destruction may never be eliminated or even diminished decisively. Humanity's drive to construct is also strong and offers at least some hope for survival, not only of the race but also of the processes leading to civilization.

To sum up, the dramas of Lorraine Hansberry explore the Africans' and the African Americans' social, economic, political, and cultural exploitation, deprivations, anger, history, and segregation during the slavery era and even after the abolition of slavery. She is a classic prototype of the evolution of a tradition that highlights the various branches of racial conflict and largely gloomy heritage in which the black womanhood represents the triple subjugation. Her women characters represent radically different world views and segments of American society.

Works Cited

Abell, Joy L. "African/American: Lorraine Hansberry's Les Blancs and the American Civil Rights Movement." *African American Review* 35. 3. (2001). Print.

Anderson, Mary Louse. "Black Matriarchy: Portrayal of Women in Three Plays." *Black American Literature Forum* 10. 3. Ed. Tasker, Witham W. Terre Haute: Indiana State University, 1976. Print.

Ashley, Leonard R. N. "Lorraine Hansberry and the Great Black Way." *Modern American Drama: The Female Canon*. Ed. Schlueter, June. London and Toronto: Associated University Presses, 1990. Print.

Bigsby, Christopher William Edgar. *Confrontation and Commitment: A Study of Contemporary American Drama 1959–66*. Columbia: University of Missouri Press, 1967. Print.

Burke, Sally. *American Feminist Playwrights: A Critical History*. New York: Twayne Publishers, 1996. Print.

Carter, Steven R. "Commitment amid Complexity: Lorraine Hansberry's Life in Action." *Multi-Ethnic Literature of the United States* 7. 3. Ed. Newman, Katharine. Los Angeles: University of Southern California, Fall 1980. Print.

Carter, Steven R. *Hansberry's Drama: Commitment amid Complexity*. Urbana and Chicago: University of Illinois Press, 1991. Print.

Carter, Steven R. "Images of Men in Lorraine Hansberry's Writing." *Black American Literature Forum* 19. 4 (1985). Print.

Cheney, Anne. *Lorraine Hansberry*. Boston: Twayne Publisher, 1984. Print.

Cooper, David D. "Hansberry's A Raisin in the Sun." *Explicator* 52. 1 (1993). Print.

Effiong, Philip Uko. "History, Myth, and Revolt in Lorraine Hansberry's Les Blancs." *African American Review* 32. 2 (Summer 1998). Print.

Gill, Glenda. "Techniques of Teaching Lorraine Hansberry: Liberation from Boredom." *Black American Literature Forum* 8. 21. Eds. Hedrick, Hannah and John F. Bayliss. Terre Haute: Indiana State University, 1974. Print.

Gunton, Sharon R. *Contemporary Literary Criticism* 17. Detroit: Gale Research Company, 1981. Print.

Hansberry, Lorraine. *A Raisin in the Sun*. New York: Random House, 1959. Print.

———. "A Raisin in the Sun." *Eight American Ethnic Plays*. Eds. Griffith, Francis and Joseph Mersand. New York: Charles Scribner's Sons, 1974. Print.

———. "Les Blancs." *Lorraine Hansberry: The Collected Last Plays*. Ed. Nemiroff, Robert. New York: New American Library, 1983. 37–128. Print.

———. "The Drinking Gourd." *Black Theatre, USA: Forty-Five Plays by Black Americans, 1847–1974*. Ed. Hatch James V. New York: The Free Press, 1974. Print.

———. "The Drinking Gourd." *Les Blancs: The Collected Last Plays of Lorraine Hansberry*. Ed. Nemiroff, Robert. New York: Random House, 1972. Print.

———. *The Sign in Sidney Brustein's Window.* New York: Random House, 1964. Print.

———. "What Use Are Flowers?" *The Best Short Plays.* Ed. Richards, Stanley. Radnor, PA: Chilton Book Company, 1973. Print.

Kanakaraj, S. "The Prophetic Vision of Lorraine Hansberry." *Modern American Literature.* Eds. Mutallik-Desai A. and T. S. Anand. New Delhi: Creative Books, 2002. Print.

Matuz, Roger. *Contemporary Literary Criticism* 62. Detroit, New York, London: Gale Research Inc, 1991. Print.

Shafee, Syed Ali. "Probing the African-American Psyche: A Study of the protagonists of Funnyhouse of a Negro and Les Blancs." *Indian Journal of American Studies* 24. 2. (Summer 1994). Print.

Washington, J. Charles. "A Raisin in the Sun Revisited." *Black American Literature Forum* 22. 1. Ed. Weilxlmann, Joe. Terre Haute: Indiana State University, 1988. Print.

Wilkerson, B. Margaret. "The Sighted Eyes and Feeling Heart of Lorraine Hansberry." *Black American Literature Forum* 17 (Spring 1983). Print.

Chapter Four
SUZAN-LORI PARKS

Life Sketch and Works

Suzan-Lori Parks, the daughter of an Army Colonel, was born in Fort Knox, Kentucky, in 1964. As a member of a military family, Parks moved often, first to West Texas and then to Germany, where she settled during her teenage years. While attending German schools, Parks began to write short stories. When she returned to the United States, she attended Mount Holyoke College, where she studied creative writing with the novelist James Baldwin. Baldwin was the first to encourage her development as a playwright. At the time Parks had the habit of acting out the characters' parts when she read her short stories in class.

Her first play, *The Sinner's Place*, was produced in 1984 in Amherst, Massachusetts. While at Mount Holyoke, Parks was a member of the Phi Beta Kappa honor society and graduated with a Bachelor of Arts degree in 1985. She also studied at the Yale University School of Drama. After college, she traveled to London to write plays and study acting. Her second play, *Betting on the Dust Commander*, was produced in 1987, followed by *Imperceptible Mutabilities in the Third Kingdom*, which won a 1990 Obie Award for Best Off-Broadway play of the year. Her play, *The Death of the Last Black Man in the Whole Entire World* (1990), explores the issues of racism and sexism that have been characteristics of her work from her earliest days as a playwright. These plays, like the others that followed, challenge the conventions of the modern theater as they address social issues such as slavery, gender roles, and poverty.

Parks won her second Obie Award for *Venus* (first produced in 1996), a dramatic account of how, in 1810, a Khoi-San woman was brought from South Africa to England to serve as a sideshow attraction. Her greatest critical acclaim to date arrived with the production of *Topdog/Underdog*, a play she began writing in 1999 and was produced Off Broadway at the Joseph Papp Public Theatre in 2001 under the direction of George C. Wolfe. It is her first play to appear on Broadway, debuted in April 2002 at the Ambassador Theatre, and, shortly, won the 2002 Pulitzer Prize for drama, thereby making Parks the first African American woman to receive that award.

Parks has received numerous awards and honors throughout her career, among them a National Endowment for the Arts Grant, a Rockefeller Foundation grant, the Whiting Writers' Award, a Kennedy Center Fund for New American Plays, and the PEN-Laura Pels Award for Excellence in Playwriting. In addition to the Obie awards and Pulitzer

Prize for drama, Parks has been awarded a Guggenheim fellowship and the prestigious MacArthur Foundation fellowship, commonly known as the Genius Grant.

Since 2000, Parks has directed the Audrey Skirball Kirn's Theatre Projects writing program at the California Institute of the Arts. Her first novel, *Getting Mother's Body*, was published in 2003 with favorable reviews. She has written two screenplays: *Anemone Me* (1990) and *Girl 6* (1996). The film version of *Girl 6* was directed by Spike Lee. She has also written another screenplay *Their Eyes Were Watching God* (2005) based on the novel of the same title by Zola Neale Hurston. Parks is writing *Hoopz*, a stage musical about a person in Harlem who travels regularly to different parts of the countries in the world.

In 2002, Suzan-Lori Parks won a Pulitzer Prize in Drama for her play *Topdog/Underdog* (2001), and her popularity has been on the rise ever since. At the age of forty-five, Parks has already written twelve plays, a novel, and a few screenplays and she is still continuing her writing today. Her work has been staged in the United States and around the world. She is considered to be one of the most innovative dramatists of her generation. Her originality occurs both at the levels of form and content in her plays. She ventures to experiment with traditional narrative styles and conventional plot.

Being well-educated and belonging to a new middle class, she no longer seeks affirmation of the dominant white culture or the approval of a purely African American audience. Instead, she produces a new direction in African American drama. She refuses to define her dramas only in terms of the politics of slavery and racism. However, this does not mean that the notion of race is not intrinsic to her work. But her work is no longer restricted to the African American experience in which African American characters are portrayed as oppressed individuals. Her dramatic works have been both praised and criticized for their ambivalent position toward traditional notions of blackness. In her work, Parks refuses to victimize her African American protagonists. In her essay, *An Equation for Black People Onstage*, Parks writes: "Can a Black person be onstage and be other than oppressed?" to question the way in which African American drama in the past has always been defined as "the presentation of the Black as oppressed" (20–21).

Parks's first history play entitled *Imperceptible Mutabilities in the Third Kingdom* (1986–1989) is her most radical experiment with indeterminacy. The play presents four separate parts, and each part has a distinct group of five characters rather than recurring characters. Once a part is finished, the characters do not appear, although their lines often do, spoken by a subsequent character played by the same actor. A cyclical history is built up over the course of the play through the bodies of five actors, who circulate through all four sections and all twenty roles in the play. Hilton Als calls it "a series of dense scenes about black life from slavery to the present, linked by the metaphor of the natural sciences" (78).

Parks's next full-length play, *Death of the Last Black Man in the Whole Entire World* (1989–1992), is structured as a classical Greek play. It has two main characters: The Black Man with Watermelon and Black Woman with Fried Drumstick. The Black Woman, widow of the last Black Man, tries to bring return her husband. But he is killed again and again—falling off a building and a slave ship, electrocution, hanging, lynching—only to be resurrected again and again. The chorus performs the Last Black Man's burial to remember his service. Alice Rayner and Harry Elam Jr. put in plain words:

> The Chorus exists, because the legacy of the Black Man must be preserved into the future. The other figures of the play, who represent spirits of black people already deceased, prevent him from passing over into their world until the significance of his life and his history is passed on to Black Woman, the only "living" character in the play. Because of this "unfinished business," Black Man exists in a luminal space between the living and the deed. He is dislocated, caught in a continual "Middle Passage." In addition, Black Man with Watermelon's plight reflects the current dislocation, fragmentation, and disillusion that Cornel West terms the "postmodern condition" of contemporary black America. (451)

Parks uses the concept of clothing as a costume in her next play entitled *Devotees in the Garden of Love* (1991). George and Lily both wear wedding gowns, though only George is a bride-to-be. She has not even met the man to whom she is to marry. Lily is not a bride, yet she also wears a gown. Lily educates George to receive her suitor and speak romantically to him. *The America Play* (1990–1993) underscores the importance of her stylistic experiments in the construction of her own African American aesthetics and in the extension of a new African American identity. Ilka Saal asserts, "To read the play as a nostalgic longing for an authentic past and unadulterated black identity means to miss its pun: while *The America Play* is a play about America, it also brazenly *plays with* ideas of America" (qtd. in Dawkins 82).

In *Venus* (1997), Parks commences the task of rearticulating the law which puts the Venus to the status of an exotic subhuman being. Venus is genuinely a decent human being who seeks to make her mark in the world. Harvey Young writes:

> *Venus* centers the story of Saartjie Baartman, the South African woman who was displayed as a freak or oddity in the early nineteenth century throughout England and France. What made her worthy of sustained attention was her ample buttocks and extended genitalia, which differed from the contemporary (black and white) French body. Following her death, Baartman's body was dissected by Dr George Cuvier, who becomes Baron Docteur in Parks's play, bottled, and put on exhibit at the Musee d' Homme but no longer on display. (39)

Her extraordinary new play, *In the Blood* (1999), is about a homeless, illiterate African American woman who self-sufficiently raises her five bastard children. Ed Siegel says,

> In "*In the Blood*", Hester meets with a number of men and women in two hours, each supposedly inhabiting a higher moral universe than that of the illiterate, unemployed young woman, though most of them betray her heedlessly. And each represents an institution—medical, religious, and political—that has abandoned women like Hester in cities all over the country. (3)

Like *In the Blood*, her next play entitled *Fucking A* (2000) has some features of classical tragedy. *Fucking A* portrays a woman named Hester Smith who is rebuked by society for her socially uncanny behavior. Throughout the play, human bodies, particularly those of women and the poor classes, are objectified as pieces of meat. In the play, the battle ground is not on the land, but it is on the human body. Carol Schafer views:

> Like Hawthorne's Hester Pryanne, Hester Smith lives on the fringes of this "kingdom" and wears the letter *A* on her chest. Hester Smith's *A* is branded into her skin, as if her body were that of a domesticated animal. This *A* weeps and stinks when a client approaches. In a capitalistic land whose slogan is "Freedom Aint Free," Hester must work as an abortionist in order to make money to buy her son's freedom. (196)

Her latest play, *Topdog/Underdog* (2001), stages the downfall of two African American brothers in which the notion of theatricality plays an important part. Michael LeMahieu writes that "*Topdog* features two characters; brothers named Lincoln and Booth, whose names prefigure the play's outcome and whose relationship drives its portrayal of "family wounds and healing" (33). In her year-long play, *365 Days/365 Plays* (2006), Parks uses her fullest energy to express her evolving construction of the Great Hole of History. It is a highly referential work to dig and explore the hole of history.

The America Play

The America Play centers on the cultural images in the history of African Americans. Parks asserts that many events in the history of African Americans have been ignored and wiped out from the consciousness of Americans, especially African Americans. It brings awareness of that invisible history into contemporary experience. For Parks, theater is a place for rewriting history. The play explores the effects of ignored experiences of the African Americans from the national history of America which propagates the beliefs, experiences, understandings, and achievements of the natives who are powerful elites. Parks tries, through historical revision, to rewrite a period of history by including the discarded experiences of African Americans. In her essay, *Possession*, she writes,

> The bones tell us what was, is, will be; and because their song is a play—something that through a production actually happens—I'm working theatre like an incubator to create "new" historical events. I'm re-membering and staging historical events which, through their happening on stage, are ripe for inclusion in the canon of history. Theatre is an incubator for the creation of historical events […]. (Parks, *The America Play* 4–5)

She continues to write, "Through each line of the text I'm rewriting the Time Line—creating history where it is and always was but has not yet been divined" (Parks, *The America Play* 5).

In writing *The America Play*, Parks has intention to awaken the contemporary African Americans to the relationship with their racial and cultural history. In her essay, *An Equation for Black People Onstage*, Parks writes,

> We have for so long been an "Oppressed" people, but are Black people only blue? As African-Americans we have a history, a future and a daily reality in which a confrontation with

a white ruling class is a central feature. This reality makes life difficult. This reality often traps us in a singular mode of expression. There are many ways of defining blackness and there are many ways of presenting Blackness onstage. (19)

Here Parks clearly states that the African Americans must see themselves in the light of their own identities as an individual and as a racial community. The African Americans should not identify themselves merely in relationship with the whites. As an author, theater is a means of communicating her vision of African American culture and society.

The America Play centers on the Foundling Father, an African American grave digger, who bears a strong resemblance to Abraham Lincoln. He loves Abraham Lincoln so much that is why he works as Lincoln Impersonator. "There was once a man who was told that he bore a strong resemblance to Abraham Lincoln. He was tall and thinly built just like the Great Man. His legs were the longer part just like the Great Mans legs. His hands and feet were large as the Great Man were large" (Parks, *The America Play* 159). The resemblance of The Lesser Known to the Great Man was profound and very deep but their livelihood was different as:

While the Great Man's livelihood kept him in Small Town. The Great man by trade was a President. The Lesser Known was a Digger by trade. From a family of Diggers. Digged graves. He was known in Small Town to dig his graves quickly and neatly. This brought him a steady business. (Parks, *The America Play* 160)

The play takes place in "A great hole. In the middle of nowhere. The hole is an exact replica of the Great Hole of History" (Parks, *The America Play* 159). The Great Hole of History is the exclusion of African American history from the canon of American history. The Great Hole of History represents all those who were marginalized throughout the American history. Parks criticized the biased history of America and she creates history by filling the Great Hole in History.

The Lesser Known believes that he is the image of Abraham Lincoln, the Great Man. He makes his living dressing up as president Abraham Lincoln and allows people to play the part of John Wilkes Booth to assassinate him for a little fee. He charges his customers a penny to take part in a reenactment of Lincoln's assassination. He claims to be a dead singer for Abraham Lincoln. He insists that he should have been present at the President's funeral. Customers come and pay him as they want to act like John Wilkes Booth. Letitia Guran says:

Before reading *The America Play*, few readers may have considered the relevance of African American's emotional involvement in the Lincoln tragedy and the rather passive role assigned to them by canonical American history in the national conflict of the Civil War, which, for them, had even more dramatic, earth-shattering repercussions than for the majority of American population. Parks strategy of rereading and rewriting this crucial episode of American history consists in selecting the Lincoln assassination scene and repeating it with African American protagonists and actors. (71)

Act first of the play centers around a man named the Foundling Father as Abraham Lincoln. He is fascinated by Abraham Lincoln. He is interested in the last days of Lincoln's life, especially his last show. He is concerned with these moments in the life of Lincoln because he wants to be perfect in his impersonation act. Before becoming the impersonator, he was a grave digger. He is ashamed of his past of grave digging due to which he is Lesser Known and wanted to be someone like the Great Man. He endeavors to get reputation by acting like someone else. He is able to get his job of Impersonating Lincoln because of his strength. He recounts:

> When someone remarked that he played Lincoln so well that he ought to be shot it was as if the Great Mans footsteps had been suddenly revealed: instead of making speeches his act would now consist of a single chair, a rocker, in a dark box. The public was cordially invited to pay a penny, choose from a selection provided pistols enter the darkened box and "Shoot Mr. Lincoln." The Lesser Known became famous overnight. (Parks, *The America Play* 171)

The second act of the play focuses on wife, Lucy, and son, Brazil, of the Foundling Father. They are totally separated from the Foundling Father. They do not see his performance but hear it off stage. When the Foundling Father left them to become the impersonator of Abraham Lincoln, they took up grave digging as the trade. Brazil comments on the livelihood of his father as:

> Digging was his livelihood but fakin was his callin. Ssonly natural heud come out here and combine thuh 2. Back East he was always diggin. He was uh natural. Could dig uh hole for uh body that passed like no one else. Digged em quick and they looked good too. This Hole here—this large one—sshis biggest venture to date. ... Uh exact replica of thuh Great Hole of History! (Parks, *The America Play* 179)

The Foundling Father was very good at digging graves. He dug the graves very quickly and neatly. But he gives up digging the graves to take up the career of an impersonator. He left Lucy and Brazil thirty years ago, so he is almost dead to them. The play, thus, explores the devastated relations in the black family of Lucy and Brazil with the Foundling Father. They go to West to search for the bones of the Foundling Father in the Great hole. Lucy insists her son Brazil to continue to dig for the things that are remarkable and worthy of memory of his father to display in the Hall of Wonders. She hopes to fill the hole where the Foundling Father lived with mementos or traces of his life. The digging is accompanied by shared memories of the departed, engendering a reconfiguration of his life. They can neither fill the holes of his biography nor recover his body. Still, Lucy and Brazil try to gather the little traces they have left of him.

Lucy's memories of Foundling Father as playing the impersonator of Lincoln, his shovel, and his tool as a digger are the most precious possessions. They dig up the trash left by the Foundling Father in the Great Hole. They unearth the objects he left behind one by one. They listen to each object for its echo hoping for a clue to their past:

BRAZIL. This could be his!
LUCY. May well be.

BRAZIL. (Rest) Whadd ya hear?
LUCY. Bits and Pieces.
… … … … … … .
BRAZIL. … Waaaaaahhhhhhhh … ! HUH HEE …
LUCY. There there, Brazil, Don't weep.
BRAZIL. … !−imiss im −WAHH. …!
LUCY. It is an honor to be of his line. He cleared this plot for us.
He was uh … digger. (Parks, *The America Play* 186)

While digging the Great Hole of History, they find an impressive variety of objects such as:

In this area here are several documents: Peace Pacts, writs, bills of sale, treaties, notices, handbills and circulars, freein papers, summonses, declarations of war, addresses, little deeds, obits, long lists of dids. And thuh medals: for bravery and honesty; for trustworthiness and for standing straight; for standing tall; for standing still. For dancing and retreating. For making do. For skills in whittling, for skills in paintin and drawing, for uh knowledge of sewin, of handicrafts and building things, for leather tannin, blacks mithery, lace makin, horseback riding, swimming, croquet and badminton, community service. For cookin and for cleanin. For bowin and scrapin. Uh medal for fakin? Huh. This could uh been his. Zsis his? This is his! This is his!!! (Parks, *The America Play* 185–86)

This inventory brings together the iconic tokens of the Foundling Father. His fame nominates them as representatives of each and every historical period with the forgotten sojourners to the Great Hole of History. The medals were won for heroism in the conduct of humble everyday activities such as standing straight, standing still, and making do.

They search for his bones in the great hole that he excavated before dying. They wanted to find the Foundling Father so that they can bury him. Hence, they are digging in the dirt to search the Lesser Known. The Great Hole of History is filled with a library of frozen memories that resemble forgotten videotapes. They find a television with a recording of Foundling Father which enables him to come back to life for his funeral. Debby Thompson writes:

We are ghosted by a history that won't stay buried. The America play, which has scenes with titles such as 'Archeology' and 'Spadework', continues the project of digging through history not to recover what 'really happened,' but to realize the power of its replications in the present. For us in the present, histories are always already replications. (169)

Lucy is Parks's mouthpiece who digs buried history of African Americans. Verna Foster says, "Through the character of Lucy—who 'digs for the truth, in the 'Great Hole of History'—contradicts the conflation of history and its representation" (qtd. in Dawkins 82). He further argues, "if there is no real history, then there is no point in [her] digging for the truth" (qtd. in Dawkins 82). Lucy and her son Brazil are homeless pilgrims in the Great Hole of History, digging for family memories and a sense of African American heritage. They are deprived of family life by racial slavery and absent husband of Lucy and father of Brazil. They are trapped in a space which strongly smells of loss and nostalgia. They are looking for a cause, for something that is missing in their lives, something to give them meaning and purpose. Brazil laments the loss of his father as:

> He left his family behind. Back East. His Lucy and his child. He waved "Goodbye." Left us tuh carry on. I was only 5. (Rest) My Daddy was uh Digger. Shes whatcha call uh confidence. I did thuh weepin and thuh moanin. (Rest) His lonely death and lack of proper burial is our embarrassment. (Parks, *The America Play* 179)

They wanted to dig up the Foundling Father's bones from the great hole. They reject the performance of mourning in favor of personal and historical loss. The great hole emblematizes the racial memory of generations of African Americans. They confront by digging into past losses. Brazil recounts his skillful enactments of grief to Lucy—at one funeral he "couldn't choose between wailin and gnashin. Weepin sobbin or moanin. Went for gnashin. More to it. …. Like I have never gnashed. I woulda tore at my coat but that's extra" (Parks, *The America Play* 176). He then suddenly erupts into spontaneous cries of sorrow as he and his mother unearth the bits and pieces of the Foundling Father's life. Brazil's genuine mourning is shattering his performer's façade and revealing the agony of a bereft son. The recovered objects provoke Brazil's scream of pain which links his grief to a historical as well as personal past. He spent his whole life digging for evidence that his father existed.

Brazil followed his father's footsteps of greatness which were always behind him. He becomes a professional mourner hired to perform a formal gesture of grieving at funerals. His gnash is a historical gesture of anguish taught to him by his father. He recalls his father teaching him to make a name for himself by conveying false emotions. Brazil does not feel emotions, but rather performs them for personal gain. When his mourning appears very sad, he is paid the better. Brazil says:

> On thuh day he claimed to be the 100th anniversary of the founding of our country the father took the son out into the yard. The father threw himself down in front of the son and bit into the dirt with his teeth. His eyes leaked. "This is how youll make your mark, son" the father said. The son was only 2 then. "this is the wail," the father said. "There's money in it," the father said. The son was only 2 then. Quiet. On what he claimed was the 101st anniversary the father showed the son "the weep" "the sob" and "the moan." How to stand just so what to do with the hands and feet (to capitalize on what we in the business call "the mourning Moment"). Formal stances the Father picked up at the History Hole. The son studied night and day. By candle light. No one could best him. The money came pouring in. On the 102nd anniversary the son was 5 and the Father taught him "the Gnash." (Parks, *The America Play* 182)

Brazil seeks to define himself in terms of the traits and talents he has inherited and learned from his father. His father has also spent his life seeking to define himself through his superficial physical resemblance to the great emancipator. Brazil walks in his father's footsteps by doing the work of digging. The father was digging holes to be used as graves, while the son digs holes to unearth memories to retract artifacts, and to acknowledge the unrecorded lives. The hole is the Lesser Known's [Foundling Father] legacy to Brazil and Lucy. It has become a proper Hall of Wonders where his own personal belongings and ornaments are buried. Brazil says:

> Welcome, welcome, welcome to thuh hall. Of wonnndersss: To our right A Jewel Box made of cherry wood, lined in velvet letters "A. L." carved in gold on thuh lid: the jewels have long escaped. Over here one of Mr. Washingtons bones, right pointer to they say; here is his likeness and here: has wooden teet. Yes, uh top and bottom pair of nibblers [...]. (Parks, *The America Play* 185)

At last, there is the reappearance of the Foundling Father on the stage. He offers an outline of the staging of the assassination of Lincoln. He performs what he calls the centerpiece of the evening. He gives a title "the Death of Lincoln" and offers a ghostly reenactment. A man dressed as Lincoln narrating the death of Lincoln:

> Uh Hehm. The Death of Lincoln!:—The watching of the play, the laughter the smiles of Lincoln and Mary Todd, the slipping of Booth into the Presidential box unseen, the freeing of the slaves, the pulling of the trigger, the bullets piercing above the left ear, the bullets entrance into the great head, the bullets lodging behind the great right eye, the slumping of Lincoln, the leaping onto the stage of Booth, the Screaming of Todd, the screaming of Keene, the shouting of Booth "Thus to the tyrants!" the death of Lincoln!—And the Silence of the nation. (Parks, *The America Play* 188)

Toward the end of the play, Lucy and Brazil go to see the Foundling Father after he performs one last reenactment. He is preparing to go to the great beyond. He is not physically going afterlife in which his consciousness and identity continue after the death of his physical body. He gets up and walks into the coffin where his son parades his dead body around. Lucy and Brazil perform the ritual of the dead body of the Foundling Father. They give him a proper burial by expressing the strong emotions which were previously blocked. Brazil realizes his role as a performer of the ritual. Lucy is also inspired by the rituals of death. She says, "It is an honor to be of his line" (Parks, *The America Play* 186). They lay the Foundling Father to rest by doing a proper burial. They symbolically lay to rest the ancestors who implicitly whisper that their dishonored bones be given a proper burial. The black mourning rites and rituals are commemoration of the dead and a source of solace for the survivors. Karla Halloway rightly observes that "such rites and rituals represent a sustaining force in black culture: Recalling the texts of our death and our dying alongside the stories of African American cultures rallies us against whatever it is that suggests we might 'fly off and leave a body'" (658).

The Great Hole figures racial memory as a wound in black consciousness. The Foundling Father's burial indicates that these wounds can be closed through the healing power of rituals and remembrance. They make a hole beneath the earth to uncover relics of the Foundling Father to ensure his proper burial. In doing proper burial through rituals, they begin a metaphorical journey of remembrance that connects them to a familial and ancestral history. The Foundling Father's rituals of mourning or death rituals enable them to partially resolve their grief. Their resolute loyalty to the Foundling Father underscores their connection to the black ancestral heritage. Despite their long-time separation from the Foundling Father, they maintained strong kinship ties by doing death rituals. They reunite with the spirit of the Foundling Father who abandoned them thirty years ago.

At the end of the play, the Foundling Father reappears as a living ghost. He is put on display as Abraham Lincoln in his coffin. Haike Frank interprets the Foundling Father's reverence for Abraham Lincoln. In his essay, "The Instability of Meaning in Suzan-Lori Parks' *The America Play*," he says, "Parks challenges the preconceived notion of African American population as minors who depend on whites for representation" (10).

Lincoln is memorialized historically as one of the American Foundling Fathers, an icon for democracy. At last, the Foundling Father says a few words from the grave about Lincoln:

> So very lovely to be here the town of—Wonderville has always be a special favorite of mine always has been a very special favorite of mine. Now, I only do thuh greats. Uh hehm: I was born in a log cabin of humble parentage. But I picked up uh few thing. Uh hehm: 4 score and 7 years ago our fathers—ah you [Lucy and Brazil] know thuh rest. Lets see now. Yes. Uh house divided cannot stand! You can fool some of thuh people some of the time! Of thuh people by thuh people and for thuh people! Malice toward none and charity toward all! Ha! The Death of Lincoln! (Parks, *The America Play* 197)

At the end of the play, Lucy narrates the Great Hole where the whole history of African Americans is buried as:

> At the Great Hole where we [Foundling Father and Lucy] honeymooned—son, at the Original Great Hole, you could see thuh whole world without goin too far. You could look in tuh that Hole and see your entire life pass before you. Not your own life but someones life from history, you know, [someone who'd done something of note, got theirselves known somehow, uh President or] somebody who killed somebody important, uh face on uh postal stamp, you know, someone from History. (Parks, *The America Play* 196)

Thus, *The America Play* deals with the suppressed cultural representations of African Americans in the mainstream history of America, because many events in the history of African Americans have been ignored and wiped out from the consciousness of Americans, especially African Americans. The play explores the effects of the ignored experiences of the African Americans from the national history of America which propagates the beliefs, experiences, understandings, and achievements of the natives who are powerful elites in America.

Venus

Venus explores the objectification and degradation of an African woman. Objectification is subordinating a human being to the grade of an object. It is the act of renouncing the humanity of fellow human beings, from any caste, creed, race, class, and nationality.

Martha Nussbaum, an American philosopher, has identified seven features that are involved in the idea of treating a person as an object:

1. Instrumentality: the treatment of a person as a tool for the objectifier's purposes.
2. Denial of autonomy: the treatment of a person as lacking in autonomy and self-determination.
3. Inertness: the treatment of a person as lacking in agency, and perhaps also inactivity.
4. Fungibility: the treatment of a person as interchangeable with other objects.
5. Violability: the treatment of a person as lacking in boundary-integrity.
6. Ownership: the treatment of a person as something that is owned by another can be bought or sold, etc.
7. Denial of subjectivity: the treatment of a person as something whose experiences and feelings (if any) need not be taken into account. (Nussbaum 257)

The humankind having power perceives or treats a person, usually a woman, as an object. It is an act of treating a woman as an animal or a thing. In a patriarchal social system, a woman is treated merely as an object of sexual pleasure. The African woman has dehumanized grades due to the European colonial powers and racial constraints. Her black body is used as a commodity without regard to her dignity. Both African men and women are objectified by the European colonial powers, but African women in comparison to African men are the most common victims of objectification. African women are degraded on the basis of their race, gender, and class. They are identified with their bodies and the standards of their appearance.

The play is based on a black woman with a large posterior from South Africa. Through the depiction of the character of Sartjie Bartman, the play exposes a lamentation for all the suffering of humanity across the world. The play sets in South Africa in the early 1800s, afterward in Europe. Sara Warner says about the play, "The play depicts the life of Sartjie [Sarah] Bartman, a Khoisan woman who was taken from South Africa to Europe in 1810, where she was exhibited as a human curiosity under the appellation 'The Hottentot Venus' until her death in 1816" (181). Lisa Mendelman's opinion about the play is that:

> Beginning and ending the play with Baartman's death, Parks envisions the totality of her experience—from Baartman's early life as a servant in Cape Town to her transformation into the Venus Hottentot to her relationship with the white doctor who fell in love with her, kept her as his mistress, and ultimately dissected her in the interest of his medical reputation. (131)

Venus was, almost nude, put on public display in London and Paris, because she was the main attraction of business for a showman who exhibited her. She was a central model for black women as otherness in the nineteenth century due to her genitalia and the abnormal bump of her buttocks. In Overture to the play, a Chorus member introduces Venus as:

> The gals got bottoms like hot air balloons./Bottoms and bottoms and bottoms pilin up like/like 2 mountain. Magnificent. And endless. An ass to write home about./Well worth the admission price./A spectacle a debacle a priceless prize, thuh filthy slut./Coco Candy colored and dressed all in all natural she likes when people peek and poke. (Parks, *Venus* 7–8)

The above introduction clears that Venus is a black colored woman who put on very little clothes. Her bottoms are so giants that they look like balloons as well as two mountains. She is a very disgusting and the only creature of her kind in the world. In the beginning, she is a poor girl in South Africa who scrubs a vast tile floor in the house of The Man and his Brother. He [the Brother] wanted to take the poor girl [Venus] to England as a black dancer at a freak show, because she is a big bottomed, novel, vigorous, and meticulous girl. He thinks that she will make a splendid freak show. He convinces Venus to make the trip to England. The two South Africans, The Man and The Brother, offered her to go to England and earn money by becoming a dancer.

> THE BROTHER. How would you [Venus] like to go to England? ... A big town. A boat ride away. Where the streets are paved with gold .... Come to England. Dance a little .... Folks watch. Folks clap. Folks pay you gold. We'll split if 50-50 .... Half for me half for you. May I present to you: "The African Dancing Princes!"
> THE GIRL. A princes. Me? .... A princes overnight. ...
> THE BROTHER. 2 yrs of work yd come back rich!
> THE GIRL. Id come back rich!
> THE BROTHER. Yd make a mint! ...
> THE GIRL. I would have a house. I would hire help. I would be rich. Very rich. Big bags of money! .... Do I have a choice? Id like to think on it.
> THE BROTHER. Whats there to think on? Think of it as a vacation! 2 years of work take half the take. Come back here rich. Its settled then. (Parks, *Venus* 15–17)

Venus Hottentot is a poor girl who works as a home servant. She is a slave who obeys every order of her white master. Being a black, poor, woman and a slave, she has also a desire to become rich and own her own house. She also wanted to hire servants in her house. But the colonial powers forbid her to fulfill her innocent desires. In her interview with Kevin J. Wetmore, Suzan-Lori Parks clears her situation about Venus. She says: "At the beginning of the play the Brothers ask Venus if she wants to go away. She's not aware of the subtleties of what they are asking or of the trap that exists for her. But she is, like a most poor people, willing to exchange her labour in order to get out of a poverty-stricken situation" (137).

The Brother and The Man are white males who have ownership over the enslaved girl. The Brother wanted to transport her to England for doing business by engaging her in a freak show. To fulfill his extreme desire, he provokes her by offering various enticements like becoming a princess and a rich woman. He sets an emotional trap in which her innocent mind gets caught. He completely colonizes her mind by putting forth the proposal of the trip to England as a vacation for two years. Jean Young says:

> A close examination of the circumstances connected with Bartman's removal from the Cape and subsequent exhibition raises serious questions regarding what Parks has described as Bartman's complicity in her own exploitation. Further, Parks's portrayal of Saartjie Bartman draws on cultural images and stereotypes commonly used to represent Black woman in demeaning and sexually debased roles, the objectified oppositional "other" measured against a white male "norm." (699–700)

It is the colonizer's mind which uses every trick to make a slave powerless. It proved to be true in regard to Venus who agrees with the proposal of the two brothers in the disguise of vultures who later use her for their own financial advantage. She is thus lured away from her home in South Africa to put on display in England with the promise of making her rich.

She is brought to England and sold to The Mother Showman who is the owner of the Eight Human Wonders that makes the shows to earn money for the Mother Showman. The girl is very happy in England at first. She gives her introduction to the chorus of the Eight Human Wonders as a very well-known exotic dancer in South Africa. She has overconfidence that she will in a short time become reputed in England and become rich very soon. But soon she is disappointed because she could not see golden streets in England. She was kept as a slave in the cage which was a cold and dark place. She feels hungry. The Brother advised her to drink more water. He tells her that he is in love with her for 12 years ago. He confesses to her that he brought her to England to make her love. He sexually exploits her.

THE BROTHER. Remember me? From way back when? About 12 yrs ago?
THE GIRL. You've growd a beard other than that you haven't changed.
THE BROTHER. I wanted you then and I want you now. That's partly why we've come here. So I can love you properly. Not like at home.
THE GIRL. Home? Love? You oughta take me shopping. I need a new dress. I cant be presented to society in this old thing.
THE BROTHER. Tomorrow I'll buy you the town. For now lift up yr skirt. There. Thats good. (Parks, *Venus* 23)

The Brother forces her to lift up her skirt and show her ass to him. He becomes very amorous to fulfill his sexual desires. Thus, in a foreign country first time, she bares her bottoms in very poor circumstances. He sold her to the Mother Showman, a freak show club owner. The Mother Showman humiliates her by saying a filthy girl. She asks the girl to take bath by scrubbing all her body, because she smells. She also asks her to take off every scrap around her woman's parts. She wanted the girl to be clean so that she can present her to the society in England. But the Girl was unaware of the new woman who treats her like a second-grade woman, as an object of show:

THE GIRL. Maam. Who are you. ...
THE MOTHER SHOWMAN. Im yr new boss. Mother-Showman and her 8 Amazing Human Wonders! Yr Number 9.
THE GIRL. Wheres my man? He had a beard.
THE MOTHER SHOWMAN. Him? Girl, he skipped town. Yr lucky I was passing through good God girl, he wasn't lying, you woulda starved to death or worse, been throwd in jail for her indecency. But its alright now, dear. Mother-Showmanll guard yr interests. Yr secrets are safe with me .... (Parks, *Venus* 30)

Venus undergoes her transmission from The Girl into The Venus Hottentot, an identity manipulated by the Mother Showman to emphasize her physique and racial identity. She is now The Venus Hottentot. The Mother Showman says:

> With yr appreciative permission for a separate admission we've got a new girl: # 9 "The Venus Hottentot". She bottoms out at the bottom of the ladder yr not a man—until you've hadder. But truly, folks, before she showd up our little show was in the red but her big bottoms friendsll surely put us safely in the black!" (Parks, *Venus* 35)

In 1807, the Slave Trade Act abolished the slave trade through the British Empire, but the law did not abolish the slavery system. The Mother Showman presents her to the English spectators in 1810 as "THE ONLY LIVING CREATURE OF HER KIND IN THE WORLD." (Parks, *Venus* 35). The Negro Resurrectionist makes comment on her exhibition in England as:

> Early in the present century a poor wretched woman was exhibited in England under the appellation of The Hottentot Venus. The year was 1810. With an intensely ugly figure, distorted beyond all European notions of beauty, she was said by those to whom she belonged to possess precisely the kind of shape which is most admired among her countrymen, the Hottentots […]. The year was 1810, three years after the Bill for the Abolition of the Slave-Trade had been passed in Parliament and among protest and denials, horror and fascination, The Venus show went on. (Parks, *Venus* 36)

The Chorus of the 8 Human Wonders is working for years, every time, gathering crowds. The initial five months in the racket were like hell without sleep and food to eat. Venus is unaware of the sexual, economic, and physical exploitation in the racket at the hands of The Mother Showman. She is unalarmed about the impending disaster of all the exploitation in her future life leading her to death. The Mother Showman presents her to the audience by humiliating her for the physic. She orders Venus as,

> Turn to the side, Girl! Let em see! Let em see! […] What a fat ass, huh?! Oh yes, this girls thuh Missing Link herself, come on inside and allow her to reveal to you the Great and Horrid Wonder of her great heathen buttocks. Thuh Missing Link, Ladies and Gentlemen: Thuh Venus Hottentot. (Parks, *Venus* 42–43)

The Mother Showman makes the marketing of the physic of Venus. She encourages the audience to view the big buttock of Venus. She scolds Venus for standing like Wooden Lady and poking out her lips. She orders her to be alive and have smiling face in front of the audience. She asks Venus to strike her feathers, smoke the pipe, and dance as to attract the audience. She introduces her to the audience as the horrific wonder with a big bum. She encourages the audience as: "What a bucket! What a bum! What a spanker! Never seen the likes of that, I'll bet. Go on sir, goon. Feel her if you like" (Parks, *Venus* 45).

Venus dances and the Mother Showman claps the time. A spectator wanders to watch and hands over a coin to the Mother Showman. The spectator takes a feel and wanders off. She convinces more and more spectators to have a feel of Venus. The Mother Showman convinces the audience once again as:

> Look extra pitiful, Girl. Yeah that's it [...]. Ladies and Gents, are you feeling lowly? Down in the dumps? Perhaps yr feeling that yr life is all for naught? I have felt that way myself at times. Come on inside and get yr spirits lifted. One look at thisll make you feel like a king! (Parks, *Venus* 45)

Several spectators are convinced to feel Venus. The Mother Showman is a real oppressor who has, being a woman, no consciousness of a woman's dignity. She repeatedly kicks Venus as her pet dog and urges the spectators to look and observe her act of kicking Venus. She also dehumanized Venus for not learning the virtue of human civilization. She says, "Ladies and Gents: The Venus Hottentot. Shes been in civilization a whole year and still hasn't learned nothing! The very lowest rung on our Lords Great Evolutionary Ladder! Observe: I kick her like I kick my dog!" (Parks, *Venus* 45). She thinks that kick is habitual to the Hottentots. The language of kick is very sophisticated to them. She goes on to kick her and the spectators erupt in wild laughter while enjoying that inhuman act.

The Mother Showman considers Venus less than a dog. Venus has only the status of a pet animal which lives only at the mercy of the master. The spectators enjoy and feel Venus but no one can see tears rolling down from the eyes of Venus. The Negro Resurrectionist comments on the grief of Venus as, "The things they noticed were quite various/ but no one ever noticed that her face was streamed with tears" (Parks, *Venus* 47).

Venus claims fifty coins a week from the Mother Showman, because she points out that she is the main attraction of the show and the other eight freaks are the second-grade wonders. The audience comes to see her not the rest. She wanted good food, a locked door, and new clothes to wear, but the ring owner does not give her anything. The Mother Showman plans to take her on a brief tour from town to town because the law forbids them to be static at one place because they create so many disturbances in the town. They traveled from one town to another town making the shows. Venus spends her two years of banishment living in a cave carved outside of the city wall. The spectators break the cage of Venus by beating with sticks. They also beat the Mother Showman who makes her to live in the cage. The spectators lead Venus to a jail cell.

The Chorus of the Spectators turns into the Chorus of the Court to look into the case of Venus. The Chorus of the Court speaks:

> We, representative of the law have hauled into court the case of a most unfortunate female, who has been known to exhibit herself to the view of the public in a manner offensive to decency and disgraceful to our country. This court wonders if she is at any time under the control of control of others, or some dark force, some say, black magic making her exhibition against her will. We ask 2 questions: Is she or was she ever indecent? And at inny time held against her will? (Parks, *Venus* 64)

The court is in the position to uncover the cause of the nude exhibition of Venus, an unfortunate black woman. The court calls upon The Mother Showman, the present keeper of Venus. She submits the certificate of baptism of Venus Hottentot as a proof that she takes good care of Venus. She also clarifies to the court that she has never been unkind to Venus. She treated Venus as her own daughter. She also clarifies that she does not put any force on Venus for nude exhibition for public.

The court calls various witnesses to prove the indecency of Venus which causes harm to the reputation of the country. The court summons a member of the society as the first witness. Witness # 1 says:

> I saw her, oh several times. Call me and my Mrs. her regular. She was always standing on a stage, 2 feet high, clothed in a light dress, a dress thuh color of her own skin. She looked, well, naked, kin I say that? The whole place smelled of shit. She didn't speak at all. My Mrs. always fainted. (Parks, *Venus* 68)

The first witness and his mistress are the regular audience of Venus. He narrates about Venus that she used to be standing always in a light dress such as her color in which she looks like naked. She used to be a silent sufferer without voice and the smelling shit.

The second witness is a widow whose husband visited Venus before his death, because he was fond of the sights. He said about Venus which the widow narrates as a witness to the court:

> She was surrounded by many persons, some females! One pinched her, another walked around her; one gentleman poked her with his cane; uh lady used her Parasol to see if all was, as she called it, 'natural.' Throughout all of this the creature didn't speak. May be uh sigh or 2 maybe when she seemed inclined to protest the pawing. (Parks, *Venus* 69)

The third witness is a noted abolitionist who protests against the public exhibition of Venus for money. He is a lover of human liberty. He criticizes the forceful migration of Venus to England as a subject of curiosity in the country. He calls her a wretched creature who is a victim of slavery. He says:

> As a friend to liberty, in every situation of life, I cannot help calling your attention to a subject, which I am sure need only be noticed by you to insure immediate observation and comment. I allude to that wretched object advertised and publicly shown for money—'The Hottentot Venus.' This, Sir, is a wretched creature—an inhabitant of the interior of Africa, who has been brought here as a subject for the curiosity of this country, for 2 cents a-head. Her keeper is the only gainer. I am no advocate of these sights; on the contrary, I think it base in the extreme, that any human beings should be thus exposed! It is contrary to every principle of morality and good order as this exhibition connects the same offence to public decency with that most horrid of all situations, slavery. (Parks, *Venus* 72)

When Venus comes out of her cage, she has been asked a question by the court whether she wanted to go home. She remains silent because she thinks that she is the main attraction in London and the European colonizers have deliberately killed her people in South Africa. When she has been threatened by the court to put her in jail for the rest of her life, she breaks her long silence in the court. The Chorus of the Court asks her, "Don't push us, Girl! We could lock you up for life! Answer this: Are you here of yr own free will or are you under some restraint?" She replied, "Im here to make a mint …. After all Ive gone through so far to go home penniless would be disgraceful" (Parks, *Venus* 75). But the court does not think that poverty is more disgraceful than the public exhibition of the nakedness of the body. Her silence transforms into a voice which asserts that she is happy in her nude exhibition in England.

The court concludes and rules out that she is clearly not under any restraint. She does it voluntarily and she is pleased with her future in receiving one-half of the profits earned through her exhibition. The court evaluates the case of Venus on the basis of her income received from the exhibition of her nude body. The court assumes that taking her away from the Mother Showman would result in the loss of her income and going back home penniless. The court rules out as:

> All rise and hear our ruling: It appears to the court that person on whose behalf this suit was brought lives under no restraint. Her exhibition sounds indecent but look at her now, shes nicely dressed. It is clear shes got grand plots and plans to make her mark and mint by playing outside the bounds so that we find her person much depraved but she sez her show is part of Gods great plan and we buy that. Besides she has the right to make her mark just like the Dancing Irish Dwarf and she seems well fed. At this time the Court rules not to rule. (Parks, *Venus* 78)

The court does not recognize the power of the keeper of Venus. She is a colonized woman and the Mother Showman enjoys absolute control over her body. So, Venus could not speak against her in the court. The Mother Showman subjected her by coercion trading her with stacks of animal skins. She forcefully displays Venus in a cage against her will. The court could not focus on the economic and physical exploitation and subjection of Venus, instead the court evaluates the case on the basis of her income from the exhibition of her nude body.

Later Venus is purchased by The Baron Docteur. He promises to take her to Paris where she will have good meals, new clothes, and a salary. She will be only exhibited to his colleagues to study her for scientific purposes. Parks in her interview with Kevin Wetmore says:

> It's a love play, and it's difficult. Later in the play, after Venus has spent time in England, the Doctor asks her 'Do you want to go to France' and she says 'yes', why? Because the Doctor's hands are clean. He has clean hands. She wants to go with the man who has clean hands and who is nice, instead of staying with the Mother-Showman who beats her and steals from her and invites men to rape her. Showing that she has this much agency is not blaming the victim. Neither does it let the victimizer off the hook. But if you hip to this you can be transfixed by her story, wounded, and then healed. Her dream of a better life is so beautiful and she just misses realizing it. She misses realizing her dream to be someone of means who could send money home and may be go home and live as a wealthy woman. (137–38)

The Baron Docteur is an anatomist. He is fascinated by Venus when he saw her in the crowd of millions. He feels a little envious when he watches freak shows of Venus in London. His love for Venus is artificial. Venus is portrayed as having control of Baron Docteur. She is in search of love with Docteur Baron. She enjoys her sexual exploitation by him.

> THE BARON DOCTEUR. You know what I want more than anything?
> THE VENUS. Me. Lets have some love.
> THE BARON DOCTEUR. After you. Guess what I want.
> THE VENUS. More me. Kiss?
> THE BARON DOCTEUR. I m an everyday anatomist. One in a crowd of millions.
> THE VENUS. Another kiss. Mmmm that's good. Sweetheart, lie back down.
> THE BARON DOCTEUR. You were just yrself and crowds come running. I was fascinated and a little envious but just a little. A doctor cant just be himself no onell pay a cent for that. Imagine me just being me. …
> THE VENUS. Lie back down. Hold me close to you. Its cold. Love me?
> THE BARON DOCTEUR. I do. …
> THE VENUS. Touch me down here.
> THE BARON DOCTEUR. In you, Sweetheart, I ve met my opposite- exact. Now if I could only match you.
> THE VENUS. That feels good. Now touch me here. (Parks, *Venus* 103–4)

It is no doubt that Venus craves for money and recognition, but above all, she strives for love. Every time she calls Baron Docteur to love her. She has submitted her body forever to him. She has a flash of romantic love with him. One day in her bedroom, she imagines her lover, Docteur as:

> He spends all his time with me because he loves me. He hardly visits her [his wife] at all. She may be his wife all right but shes all dried up […]. He will leave that wife for good and we'll get married […]. And we will lie in bed and make love all day long […]. The Docteur will introduce me to Napoleon himself […]. When Im Mistress I'll be a tough cookie. I'll rule the house with an iron fist and have the most fabulous parties. Society will seek me out: Wheres Venus? Right here! […] Every afternoon I'll take a 3 hour bath. In hot rose water. After my bath they'll pat me down. They'll rub my body with the most expensive oils perfume my big buttocks and sprinkle them with gold dust! (Parks, *Venus* 135)

Docteur Baron is greedy and selfish in romantic relation with Venus. Being a married man, he commits adultery with Venus. He is immoral and uses Venus for his sexual gratification and for his research on her anatomy. When she is pregnant twice, he advises her for an abortion because he fears for the spoil of his family life, career, and reputation. He says, "I ve a wife. A career. A reputation. Is there anything we can do about it, we together in the privacy of my office. I ve got various equipments in here we could figure something out" (Parks, *Venus* 128).

Thus, Venus is delineated as a free and liberated woman who enjoys her status as a sex object. The Baron Docteur exploits her sexually by showing his false love for her. He has a wife, but he pretends to love Venus more than his wife. He wanted to study and analyze her entire physique. After her utilization for his scientific purpose, he wanted to send her back to her native country. When he says to Venus that, "You can't stay here forever you know .... I've got a wife. You've got a homeland and a family back there," she replies, "I don't wanna go back inny more. I like yr company too much. Besides, it was a shitty life" (Parks, *Venus* 105).

The Docteur initially desires for physical intimacy with her. Consequently, his desire for physical intimacy results in a scientific interest in her body. He focuses on her exterior to achieve reputation through the scientific discovery of her body. His analysis of Venus's exterior body which is recorded in a notebook and read by the Negro Resurrectionist explores his genuine interest in Venus. He gives a detailed and ugly description of her breast:

> She usually lifted and tightened beneath the middle part of her dress, but, left free, they [her breast] hung bulkily and terminated obliquely in a blackish areola about 1 and ½ inches in diameter pitted with radiating wrinkles, near the center of what was a nipple so flattened and obliterated as to be barely visible: The color of her skin was on the whole a yellowish brown, almost as dark as her face. (Parks, *Venus* 109)

He investigates and measures various parts of her body. Venus is an image of a woman whose dead body is kept in a mortuary to study anatomy for science students. Her body is marked as the "Other" by social and racial construction. The Docteur as an anatomist looks at her body and masturbates. Her commodification relates to the intersections of socially defined ideas of racial and sexual identity. Her biological distinctiveness is incorporated into the discourse of science and racial domination. The Docteur presents his racially and sexually dominated study of the body of Venus at a conference in Tubingen. He reads his notebook:

> In regards to the formation of buttocks we make the following remarks: The fatty cushion [...]. Steatopygia was 9 inches deep [...]. Her buttocks had nearly the usual origin and insertion but the muscular fibers were surprisingly thin and flabby and very badly developed thus showing that the protuberance of the buttocks so peculiar to the Bushman race is not the result of any muscular development but rather totally dependent on the accumulation of fat. (Parks, *Venus* 147)

The Grade-School Chum, a school friend of the Baron Docteur, is one more villain who wants Baron to get rid of Venus, because she causes the spoil of Baron's family life and reputation. He considers Venus a subhuman being who is not a type of Baron. He advises Baron to dissect her "So get rid of her! Break with her! Kick her out on her fat ass!" (Parks, *Venus* 131). Though Baron is under the strong instinct of Venus, he is finally convinced to dissect her. The Grade-School Chum puts a pill in the mouth of Baron to clear his head from the impression of Venus. He advises Baron to put Venus in jail for indecency. He takes Baron away by leaving Venus alone.

There is a riot among the spectators when they assemble around Venus. She takes a chance to flee away, but she is caught and imprisoned in a chain like a dog. The Negro Resurrectionist seats beside her as a guard. The Grade-School Chum approaches the Negro Resurrectionist to take the body of Venus after her death. The Grade-School Chum says, "A friend of mine in the medical profession is very interested in the body of yr ward. After she 'goes on' for scientific analysis only of course" (Parks, *Venus* 151).

The Negro Resurrectionist, in the last scene, announces that Venus is dead. There is a discussion about the cause of the death of Venus. Baron has given reason that Venus died from a sexually transmitted disease. The Grade-School Chum declares that she is killed by exposure. Worthen W., in his essay, "Citing History: Textuality and Performativity in the Plays of Suzan Lori Parks," says about the ending of the play that, "At the end of the play, The Venus is only reflection of peculiar desire, the desire to fashion the … self through the projection of a fictive 'Other' " (14).

Thus, there is a tragic end for Venus who is completely objectified in the hands of dominating powers throughout the play. The play explores the anger at human oppression especially black women at the hands of oppressors in every face having power.

In the Blood

Suzan-Lori Parks, in her response to a Forum on Black Theatre initiated by The Theatre Journal in 2005, says, "A black play employ the black not only as a subject but as a platform, eye, and telescope through which it intercourses with the cosmos" (qtd. in Guran 65). For Parks, black play is a medium through which the black characters expose their troublesome experiences in the history of the United States. The play, *In the Blood*, captures such troublesome experiences in the life of a black woman. Parks presents an image of a black woman who is brutally victimized by the racist system and white patriarchal social order. Hester La Nigrita is a mother of five children from different men. As a result, she is branded as a slut by the community. She is oppressed by evils in the society such as poverty, discrimination, sexual harassment, hypocrisy of black patriarchy, and violence. Hester, the protagonist, is oppressed by Reverend D and the Welfare Lady, who are African Americans, as well as the Doctor and Amiga Gringa, who are the whites.

Hester works insistently to establish a new life for herself and for her homeless family. She is at war with poverty and the society which has no mercy for the poor. She faces financial scarcity to raise her five children because she has no financial help from her children's fathers. She has no family home so she lives a struggling life under a bridge with five children. Being an illiterate black woman who cannot read and write, she is excluded from the society. People call her slut, an immoral woman who is a burden to the society. In the Prologue to the play, she has been described by the Chorus as:

SHE DONT GOT NO SKILLS / CEPT ONE / SHE MARRIED? / … … … / SHE OUGHT BE MARRIED / THATS WHY THINGS ARE BAD LIKE THEY ARE / CAUSE OF / GIRLS LIKE THAT. … / SOME PEOPLE HAVE / BAD LUCK / SHE OUGHTA GET MARRIED / TO WHO? / THIS AINT THE FIRST TIME THIS HAS HAPPENED TO HER / NO, / THIS IS HER FIFTH / FIFTH? / SHE GOT HER FIVE OF THEM / FIVE BRATS / AND NOT ONE OF THEM GOT A DADDY / ………… / SHE KNOWS SHES A NO COUNT / SHIFTLESS / HOPELESS / BAD NEWS / BURDEN TO SOCIETY / HUSSY / SLUT. (Parks, *In the Blood* 5–6)

These vultures of the society are the oppressors of Hester who ostracize her as the other. She has been made a social outcast by these oppressors.

At the beginning of the play, she enters holding a newborn baby in her arms that she raises toward the sky. She says her new born baby as "My treasure. My joy" (Parks, *In the Blood* 7). All of her children are her treasures, because human beings have more worth than money. She has five illegitimate children named as Jabber, Bully, Trouble, Beauty, and Baby. She is suffering in a society that has no sympathy for adulteress. She is a homeless mother trying to earn money to feed her helpless children. She is exploited by the friends who are supposed to help her in her hostile condition. However, she never loses hope. Hester has excessive love for her children. She is the complete epitome of a black mother which is presented in the history of African Americans. As a self-sacrificing mother devoted to her children's survival, she protects, nurtures, and cares for her children at any cost.

She asks her eldest son, Jabber, to read the bad word "SLUT" scrawled on a wall of her house under the bridge. But Jabber pretends that he cannot read the word to protect the feeling of his mother because he knows the meaning of the word.

HESTER. Read that word out to me, huh? I like it when you read to me.
JABBER. Dont wanna read it.
HESTER. Cant or Wont?
JABBER. … Cant. (Parks, *In the Blood* 11–12)

He knows what the word says, but he will not say it. It is that ugly word which branded her as an immoral outcast woman living in isolation from society. It is the society, the bad boys, who humiliate her by writing the word on the wall. This word, she knows, the meaning of which hurt her feelings. But she is unfortunate to live with these humiliating feelings, because she has no option to look after and survive her five children. She says,

> We know who writ it up there. It was them bad boys writing on my home. And in my practice place. Do they write on they own homes? I don't think so. They come under the bridge and write things they don't write nowhere else. A mean ugly word, I'll bet. A word to hurt our feelings. And because we aint lucky we gotta live with it. 5 children i got. 5 treasures. 5 Joys. But we aint got our leg up, just yet. So we gotta live with mean words and hurt feelings. (Parks, *In the Blood* 12)

She is born as a black woman to suffer because she is illiterate. Jabber tries to teach her to read and write. She practices writing the alphabet on the wall of her home. Reading and writing can make her a member of civilized society. But she has no enough time and energy to practice. She has got only the alphabet "A." She repeatedly writes the alphabet "A" on the wall. She has a precious love for her children so she remains hungry all the day, but she feeds her children full of stomach. The soup she makes for her children is "a very special blend of lerts and spices. The broth is chef Mommies worldwide famous 'what have you' stock. Theres Carrots in there. Theres meat. Theres oranges. Theres pie …. Theres pumpkin and cherry too. And steak. And mash potatoes for Beauty. And Milk for Baby" (Parks, *In the Blood* 17–18)

Deborah Gies comments on her brilliance as, "Hester has a gifted imagination seen especially when she helps the children to enjoy the meager soup that she feeds them for dinner be telling them that it has everything they love in it" (83). She sees that the pot of soup is empty. She has a wave of pain due to her hunger. She speaks to herself, "You didn't eat, Hester. And the pain in yr gut comes from having nothing in it …. Kids ate good though. Ate their soup all up. They wont starve" (Parks, *In the Blood* 22). All the children swallow down their soup quickly. Very quickly they empty their bowls. Being very hungry, Hester does not eat anything. When asked by Jabber, she answered him that I will eat later. By saying so she tries to avoid Jabber from noticing her hunger. She turns to a story to let her children sleep. She tells them a story which has some allusions to their own lives:

> There were once these five brothers and they were all big and strong and handsome and didn't have a care in the world. One was known for his brains so they called him Smarts and one was known for his muscles, so they called him Toughguy, the third one was a rascal so they called him Wild, the forth one was as good looking as all get out and they called him Looker and the fifth was the youngest and they called him Honey child cause he was as young as he was sweet. And there was this princess. And she lived in a castle and she was lonesome and looking for love but she couldn't leave her castle so she could not very far so every day she would stick her head out her window and sing to the sun and every night she would stick her head out and sing to the moon and the stars: "Where are you?" And one day the five brothers heard her and come calling and she looked upon them and she said: "There are five of you, and each one is wonderful and special in his own way. But the law of my country doesn't allow a princess to have more than one husband." And that was such bad news and they cried. Until the Princess had an idea. She was after all the Princess, so she changed the law of the land and married them all […]. And with Bro Smart she had a baby named Jabber. And with Bro Toughguy she had Bully. With Bro Wild came Trouble. With Bro Looker she had Beauty. With Bro Honeychild came. And they was all happy. (Parks, *In the Blood* 19–20)

In the above story, she changes the original script of a fairy tale to render the respectable status of her five illegitimate children. She glorifies herself in the story as a Princess having five legal husbands. She also has five children having a legal father for each. She is dreaming of a happy life living all together. But in reality, it is a hallucination of a happy family which is poverty ridden. And the five illegitimate children are without happiness in their life. It is clear that the mother is not only hungry for food but also for the love of a passionate husband. She is a woman who has nowhere a man neither to love her nor to take care of her with her children.

The play addresses the issue of adultery. It shows that the poor, helpless black mother of five illegitimate children (five treasures) commits adultery. In the society she is identified as a SLUT. She is not an adulterous woman committing the immoral crime as a professional but she has a romantic passion for the men who come into her life. She needs the man as her husband and the father of her children to help them. The people in her life commit adultery and the blame and stigma are adhered to her as a slut.

Amiga Gringa is a poor white woman and friend of Hester who claims that she is also suffering from sexual oppression like Hester. In fact, she is also a part of Hester's victimization by stealing money from her. She gives Hester five bucks for a man's watch which Hester has given her to sell.

> HESTER. Wheres the rest?
> AMIGA GRINGA. Thats it.
> HESTER. 5 bucks?
> AMIGA GRINGA. It wast a good day. Some days are good some days are bad. I kept a buck for myself.
> HESTER. You stole from me.
> AMIGA GRINGA. Don't be silly. We're friends, Hester.
> HESTER. I shoulda sold it myself.
> AMIGA GRINGA. But you had the baby to watch.
> HESTER. And no ones gonna give money to me with me carrying Baby around. Still I could got more than 5. (Parks, *In the Blood* 27)

Amiga views the children as a burden on the mother, Hester. The kids are the cause of hunger for Hester according to Amiga. So, she advises Hester to sell her children to rich people and get money from them. In an open market, she cannot get money by carrying the burden of kids. But the children are the treasures and everything for Hester. She is ready to sacrifice everything in her life. Therefore, she gets her legs up instead of selling the children:

> AMIGA GRINGA. The dangers I incur, working with you. You oughta send your kids away. Like me. I got 3 kids. All under the age of 3. And do you see me looking all baggy eyed, up all night shining little shoes and flattening the shirts and going without food? Theres plenty of places that you can send them. Homes. Theres plenty of peoples, rich ones especially, that cant have kids. The rich spend days looking through the news paper for ads where they can buy one. Or they go to the bastard homes and pick one out. Youd have some freedom. Youd have a chance at life. Like me.
> HESTER. My kids is mine. I get rid of em what do I got? Nothing. I got nothing now, but if I lose them I got less than nothing.
> AMIGA GRINGA. Suit yrself. You wouldn't have to send them all away, just one or two or three.
> HESTER. All I need is a leg up. I get my leg up I'll be ok. (Parks, *In the Blood* 27–28)

Amiga earns money by selling her children. She convinces Hester to follow the way of selling her kids to get money. She uses her body as a tool to get money. She is a poor woman but she refuses to work hard to earn money and sustain her kids. She does not wish to do the work having less earnings. However, she criticizes Hester for her sewing clothes as a profession. She calls it a foolish work which makes Hester a slave. When Hester offers her the job of sewing, she replies, "Oh no. Thats not for me.

If I work, Hester, I would want to be paid a living wage. You have agreed to work for less than a living wage. May as well be a slave. Or an animal .... If you do well shes [The Welfare Lady] gonna let you be her slave for life. Wouldnt catch me doing that. Chump work ..." (Parks, *In the Blood* 66).

Amiga has sympathy for Hester and her poverty. She dislikes the living place of Hester which is under a bridge. She wants to drag Hester out of poverty and hardship. But the way and the scheme to earn money is an immoral act of selling the body and the product of her body. In her confession, Amiga speaks:

> I had me some delicious schemes to get her out of that hole she call home. Im doing well for myself working my money maker. Do you have any idea how much cash I'll get for the fruit of my white womb?/Grow it. Birth it. Sell it./And why shouldn't I?/(Rest)/ Funny how a woman like Hester driving her life all over the road most often chooses to walk the straight and narrow. (Parks, *In the Blood* 71)

Being a poor mother, Hester does not consent to Amiga to sell the fruit of her womb that is five treasures for her. Her children are not a burden for Hester, but they are the treasures for her. She is not an adulterous woman in reality. It is the society of which she is a member that leads the helpless woman to this kind of immorality. She sacrifices the virtue of a woman for the sake of the betterment of her children. With Amiga, she had a sexual encounter of which they made a movie to sell for money. Amiga's confession is about the sexual experience with Hester to make money together. Amiga confessed, "In my head I got it going on. The triple X rated movie: Hester and Amiga get down and get dirty. Chocolate and vanilla get into the ugly. We coulda done a sex show behind a curtain then make a movie and sell it for 3 bucks a peek" (Parks, *In the Blood* 71). Amiga's offer of help for Hester leads her to pornography. Amiga is a professional prostitute. She is having American materialistic dreams. She cajoled Hester to have a sexual show to get money.

Another woman in addition to Amiga who causes oppression of Hester is the Welfare Lady, a black woman. She represents the welfare system of the government. She blames Hester for her poverty and homelessness. She does not think Hester as a part of that society which should take care of Hester as a poor woman. The Welfare Lady gives Hester the job of sewing clothes to help her economic welfare. Hester is an unskilled worker in sewing so she needs training in sewing clothes. If it is an honest help to Hester, she must have training given by the welfare system. But the Welfare Lady does not teach her how to sew. The welfare system is a barren help for Hester, because it is just for the sake of show, not an authentic concern for the poor and needy people in the society. Hester says to the Welfare Lady, "My lifes my own fault. I know that. But the world don't help, maam" to which the Welfare Lady replied, "The world is not here to help us, Hester. The world is simply here. We must help ourselves" (Parks, *In the Blood* 59).

Hester is dissatisfied with the people who surrounded her. She knows that she has committed five mistakes. She has five bastard children and the men in her life are responsible for her plight. They must have some responsibility for their children. It is their moral concern to look after the children and the mother.

The world is helpless for her and the charge of her deplorable condition goes to the men in her life. The welfare system is also simply here having no genuine concern for the plight of Hester. She has to rise up herself with the hard work for her welfare without the help of the people surrounding her. The fault of Hester is that she does not know the difference between honest love and lovemaking. She admits her fault and considers herself responsible for her plight. But in some way, it must be considered that the men who deceived her in love are responsible for her plight.

Hester is an unmarried woman in the society having five bastard children. Being an unmarried woman with five bastard children is not considered morally decent womanhood. Therefore, she is not accepted by the society. She is considered a low-class woman in the society. In her confession, the Welfare Lady considers Hester as an inferior woman:

> And I should emphasize that she [Hester] is a low-class person. What I mean by that is that we have absolutely nothing in common. As her caseworker I realize that maintenance of the system depends on a well-drawn boundary line and all parties respecting that boundary. And I am, after all, I am a married woman. (Parks, *In the Blood* 62)

Though Hester is immoral as an unmarried woman, she is the best and most devoted woman as a mother of five bastard children for caring them. She bears all the suffering and takes the responsibility of her children. When the Welfare Lady says, "5 bastards is not good. 5 bastards is bad" (Parks, *In the Blood* 58). She becomes furious and raises her club to strike the Welfare Lady.

The Welfare Lady's opinion is that she is a married woman and marriage is a system which has a boundary line. Married women respect the boundary line. Accordingly, they are superior to unmarried women having kids. She, being a married woman, has also crossed the boundary line by having a threesome sexual encounter with her husband and Hester, because they wanted a little spice. In her Confession, she admits that:

> And Hester, she came to tea [...]. She came over and we had tea [...]. Hubby sat opposite in the recliner hard as Gibraltar. He told us what he wanted and we did it. We were his little puppets. She was surprised, but consented [...]. Just light petting at first. Running our hands on each other than Hubby joined in and while she and I kissed Hubby did her and me alternately. The thrill of it—[...]. I was so afraid I'd catch something but I was swept away and couldn't stop. She stuck her tongue down my throat and Hubby doing his thing on top my skin shivered. She let me slap her across the face and I crossed the line. (Parks, *In the Blood* 61–62)

The Welfare Lady and her husband have used Hester for their selfish sexual gratification. These representatives of the welfare system exploit her sexually. They do not have any genuine concerns for the poor blacks but they are doing the welfare as their duty to the society. The Welfare Lady says, "I care because it is my job to care. I am paid to stretch out these hands. To you" (Parks, *In the Blood* 55). The Welfare Lady behaves very cruelly with Hester. She blames Hester for her poverty. She accuses her children as truant, criminal, and robber. She goes on accusing Hester's daughter of committing a generational sin of adultery by being pregnant. The Welfare Lady says:

> The welfare of the world weighs on these shoulders, Hester [...]. We at Welfare are at the end of our rope with you. We put you in a job and you quit. We put you in a shelter and you walk. We put you in school and you drop out. Yr children are also truant. Word is they steal. Stealing is a gateway crime, Hester. Perhaps your young daughter is pregnant. Who knows. We build bridges you burn them. We saw safety nets, rub harder, good strong safety nets and you slip through the weave. (Parks, *In the Blood* 54)

The Doctor is also a part of the exploitation of Hester through the gratification of sexual desire. He is the representative of the health agency of the social welfare system of the poor blacks. He carries his roadside practice on his back like a hawker with a sandwich board. He treats Hester in an inhuman way when he quickly and thoroughly examines her in the street. He asks Hester, "In a minute. Gimmie the spread & squat right quick. Let's have a look under the hood" (Parks, *In the Blood* 39). In the street, Hester spreads her legs and the Doctor slides between her legs to look up into her privates with a flashlight. This is a very inhuman treatment given by the Doctor to Hester. As a representative of the health agency, he is responsible for Hester's disease. He checks up her and says:

> Every blemish on your record is a blemish on mine. Take yr. Guts for instance. Yr pain could be nothing or it could be the end of the road—a cyst or a tumor, a lump or a virus or an infected sore. Or cancer, Hester. Undetected. There youd be, lying in yr coffin with all yr little ones gathered around motherlessly weeping and the Higher Ups pointing their fingers at me, saying I should of saved the day, but instead stood idly by. You and yr children live as you please and Im the one. The Higher Ups hold responsible [...]. (Parks, *In the Blood* 37)

He is such a cruel Doctor who wishes to subvert Hester's womanhood. For the pain in the guts of Hester, he held herself responsible for having many children. To control her birth rate, he tells her to remove her sexual organ to make her unable to have babies. He thinks that sterilization of Hester by removing her uterus and ovaries is the best treatment for Hester's disease.

> DOCTOR. When I say removal of your "womanly parts" do you know what parts Im talking about?
> HESTER. Yr gonna take my womans parts?
> DOCTOR. My hands are tied. The Higher Ups are calling the shots now./(Rest)/ You have 5 healthy children, itll be for the best, considering.
> HESTER. My womans parts.
> DOCTOR. I ve forwarded my recommendation to yr caseworker. Its out of my hands. Im sorry. (Parks, *In the Blood* 43)

The Doctor has already recommended her caseworker, a social worker who is employed by the government agency, to remove her womanly parts. The Doctor seems to be caring for Hester's life, because he has to care about her within the welfare system. He takes every advantage of her to satisfy his own sexual desire. In his confession, he says:

> I was lone some and she [Hester] gave herself to me in a way that I had never experienced even with women I ve paid she was, like she was giving me something that was not hers to give me but something that was mine that I'd lent her and she was returning it to me. Sucked me off for what seemed like hours but I was very insistent. And held back and she understood that I wanted her in the traditional way. And she was very giving very motherly very obliging very understanding very phenomenal. Let me cumm inside her. Like I needed to. (Parks, *In the Blood* 44–45)

Reverend D is the father of Hester's last child, Baby. He enjoys his latest position/power of Priest. He is a representative of the church which is the symbol of salvation. He is a man who has given up all the materialistic pleasures in the world. He has also the responsibility of social welfare through his religious preaching. He shows the ways to the poor toward a better life. He says:

> I am a man who crawled out of the quicksand of despair. I am a man who has pulled himself out of that never ending gutter—and you notice friends that every city and every town got a gutter. Aint no place in the world that don't have some little trench for its waste. And the gutter, is endless, and deep and wide and if you think you gonna crawl out of the gutter by crawling along the gutter you gonna be in the gutter for rest of your life. You gotta step out of it, friends and I am here to tell you that you can. (Parks, *In the Blood* 47)

Reverend D is a preacher who preaches the people to come out of the gutter. He preaches the morality to people. He is an ecclesiastical man in the church of the state. Being a representative of a religious institution, he must hold a moral character as he preaches, but he is a big hypocrite of false virtue of religion. When Hester goes to him with hiding her face by holding the picture of Baby, the son of Reverend D, he does not identify them:

> HESTER. This child here don't know his daddy.
> REVEREND D. The ultimate disaster of modern times. Sweet child. Yours?
> HESTER. Yes
> REVEREND D. Do you know the father?
> HESTER. Yes.
> REVEREND D. You must go to him and say, "Mister, here is your child!"
> HESTER. Mister here is your child!
> REVEREND D. "You are wrong to deny what God has made!"
> HESTER. You are wrong to deny what God has made!
> REVEREND D. "He has nothing but love for you and reaches out his hand every day crying wheres daddy?"
> HESTER. Wheres daddy?
> REVEREND D. "Wont you answer those cries?"
> HESTER. Wont you answer those cries?

REVEREND D. If he don't respond to that then hes a good-yor-nothing dead beat, and you report him to the authorities. Theyll garnish his wages so at least you all wont starve …. You should go to yr childs father and demand to be recognized.
HESTER. Its been years since I seen him. He didn't want me bothering him so I been good.
REVEREND D. Go to him. Plead with him. Show him this sweet face and yours. He cannot deny you. (Parks, *In the Blood* 47–49)

According to Reverend D, nonidentity of father is the disaster of modern times. He advises Hester to go to the father of the child and ask him to identify the child because he is crying for daddy. If the father denies identifying them, she must give him to the authorities that will take some amount from his wages and give her to feed the child. But when Hester reveals her identity by uncovering her face, he shows his double-faced preacher. He does not recognize his past illegal relations with her and subsequently the father of the baby. He thinks that she is an adulterous woman who is under the impression of his priestly position to rob him economically. He promises her to give money to save her from starving from all sorts of special agencies. The religious institution is corrupted in the hands of a nonethical man like Reverend D. He promises to bribe her for not revealing his name to the authority as the father of the child.

REVEREND D. Do the authorities know the name of the father?
HESTER. I don't tell them nothing.
REVEREND D. They would garnish his wages if you did. That would provide you with a small income. If you agree not to ever notify the authorities, we, could, through my institution, arrange for you to get a much amount of money. (Parks, *In the Blood* 50–51)

Hester's suffering takes an enormous turn with each character. Reverend D, being a religious man, has the responsibility of Hester and her children, but without giving any financial assistance to her, he threatens her for not disclosing his name as the father of her youngest child. Though he preaches about charity and social welfare of the poor in the society, he does nothing for the economic upliftment of Hester. He hates Hester for her being hungry with her children. In his confession, he discloses his dissatisfaction and detestation with Hester:

> She was one of the multitudes. She did not stand out […]. The intercourse was not memorable. And when she told me of her predicament I gave her enough money to take care of it […]. In all my days in the gutter I never hurt anyone. I never held hate for anyone. And now the hate I have for her and her hunger. (Parks, *In the Blood* 79)

Chilli is the first man in the life of Hester. He is the father of Hester's eldest son, Jabber. He comes back after changing his name because he did not want to be identified by the welfare. When he meets Hester, he is too happy to see her, because he wanted to marry Hester. Long ago he was in love with her and had romance with her in the past. But he was poor and infatuated with narcotics. He in his confession narrates his love for Hester:

> I was her first and zoom to the moon if we wanted and couldnt nothing stop us. We would go fast and we were gonna live forever and any mistakes we would shake off. We were Death Defying we were Hot Lunatics careless as all get out and she needed to keep it and needed to leave town. People get old that way [...]. We didn't have a car and everything was pitched toward love in a car and there was this car lot down from where we worked and we were fearless late nights go sneak in those rusted Buicks that hadnt moved in years. I would sit at the wheel and pretend to drive and she would say she felt the wind in her face surfing her hand out the window then we'd park without even moving in the full light of the lot making love. She was my first. (Parks, *In the Blood* 97–98)

But this time he is a rich man and has earned money by changing his name, but his life is loveless. He proposes Hester to marry him by offering her a wedding dress. She is very ecstatic to see her dream of a wedding turning out to be true. She wears the dress and gets out her special shoes to wear and gets ready for the happiest moment in her life. Chilli thinks that Hester is a Virgin Mary woman and her son as Jesus. But when he knows that Hester is not a Virgin Mary figure, because she has five bastard children, he revokes his proposal of marriage. He takes back the marriage ring, her veil, and dress. He elaborates his thinking about Hester as:

> I'm thinking this through. I'm thinking this all the way through. And I think—I think— [...]. I carried around this picture of you. Sad and lonely with our child on yr hip. Struggling to make do. Struggling against all odds. And triumphant. Triumphant against everything. Like–hell, like Jesus and Mary. And if they could do it so could my Hester. My dear Hester. Or so I thought [...]. But I don't think so. (Parks, *In the Blood* 96)

At the end of the play, when Hester demands Reverend D some money, he brutally twists her hand and calls her, "Slut, ... Don't ever come back here again! Ever! Yll never get nothing from me! Common Slut. Tell on me! Go on! Tell the world! I'll crush you underfoot" (Parks, *In the Blood* 103). Jabber watches this struggle and the inability and helplessness of his mother. He clarifies his mother that the bad boys were writing the bad word "Slut" on their wall, which he could read but he did not want to read. By knowing this, Hester becomes very furious about the identity the society has given her. At last, she could not bear her stress and frustration. When Jabber repeats the word "Slut" again and again, Hester quickly raises her club and hits him brutally. He cries out and falls down dead. She stands alone wet with her son's blood. She cradles his body with grief.

In her confession, Hester clarifies that she had committed five mistakes by giving birth to five fatherless children which she believed before as five treasures. She confesses, "Never shoulda had him./Never shoulda had none of them./Never was nothing but a pain to me: 5 Mistakes!" (Parks, *In the Blood* 106). Thus, Hester is a tragic character for whose downfall all the characters are responsible. She has been sexually exploited by everyone whom she knows. These people have taken advantage of her body as a commodity. She suffers because of the poverty and the patriarchal social system. Throughout the play, she wants to get up but every time she is pulled down by the social system.

Fucking A

Suzan Lori Parks's *Fucking A* is encouraged by the novel, *The Scarlet Letter*, written by Nathaniel Hawthorne in 1850. The play has several similarities with the novel such as the name of the main character, Hester. Both Hesters are branded as "A." Hawthorne's Hester is branded for adultery and Parks's Hester is branded as an abortionist. These identities are given to them by the society in which they are living. Hester Smith in *Fucking A* is a woman excluded by the society for her socially aberrant behavior. Parks on the title page describes the play as "an otherworldly tale involving a noble mother, her wayward son, and others. Their troubled beginning, their difficult end" (Parks, *Fucking A* 113).

Hester is glorified as a noble mother who faces troubles and will have a disastrous end. The play sets in a small town in a small country in the middle of nowhere. The play reveals the dark and bleak world where Hester strongly aspires to take revenge. It also deals with sexuality and fertility of women which is dominated by white patriarchy and power politics. Parks criticizes the modern American society for the oppression and suffering of lower classes.

Hester is most likely an African American woman living in the racist era of America. The play centers on Hester Smith whose son has been sent to jail by the First Lady of the city for stealing meat when he was hungry. She is a poor woman living in the surrounding of an oppressed world wearing the letter "A" on her chest, as if she were a domesticated animal. Throughout the play, human bodies, particularly women and poor classes, are objectified as pieces of mark.

The goal of Hester is to free her son who has been imprisoned for stealing meat to assuage his hunger. He was sent to prison just because he was poor and hungry, when Hester was working for the First Lady's family. She was given choice between prison and becoming an abortionist. Hester says, "[I] scrubbed floors for the Rich Family but then Boy stole from them and they came down extra hard on me. It was either prison or—employment as an abolitionist" (Parks, *Fucking A* 132). She is a strong and determined woman to work as an abortionist to see her son again, even through a disgraced occupation. When she goes to the Freedom Fund to set her son free, The Freedom Fund Lady says "Freedom Ain't Free!" (Parks, *Fucking A* 131), which is the maxim of capitalistic American society. Therefore, Hester must work as an abortionist to make money to buy her son's freedom.

Canary Mary is a white whore. She is a poor woman earning her daily living through prostitution. She is a pet woman of the Mayor and desires to become a rich woman. She is very happy that the Mayor is leaving the First Lady by accepting her. That is why she is not willing to accept any poor handsome man as a customer. When Hester asks Canary if she would marry her son after she has bought his freedom, she says,

"The Mayor owns my exclusive rights so I wouldn't have no time for a poor man even if he was handsome. Although poor men got a beauty to them. But nope. The son of an abortionist. I'd turn my nose up" (Parks, *Fucking A* 122).

Canary is a lower-class woman who sells her body as a commodity to the noneffective leader of the ruling class who has power of the city, but he is not able to have a lawful successor to his kingdom. She supplies the gold coin to Hester which she uses to pay for a visit to her son. However, the Boy has been misplaced by the prison management. They attempt to substitute for him another prisoner, Jailbait who grabs the basket from Hester and begins to eat like an animal. She has branded her son so that she easily recognizes that Jailbait is not her son. Jailbait says that he has killed Boy Smith. Jailbait proceeds to kiss and rape her. She becomes dumb with grief and disbelief of her son's death. She lets him do what he wants. She sings "My Vengeance" cursing the Rich Girl:

> The low on ladder
> The barrels rock bottom
> Will reach up and strange
> The Rich then God not them.
> She'll mourn the day
> She crushed us underfoot.
> Her Rich Girl wealth
> Will no stop me from put-
> ing my mark on her
> And it will equal what we've paid.
> My Vengeance will show her
> How a true mother is made. (Parks, *Fucking A* 184)

At the beginning of the play, Hester and Canary celebrate the conflicting marital life of the Mayor of the city and his wife, the First Lady of the city. Canary confides to Hester that the Mayor is cheating on his wife and one day he will choose her as his mistress. The First Lady is childless. She has taken every medicine to get pregnant and give birth to a child. The Mayor is very ambitious to have a heir to his position. But the First Lady is unable to fulfill his dream and ambition. She is a rich woman and the Mayor loves her ancestral property. Hester shouts at the First Lady because she had caught Hester's son stealing meat. She was working for the First Lady's family many years ago in the past. Now the First Lady is married to the Mayor. She is having trouble in conceiving a child. Canary discloses that the First lady is not able to bear a child and the Mayor is ready to leave her. The conversation between Canary and Hester indicates that they are very happy by knowing this:

> CANARY. Drink with me. Come on. Things are getting worse between the Mayor and his wife. Lets celebrate.
> HESTER. Cheers (They Drink)
> CANARY. The wifes at the end of her rope. He hates her. Her days are numbered.
> HESTER. But he loves her money so her money buys her time. The Rich Bitch. (Parks, *Fucking A* 119)

Hester calls the First Lady a Bitch, because she is very angry and bitter about her. She expresses her anger by cursing the First Lady like she may never conceive and her womb may dry up and shrivel. She is not ready to forgive her for sending her son to prison. Hester says, "Not until my boy comes home. Im not a true mother otherwise. When he comes home then maybe I'll forgive her but not before" (Parks, *Fucking A* 120).

The Mayor, a patriarch, is the representative of the higher class and the power. He plans to assassinate his wife, the First Lady. He cheats on his wife by indulging in an extramarital affair with Canary who is a prostitute. He is strongly possessed by his ambition to have an heir to his position. The people elected him as the head of the state for the rest of his life. They expect him to have a son to lead the state for the rest of his life. But the people look at him as an ineffective man. He says:

> And Im the Mayor. The people look up to me. They look up to me and they see my right-hand dangling. Where I should be holding the hand of my son, or perhaps have my arm resting proudly on the young man's shoulder my right hand is only dangling. Empty. And they see it. And they begin to wonder what kind of man I am. I promised them a greatness that would last a hundred-thousand years but my right hand is dangling empty, woman. (Parks, *Fucking A* 128)

He has thoroughly examined himself. There is no question of his ineffectiveness. He blames his wife for her inability to have a fertile womb. People see her inability as a kind of disloyalty. For that, she has gone through every medicine to conceive. She says, "Ive tried. I went to Europe. Saw all those doctors. All of them poking at me. All of them overcharging me because they all knew I was foreign. All the pills they gave me. Suitcases full. And I take them. I take them every day. Ive tried" (Parks, *Fucking A* 128). She is a disgrace to the nation. Everyone agrees to move her from the townhouse to the country house. The Mayor is a treacherous man who secretly plans to murder her. After her death, he will get all her wealth. And he will remarry on the demand of the people of the state. Besides having a whore, Canary, he will have a new wife every night. Mayor says:

> My wife will die a tragic death. I will stand like the soldier that I am as they put her in the deep dark ground. My chest will heave in sadness but no tears will fall. I am their Soldier-Mayor. Not a tear will fall. She will have left me all her money. I will hang my head and the people will want me to lift my head up. The people will demand that I remarry [...]. They will demand that I remarry a woman of a—of a certain background. My heart will be split in two. Each night with my new wife I will dream of you [Canary]. I am their humble civil servant. I cannot let them down. (Parks, *Fucking A* 151)

Ultimately, The First Lady is pregnant by Hester's son, Monster (Boy). The Mayor is very happy with the news of his wife's pregnancy. She asks him to keep it hush-hush, but he feels it necessary to share the news with everyone to prove his ability. He has the honor that his wife has made him a father. They are reconciled again.

But the First Lady knows that the Mayor is not the father of the child. It is Hester's son, Boy. She, being a married woman, has shown infidelity to her husband. Being a rich woman, she is an immoral woman who has committed adultery. But it was for her salvation. She sings, "My Little Enemy" as:

> They say Fidelity
> Is the most important thing
> When yr married.
> But its such a pricey luxury.
> When yr up against the wall
> Yll take a poke from some poor slob.
> The child Im growing will be my salvation.
> Who knows, he may grow up to rule the nation.
> And my husband, blind with happiness,
> Will never guess
> The enemy in his army. (Parks, *Fucking A* 191)

When Canary tells the news of reconciliation of the Mayor and the First Lady, Hester is furious to see the happiness in their life. She wants to take revenge of her son's imprisonment caused by the First Lady and her separation from her son long ago. She says to Canary, "I could cut her head off …. Youd put sleeping powder into her bedtime snack. I'd sneak into her big house, find her room, and cut her head off" (Parks, *Fucking A* 192). She continues to say her different ways of killing the First Lady: "I could follow her on one of afternoon constitutionals and jump out from behind a tree and strangle her with my bare hands …. Take my knife and stab her till theres nothing left of her but wounds. Then we'd be equal …. I could slit her throat" (Parks, *Fucking A* 193).

With the help of Canary, she plans to kill her (First Lady's) child. But it would be disastrous for Canary to help Hester directly in the plan. However, Hester gets the help of Butcher. The Butcher and Canary hold the First Lady and bring her to the house of Hester where she aborts the First Lady's child. She does not know that it is her own grandchild which she is about to abort. Then she thinks that she is a real mother who has taken the revenge of her son's death. The notion of womanhood is sacrificed for the sake of the notion of motherhood. Mother's excessive love is much more powerful than the bond between two women.

It is class consciousness that leads toward the destruction of womanhood. The woman of the higher class (White) shows less interest in the concerns of women in the lower class (Black). As a result of this, the lower-class women like Canary and Hester generate negative perceptions about the rich women like the First Lady. Parks focuses on the intersectionality in the conflict between class and gender. Poverty is the root cause of evils in the society which leads to various issues like crimes, robbery, rape, and exploitation.

When the son of Hester was sent to prison for stealing, Hester knew that she would not see him again for a very long time. She would not recognize him by his looks after a long time. So, her solution was to mark him and herself. She shows Butcher her bite mark scar on the inside of her left forearm. She clarifies the Butcher about her wound as:

> When they comed to take him away, Just before they took him, I bit him. Hard. Right on the arm just here. I bit hard. Deep into his skin. His blood in my mouth. He screamed but then he was screaming anyway. After they tooked him away I went and bit myself. Just as hard and in the same place exactly. See the mark I got? My boys got one too. Identical. (Parks, *Fucking A* 166)

She believes that physical mark will never lie. It will reveal the truth like a never changing birthmark.

The play follows Hester's journey to see her son again. She has not seen her son, Boy (as she used to call him as a child), for twenty years. She discusses about the physique of the grown-up Boy. She describes Canary what she heard from the Freedom Fund Lady as:

> HESTER. Who knows what he looks like now. Hes alive. Freedom Fund assures me of that. All growd up, that's for sure. And tall. And a beard. And a deep voice. And a smile in his eye like his dad had and—
> CANARY. Handsome.
> HESTER. If he takes after his dad hes good looking but don't you go getting any ideas. Hes good boy and when I finally buy his freedom he'll be looking for a wife. (Parks, *Fucking A* 122)

She is dreaming about the day she can see her son again. She writes a letter to her son about her reunion picnic. For that, she is saving her fees of abortion to pay for an outing with him. She is a strong and determined mother to do the disgraced profession.

The basic idea of the play is a mother's love for a child. Every day she has women who come in to get rid of themselves of an unwanted child. She helps the women who do not love their children. She earns and saves everything to have a small picnic with her son after releasing from jail. She collects all her earnings to Freedom Fund Lady to see her son free from jail. She says, "If Im lucky by the end of next year I'll have paid enough for me and Boy to have a reunion picnic. Thatll take 500 coins" (Parks, *Fucking A* 121).

Hester is branded as an unacceptable member of the community for her trade as a baby killer or abortionist. She performs a much-needed function of the higher-class society. Everybody refers to her as untouchable by using TALK—a special, unintelligible language. She is separated from her proper community for living the life of an abortionist. Along with the Butcher, she seems the only one who has blood on her hands. Through the course of the play, most of the characters prove to be tainted by crime. Most of the characters bear no responsibility for violating social or moral ethics. Deborah Geis observes, "the tragic clash between Hester's attempts to 'Prevail and Endure' and the myriad forces of society that work against her" (qtd. in Kurahashi 780).

Hester is ostracized by society for her socially aberrant behavior. She wears the letter A on her chest. The letter is branded into the skin. She always sits or stands by pulling her left shoulder, because she does not like the people staring at her. She explains the reason of branding A:

> The brand comes with the job is all I know. "And the brand must be visible at all times." That's the law. Everyone knows what I do—but then, my A is also like a shingle and a license, so nobody in needll ever get suckered by a charlatan. / (Rest) / Go to prison or take this job. That was my choice. Choose A or choose B. I chose A. (Parks, *Fucking A* 165)

She has chosen to be an abortionist rather than going to prison. She lights candles for killing the baby and washes the blood from her tools and her hands. She has no shame in the bloody apron which she wears while aborting the child. Her goal is to free her son. She works continually to support herself and her child. She tells in a working woman's song:

> Its not that we love
> What we do
> But we do it
> We look at the day
> We just gotta get through it.
> We dig our ditch with no complaining.
> Work in hot sun, or even when its raining
> And when the long day finally comes to an end
> We'll say:
> "Her is a woman who does all she can." (Parks, *Fucking A* 122–23)

She is a hardworking poor black woman. Before working abortionist, she would scrub the floors for the rich family. Being very hungry, her Boy stole a piece of meat. Her all troubles are due to the little Rich Girl [the First Lady] who caught him and sent him to jail. Hester says:

> If only that Rich Little Bitch hadn't told on him! We worked for them. They treated us worse than animals. He was only hungry! He stole some meat and she seen him and he seen her seeing him and begged her not to tell, one child to another, but she told. Went and snitched on my Boy and they took him away. (Parks, *Fucking A* 134)

If she had not sent him to prison, he would have grown up a good son under the guidance of his mother. The prison has changed his perspectives on life.

The lives of Hester and Monster signify the tragic stories of African Americans victimized by the racist society. In this society, the black women were denied the status of the motherhood of their own children. They have to endure constant abuses in the society. The marginal status of Hester and Monster in the society clearly reflects the interrelationship between race and gender. He is not dead, but he has become a Monster in the prison system. He has escaped from prison and is on run.

The hunters plan to savagely torture Monster once they capture him. They have set the dogs to catch him. They want to show him what the hunters can do to him when he is captured.

> THIRD HUNTER. [A run through] is the best thing to do to a convict [Monster] when you catch him. If gets the loudest screams.
> FIRST HUNTER. You get a hot iron rod and run it up his bottom and out his throat.
> THIRD HUNTER. Then you stick the rod in the ground and let him wiggle on the stick. (Parks, *Fucking A* 173)

Monster is being chased by the hunters. He runs into the house of Hester. They find out that they are mother and son. The hunters are getting close, because the barking of their dogs grows louder. Monster tells Hester that if he is caught, they will not kill him but torture him mercilessly to death. Monster says, "I heard once how they cut one gut balls off and let him watch the dogs eat them and then they cut his fingers off and the dogs ate those and he had to watch. His fingers and then his toes then his feet then his hands" (Parks, *Fucking A* 209). He begs Hester to kill him. Hester plans to save her child from being tortured:

> Hester: We'll turn the lights and they'll think nobodys home and they'll go away. They'll go look somewhere else. They'll go away. They ll go away wont they?
> Monster: I don't think so.
> Hester: Theyll come to the door and I'll tell them I aint seen you. "What the hell would I be doing seeing a villain like that," I'll say. Then thayll go away, They yll run out the back.
> Monster: They wont go away. Theyre hunters. They hunt. They can smell me. Theyre hunters and they can smell me. They wont go away. They'll do what they got to do to catch the Monster. (Parks, *Fucking A* 217)

This is the most pathetic incident in the play that arouses the seeing of pity and terror. Hester was tirelessly aspiring to the reunion with her son throughout the play. When she meets her son, instead celebrating the happy moment of the reunion, she has to kill her son. If he survives, he will have to endure endless torture till his death. The degree of torture is equivalent to the multiple deaths not only of her son but also of her. When the sound of dogs barking gets louder, Monster urges his mother to save him from the torture by killing him. Monster says:

> When they catch me they'll hurt me. Run me through and plant me in yr front yard so you can hear me scream. They catch me and they'll run me through. You hide me they'll run you through too. I wonder how much itll hurt? They'll keep me alive and cut me up and I wonder how much itll hurt? [...]. Hear the dogs? Take the gun. Shoot me with it. (Parks, *Fucking A* 218)

At first, she calls him silly and refuses to kill her son. She has been killing other people's children in her life, but she cannot dare to kill her own son. Even the killing of her son by her was better for him than his torture by the hunters. She finally decides to save him from the pain of torture. She chooses that the best thing she can do for her son is to give him a swift and painless death. Otherwise, he will be captured and have to endure all the agonizing torture. Hester in a tremendous grief says, "I have a way t do it that wont hurt. (Rest) Give me yr knife. Sit in my lap" (Parks, *Fucking A* 219). She slits his throat like a pig, which the Butcher has told her is the less painful way. Monster dies instantly. At the end of the play, as stage direction states:

> She sits in a chair. He hands her his knife and sits on the floor in front of her with his back toward her stomach. She gently pets his head. Then with a quick firm motion, she slits his throat like Butcher taught her. He dies. She holds him in her lap. The sound of dogs barking and Hunters voices are now deafening. Theyre right outside her door. They force their way in. They stand around looking at Hester and Monster. The dogs bay outside. (Parks, *Fucking A* 220)

When the Hunters see that Monster is dead already, they are disappointed. Though Monster is dead, they still leave away dragging his dead body, because it is still warm. And with warm dead body, they can have plenty of fun still. Hester sits alone in her house and drops the knife in the wash bucket. She lights another candle. But very soon, she picks up her abortion tools, puts on her apron, and goes back to continue her work. She has been forced to fill the undesirable role of abortionist and has been branded with an A on her chest, in order to atone for the crimes of her son who has been put in prison as a child after stealing some food. Throughout the play, this Hester saves money to buy her son's freedom from prison. She does not commit a crime, but she is punished for the sin of another: her son, Boy. The back story to the action we see on stage involves an impoverished child who is incarcerated for stealing food and a mother who must also atone for his crime by either going to prison or performing community service.

In *Fucking A*, Hester Smith shares a portion of her son's penance and pays money toward his freedom. The protagonist's unfortunate situation raises questions about how much we can blame on parenting. Moreover, the severity of Boy's crime, stealing food, diminishes in the context of "the poverty of the world of the play" (Parks, *Fucking A* 115). Boy's own penance, rather than purifying him, entirely alters his identity, turning him into a monster. These elements of *Fucking A* work to blur the distinctions between sin and morality, and to question the contemporary functions of penance and penitence.

In the course of the play, Hester is told that her son is dead and vows to take revenge on the First Lady who was responsible for his incarceration. The audience, however, is made aware that Boy—or Monster as he is now known—is actually alive. He escapes from prison. He has an affair with the First Lady through which she becomes pregnant. The First Lady is married to the Mayor and passes the unborn child off as her husband's. Hester enacts her revenge by kidnapping and drugging the First Lady, after which she forcibly aborts the fetus. Meanwhile, Hester has failed to recognize the dangerous criminal, Monster, as her son. There is a moment of irony in which she describes him as evil and states that his mother is probably dancing.

However, Hester eventually discovers the Monster's true identity. Hester's ensuing infanticide is depicted as a final and tragic act of love in which she gives her son a quick and painless death to save him from the worse fate of prolonged torture. Hester has wiped out her own bloodline through two murderous acts motivated by an intense love for her son. Parks promotes enquiry regarding rightness, rights, life, and the body through the complexity of *Fucking A*'s paradoxes.

Abortion is offered for consideration through Hester's occupation, the "A" that is branded on her chest and the way in which she unwittingly kills her unborn grandchild. Hester's friend Canary describes the protagonist's profession as "one of those disrespectable but most necessary services" (Parks, *Fucking A* 121). Here and as the plot develops, Parks reveals the contradictions of abortion. It allows women to control over their bodies, but it is still a source of stigma and shame. Hester's mark points to the real-life burden placed on those who administer the procedure.

Canary's dialogue and the regular callers who avail of Hester's services show that abortion might be necessary for women's autonomy. Yet, the coercive way in which Hester aborts the First Lady's unborn child, not realizing that the baby is her son's, reveals the potential misuse of the act. On the other hand, there is in the play a certain understanding for the taking of life in some contexts. Hester's tender murder of her son, at his request and to save him from a more grueling end, points to issues such as assisted suicide. *Fucking A* suggests reasons both for and against controversial acts that affect human life.

Thus, *Fucking A* clearly marks the crucial repercussions of race, gender, and class on the African American men in general and African American women in particular. The play is an account of the modern social ideals that are the roots of the oppression and suffering of subordinate classes in American society. Hester Smith, a poor black woman, is banded with the letter "A" on her chest, as if she were a domesticated animal, by the society for her socially disgraced occupation of an abortionist. She is a self-sacrificed mother who tries to save her son. On the contrary, there are so many rich mothers belonging to the higher class, especially white women who want to kill their children in their womb. This suggests that the society in which Hester lives violates the moral standards and ethics of the society. This society considers Hester as untouchable because she is a baby killer. Being poor, she doesn't continue the profession of abortionist for her material welfare, but to buy the freedom of her son. The suffering of Hester and Monster, her son, signify the tragic stories of African Americans who are victimized by the racist white society. In this society, the black women were denied the status of the motherhood of their own children.

Topdog/Underdog

Topdog/Underdog explores the plight of African American males in conditions of family dysfunction, urban poverty, and social oppression. It is about competition, reversals, and mirror images that reflect the true self. It tells the story of two brothers: Lincoln and Booth who have been abandoned by their parents. Thus, they have had to depend upon each other for survival since they were teenagers. They are trying to cope with the loss of their parents. They are struggling for earning their livelihood. The play deals with the question of identity of two African American brothers. The play is set in a dirty and unpleasant house in an apartment with no running water.

The play unfolds a bleak, disturbing, and disrupted family and devastation in black urban society in America. It also explores the social and psychological conflicts between the two African American brothers that ultimately result in fratricide. Suzan-Lori Parks gives a flash in the lives of two African American brothers, Booth and Lincoln. In the introduction to the play, Parks writes "This is a play about family wounds and healing. Welcome to the family" (Parks, *Topdog/Underdog* 4). The play repeats and revises the assassination of Abraham Lincoln at the arcade where the black Lincoln impersonator is shot at all with a top hat, false beard, a black frock coat, and a white face mask. Throughout the play, the brothers reveal parts of their past that have shaped their present situation. The play deals with the recovery of African American history and cultural memory.

All the scenes in the play are set in the boarding house room. Any action that occurs outside of the room is reported by either Lincoln or Booth. Officially, it is Booth's room and Lincoln is staying as his guest. Since Lincoln is the only one with a steady salary, he is responsible for paying the rent. The arcade where Lincoln works is a tourist attraction. Lincoln works as Abraham Lincoln impersonator. He dresses up like Abraham Lincoln and wears white face paint. He sits pretending to watch a play and tourists pretend to assassinate him. Abraham Lincoln is not a character in the play, but he is important for two reasons. First, the main characters are named after him and his assassin John Wilkes Booth. Second, Lincoln, the character in the play, has a steady job in which he impersonates Abraham Lincoln.

The play has a strong sense of history with the names of its characters. Throughout the play, the brothers reveal portions of their past that have shaped their present situation. The death of Lonny, a friend of Lincoln, is influenced by Lincoln's decision to stop dealing with three-card monte. When Booth shows Lincoln the ring he boosted, he reveals a past relationship with Grace, his girlfriend that has been nothing short of disappointing. During an outburst of anger, Booth reveals why he slept with Lincoln's wife Cookie. Moreover, the one item that the brothers have recovered from their days as a family is a raggedy photo album. It contains a link to a past that, though turbulent, still held hopes and dreams for the future. In her essay, *Possession*, Parks writes:

> Since history is a recorded or remembered event, theatre, for me, is the perfect place to "make" history—that is, because so much of African American history has been unrecorded, dismembered, washed out, one of my tasks as playwright is to—through literature and the special strange relationship between theatre and real life—locate the ancestral burial ground, dig for bones, find bones, hear the bones sing, write it down. (4)

The play scrutinizes American history as both a moral wound and a theatrical performance. It repeats and revises the assassination of Abraham Lincoln at the arcade where the black Lincoln impersonator is shot at all with a top hat, false beard, a black frock coat, and a white face mask. On April, 9, 1865, the Army of Northern Virginia, the main Army of Confederacy, surrendered to the Army of Potomac at Appomattox court house. Booth attended a speech at White House on April 11, 1865, in which Lincoln supported the idea of enfranchising the former slaves. Furiously provoked, Booth decided to assassinate Lincoln. He was a Confederate sympathizer and an ardent believer in the supremacy of the white race over the black. Booth was a supporter of black slavery. He believed that Lincoln was determined to overthrow the Constitution and destroy his beloved south. Lincoln's speech outlined some of his ideas about reconstructing the nation and bringing the defeated Confederate States back into the Union. Lincoln also indicated a wish to extend the franchise to some African Americans—those who fought in the Union ranks during the war and expressed a desire that the southern states would extend the vote to literate African Americans.

The dramatic persona lists two brothers, Lincoln as the Topdog and Booth as the Underdog. Their names correspond to the roles in the national hierarchy of President Abraham Lincoln and the southern actor John Wilkes Booth. Lincoln as the elder brother is the dominant brother in the relationship, because he was formerly a highly successful three-card monte hustler. They live together in a shabby apartment which is described in the stage direction as, "A seedily furnished rooming house room. A bed, a reclining chair, a small wooden chair, some other stuff, but not much else" (Parks, *Topdog/Underdog* 11). It indicates that there is a lack of space and sufficient material possessions required for two brothers. Lincoln quits playing three-card monte. He now works at an amusement park performing the death of Abraham Lincoln in white face. Booth attempts to learn his brother's former trade as a three-card monte hustler.

The play opens on a Thursday evening in a boarding house room. Booth is practicing his three-card monte routine over a board which is supported by two milk crates. He practices his patter imagining that he has won a large sum of money. While Lincoln, a black man in his later 30s, comes in. Stage directions say, "He is dressed in an antique frock coat and wears a top hat and fake beard, that is, he is dressed to look like Abraham Lincoln" (Parks, *Topdog/Underdog* 12). Booth tells Lincoln to take off his disguise because he fears that Lincoln's getup will scare Grace, with whom Booth has a date the next day. Booth claims that Grace is in love with him, and that no man can have her the way he can. Booth then shows Lincoln a ring of diamond he plans to give Grace. The ring is stolen, but it is smaller than the one he gave her when they were together two years before.

Lincoln is a reformed card sharp. Once upon a time, he was an expert in the three-card monte scam. After the death of his friend Lonny, he gives up the cards and takes the job of Abraham Lincoln impersonator. Booth aspires to be an expert in three-card monte. He creates his identity as "3 card." He insists Lincoln to teach him, but Lincoln initially resists teaching him:

LINCOLN. I cant be hustling no more, bro.
BOOTH. What you do all day aint no hustle?
LINCOLN. Its honest work.

BOOTH. Dressing up like some cracker as white man, some dead president and letting people shoot at you sound like a hustle to me.
LINCOLN. People know the real deal. When people know the real deal it aint a hustle.
BOOTH. We do the Card game people will know the real deal. Sometimes we will win sometimes they will win. They fast they win, we faster we win.
LINCOLN. I aint going back to that, bro. I aint going back.
BOOTH. You play Honest Abe. You aint going back but you going all the way back. Back to way back then when folks was slaves and shit." (Parks, *Topdog/Underdog* 26–27)

Here Lincoln distinguishes between honest work and a hustle. He insists that his work of playing Honest Abe is a honest job. Booth claims that Lincoln's current job resembles a hustle. Booth knows that Lincoln only plays as being honest. It is a play which is no less a hustle than the three-card monte. Lincoln takes money from a child in exchange for Honest Abe's autograph. His playing perpetuates a history of exploitation and oppression of African Americans. The play exhibits economic disparity in wages between African Americans and white Americans:

LINCOLN. They said thuh fella before me—he took off the get up one day, hung it up real nice, and never came back. And as they offered me thuh job, saying of course I would have to wear a little makeup and accept less than what they would offer a—another guy—.
BOOTH. Go on, say it. "White." They'd pay you less than they'd pay a white guy. (Parks, *Topdog/Underdog* 34)

The two African American brothers are abandoned by their parents at an early age. Subsequently, they struggle to make new life which will lead them out of poverty. Throughout the play, Booth taunts Lincoln for playing Abraham Lincoln's assassination for a lower wage than a white man gets. Lincoln is a master of Con game three-card monte. He has abandoned a life of crime for a more respectable job of impersonating Abraham Lincoln at an arcade. On the other hand, Booth earns his living as a petty thief. He wishes to imitate his elder brother's success by learning how to throw the cards. He finds Lincoln's current work slavish because he performs in white face. Booth, therefore, accuses Lincoln of his dishonesty for his black race. His personal identity is reflecting his racial identity. Here, Lincoln establishes his own identity by concealing his own black race. He has white-washed the African American history for earning money. But for Lincoln, his real job is something more than a hustle: "I don't gotta spend my whole life hustling. Theres more to Link than that. More to me than some cheap hustle. More to life than cheating some idiot out of his paycheck or his life savings" (Parks, *Topdog/Underdog* 60).

However, Lincoln is proud of his job as Lincoln Impersonator and of being the one who daily supplies the food to the family of two brothers. This gives him a sense of identity and value that he struggles to maintain after he is fired as Lincoln. He maintains,

"They didn't fire me cause I wasn't no good. They fired me cause they was cutting back. Me getting dismissed didn't have no reflection on my performance. And I was a damn good Honest Abe considering" (Parks, *Topdog/Underdog* 91).

They have no links to family or any other member in the community, because they thoroughly live in social isolation. They bring up some characters in their conversation which indicate their relationship. But no character has a real relationship with either of the brothers. They lack social and family bonds as well as community relations. This social isolation of the brothers embodies a process in the contemporary black urban living. Carnel West has precisely described that:

> Post-modern African American community in the U. S. A. has witnessed the collapse of meaning in life—the eclipse of the hope and absence of love of self and others, the breakdown of family and neighborhood bonds—that leads to the deracination and cultural denudement of urban dwellers, especially children. We have created rootless, dangling people with little link to the supportive networks … that sustain some purpose in life. (qtd. in Bush 77)

Thus, the play demonstrates the loss of the African American ideal of brotherhood in the American society. Becoming alienated from their ancestral heritage, Lincoln and Booth take combative roles about one another.

The family life of the brothers is determined by some impulsive forces. Booth remains devoted to the perfectness of his family in childhood. He refuses to work, earn, and spend money. He prefers to steal. He believes that excessive work and consumerism destroyed his parents' marriage. In contrast, Lincoln is not worried at all about his family's past. He is willing to perform any role that will give him money to survive. His role of Lincoln's impersonator destructs his identity. He is eager to spend money as he earns it. When their parents separate, they give five hundred dollars to each of the brothers.

> BOOTH. When moms splits she gives me 5 hundred- dollar bills rolled up and tied up tight in one of her nylon stockings. She tells me to put it in a safe place, to spend it only in case of an emergency, and not to tell nobody I got it, not even you. 2 years later Pops splits and before he goes—.
> LINCOLN. He slips me 10 fifties in a clean handkerchief: "Hide this somewhere good, don't go blowing it, don't tell no one you got it, especially that Booth."
> (Parks, *Topdog/Underdog* 73)

Booth has a constant desire for his parents' reunion. Lincoln considers a family as an arrangement that can be reproduced at will with different participants:

> BOOTH. Theyd been scheming together all along. They left separately but they was in agreement. Maybe they arrived at the same place at the same time, maybe they renewed they wedding vows, maybe they got another family.
> LINCOLN. Maybe they got 2 new kids. 2 boys. Different than us, though. Better.
> (Parks, *Topdog/Underdog* 73)

Booth strongly relies on Lincoln because he is the only person who shared his mother with him. He wants to reestablish the broken familial bonds. Booth wants to work the three-card monte scam with Lincoln to reestablish the close bond which the brothers formed after their parents' desertion. He wishes to return to the lost familial harmony of his childhood by using the assigned roles within the three-card monte. In this regard, he pleads with Lincoln to become a three-card monte dealer again and to accept him as a partner:

> BOOTH. I didn't mind them leaving cause you was there. That's why Im hooked on us working together. If we could work together it would be like old times. They split and we got that room downtown. You was done with school and I stopped going. And we had to run around doing odd jobs just to keep the lights on and the heat going and thuh child protection bitch off our backs. It was you and me against thuh world, Link. It could be like that again. (Parks, *Topdog/Underdog* 74)

Booth again raises the idea of the brothers working as a team. He has visions of making easy money, but Lincoln reminds him that there is more to making money at three-card monte than finding a mark. Booth provokes Lincoln into accepting his proposal by reminding him that their success would attract women. Lincoln questions Booth's relationship with Grace, his girlfriend, which does not seem all that secure. Booth appeals to Lincoln's sense of egotism by reminding him that at one time he was the best three-card dealer in the city. Lincoln, however, states that he does not touch the cards anymore. Booth tries another way by reminding him of how he discovered their mother packing her things to leave. Booth tells Lincoln that their mother asked him to look out for his elder brother.

Lincoln has abandoned his game of three-card monte for an hourly-wage job at a local arcade. He hates the violent and exploitative street culture of hustler. He has pride in his perfection of the skills in hustler which gave him fame in the society. He says:

> Hustling. Shit, I was good. I was great. Hell I was the be all and end all. I was throwing cards like throwing cards was made for me. Made for me and me alone. I was the best anyone ever seen. Coast to coast. Everybody said so. And I never lost. Not once. Not one time. Not never. That's how much them cards was mines [...]. (Parks, *Topdog/Underdog* 59)

The play focuses on family identity, fraternal interdependence, and the struggles of everyday African American life. The play chronicles the adult lives of two African American brothers as they cope with women, work, poverty, gambling, racism, and their troubled upbringings. Lincoln was three years older than his brother. He was of sixteen years and Booth thirteen years when their family broke up. This break-up affects Booth more than Lincoln who had got up on his own feet somehow. But Booth was still in need of a protective cocoon of a family life.

Booth is a thief. He steals two new suits from a departmental store, which earns more money in one day that they cannot earn in their whole life. He claims that the clothes would bring out Lincoln's former swagger. He says to Lincoln, "You look sharp too, man.

You look like the real you. Most of the time you walking around all bedraggled and shit. You look good. Like you used to look back in thuh day when you had Cookie in love with you and all the women in the world was eating out of yr hand" (Parks, *Topdog/Underdog* 34). Booth implies that the real Lincoln is the cardsharp who dresses sharply. The new clothes cause Lincoln to reflect on the relationship between exterior appearance and his interior identity. Foster Verna writes, "the black Lincoln demonstrates the African American's attempts to create or repossess his place in history" (32).

The play centers on the African American men who are completely caught up in masculine jealousy. The two brothers in the play have brought forth the image of contemporary African American manhood who are caught in an inferiority complex. Booth builds his image on his sexual expertise which fails him. He reacts violently against his brother who he identifies as his rival for sexual and financial privileges. Susan Faludi says:

> Male traditions and changing male roles in the workplace and home have undermined men's faith in themselves. She [Parks] focuses on the social world in which men live, and concludes that our society is a 'culture of ornament' in which manhood is defined by appearance, by youth and attractiveness, by money and aggression. (38)

In the play, Lincoln and Booth struggle for self-affirmation which suggests their inability to work in the society. However, the society has not given up its hold on the two brothers. They are locked up with the racial inheritance of the broken family system of the African Americans. Their inheritance is the memories of what might have been happy childhood memories with the family which are destroyed by Booth's witnessing his mother with another man. His dream of a happy family is destroyed by his mother making off with that man and abandoning him. And his father had left two years later.

Lincoln, the elder brother by four years, takes over the role of his caretaker. Being adults, they live together in a room and Lincoln brings and serves food to Booth. Booth boasts of his sexual ability with Grace, his girlfriend, and the rape of Cookie who is the ex-wife of his brother. Lincoln has taken over the parental role for Booth. So, the rape of Cookie by Booth symbolizes the rape of his own mother like oedipal situation.

The two brothers did not have the ideal role models before them set up by the African American patriarchal society. Their mother was a slut and father was a drunkard. Their parents taught them a desire for sex and liquor. Booth has seen his mother with her lover and Lincoln has heard and observed his father with other women at night. Lincoln has enjoyed certain initiating favors right beside his snoring sexually quenched father. He explains to Booth, "One of his ladies liked me, so I would do her after he'd done her. On thuh sly though" (Parks, *Topdog/Underdog* 90).

In the slavery system, the African American man was wiped out of his masculinity. Their family life was destructed due to racial slavery. The African American men were made effeminate to keep their wives with themselves physically. Lincoln was also unable to have his wife Cookie due to his inability to sustain and maintain his wife and family. Laura Dawkins puts that the figure of Lincoln in *Topdog/Underdog* illustrates "how the black man's adoption of fabricated masculine identities—and, most importantly, his inability to relinquish the adopted roles—alienates him from the African American heritage" (84). This domestic and social isolation of the brothers embodies a process of family disruption in the contemporary African American life in urban areas. This unfolds the bleak, disturbing, and disordered family and the desolation of relationship in African American society in America which creates the social and psychological conflicts between the two African American brothers that ultimately results in fratricide. In *Topdog/Underdog*, Parks creates a multifaceted portrait of her African American protagonists, giving them a voice of their own.

In brief, dramas of Suzan-Lori Parks focus on the African American people's exploitation in general and African American women in particular. Moreover, her plays throw light on how the African and African American men and women try to gain self-awareness and self-identity as the African Americans by rewriting their history and culture. Her plays also pictured how African American men and women face racism, sexism, and classism in America. Through her plays, Parks emphasizes the reshaping of African American identities in questioning dominant ideologies that perpetuate racism in America.

Works Cited

Als, Hilton. The Show-Woman: Suzan-Lori Parks's Idea for the Largest Theatre Collaboration Ever." *The New Yorker* 2006. Print.
Bush, Jason. "Who's Thuh Man? Historical Melodrama and the Performance of Masculinity in Topdog/Underdog." *Suzan-Lori Parks: A Casebook*. Eds. Wetmore, Kevin J. and Smith-Howard, Alycia. Oxon: Routledge, 2007. Print.
Dawkins, Laura. "Family Acts: History, Memory, and Performance in Suzan-Lori Parks's The America Play and Topdog/Underdog." *South Atlantic Review* 74. 3 (Summer 2009). Print.
Faludi, Susan. *Stiffed: The Betrayal of the American Man*. New York: William Morrow, 1999. Print.
Foster, Verna. "Suzan-Lori Parks's Staging of the Lincoln Myth in the America Play and Topdog/Underdog." *Journal of American Drama and Theatre* 17. 3 (Fall 2005). Print.
Frank, Haine. "The Instability of Meaning in Suzan-Lori Parks's The America Play." *American Drama* 11. 2 (2002). Print.
Gies, Deborah. "Hawthorne's Hester as a Red-Lettered Black Woman: Suzan-Lori Parks's In the Blood and Fucking A." *Journal of American Drama and Theatre* 16. 2 (2004). Print.
Guran, Letitia. "Suzan Lori-Parks: Rearticulating the Laws of Race and Gender in African American History." *South Atlantic Review* 76. 2 (Spring 2011). Print.
Halloway, Karla F. C. "Cultural Narratives Passed on: African American Mourning Stories." *African American Literary Theory: A Reader*. Ed. Napier, Winston. New York: New York University Press, 2000. Print.
Kurahashi, Yoko. "Review of Deborah Geis's Suzan-Lori Parks." *African American Review* 43. 4 (Saint Louis University, Winter 2009). Print.
LeMahieu, Michael. "The Theatre of Hustle and the Hustle of Theatre: Play, Player, and Played in Suzan-Lori Parks's Topdog/Underdog." *African American Review* 45. ½ (Spring/Summer 2012): 33–47. Print.
Mendelman, Lisa. "Resonant Silence: Love, Desire, and Intimacy in Suzan-Lori Parks's Venus." *GRAMMA* 17. 1 (2009). Print.
Nussbaum, Martha. "Objectification." *Philosophy and Public Affairs* 24. 4 (1995).
Parks, Suzan-Lori. "An Equation for Black People Onstage." *The America Play and Other Works*. New York: Theatre Communications Group, Inc., 1995. Print.

———. "Fucking A." *The Red Letter Plays*. New York: Theatre Communications Group, Inc., 2001. Print.

———. "In the Blood." *The Red Letter Plays*. New York: Theatre Communications Group, Inc., 2001. Print.

———. "Possession." *The America Play and Other Works*. New York: Theatre Communications Group, Inc., 1995. Print.

———. "The America Play." *The America Play and Other Works*. New York: Theatre Communications Group, Inc., 1995. Print.

———. *Topdog/Underdog*. New York: Theatre Communications Group, Inc., 2001. Print.

———. *Venus*. New York: Theatre Communications Group, Inc., 1997. Print.

Rayner, Alice, and Harry Elam, Jr. "Unfinished Business: Reconfiguring History in Suzan-Lori Parks's Death of the Last Black Man in the Whole Entire World." *Theatre Journal* 46 (1994). Print.

Schafer, Carol. "Staging a New Literary History: Suzan-Lori Parks's Venus, In the Blood and Fucking A." *Comparative Drama* 42. 2 (Summer 2008). Print.

Siegel, Ed. "Ambitious Blood Enriches an Old Tale." Boston Globe 28 March 2002, D3. Print.

Thompson, Debby. "Digging the Fo'-Fathers: Suzan-Lori Parks's Histories." *Contemporary African American Women Playwright: A Casebook*. Ed. Kolin, Philip C. New York: Routledge, 2007. Print.

Warner, Sara L. "Suzan-Lori Parks's Drama of Disinterment: A Transnational Exploration of Venus." *Theatre Journal* 60. 2 (May 2008). Print.

Wetmore, Kevin J. "It's an Oberammergau Thing: An Interview with Suzan-Lori Parks." *Suzan-Lori Parks: A Casebook*. Eds. Wetmore, Kevin J. and Alycia Smith. Howard, Coxon: Routledge, 2007. Print.

Worthen, William B. "Citing History: Textuality and Performativity in the Plays of Suzan-Lori Parks." *Essays in Theatre* 18. 1 (1999). Print.

Young, Harvey. "Choral Compassion: In the Blood and Venus." *Suzan-Lori Parks: A Casebook*. Eds. Wetmore, Kevin J. and Alycia Smith-Howard. Oxon: Routledge, 2007. Print.

Young, Jean. "The Re-objectification and Re-commodification of Saartjie Baartman in Suzan-Lori Parks's Venus." *African American Review* 31. 4 (Winter 1997). Print.

Chapter Five

CONCLUSIONS

The dramatic movement of African American women is a consciousness of victimization that one is oppressed, because one is African American, female, and poor. Through their plays, Alice Childress, Lorraine Hansberry, and Suzan-Lori Parks have revealed the social, economic, political, cultural, and educational oppression of African Americans in general and especially the African American women in the racist white society. They have defined and captured the African, African American, and especially African American women's experiences in their dramas. They have highlighted their existential troubles to reveal African and African American life, history, and culture. These dramatists have demolished the distortions which were in existence pertaining to their history, culture, civilization, and the life style in general and African American women in particular. They have launched a protest against racism, sexism, and classism.

The images of African American women in the plays written by African American men are generally different from the images of African American women in the plays by African American women. In her essay, "Images of Black Women in the Plays by Black Playwrights," Jeanne Marie A. Miller states that:

> In the plays written by black males, black women's happiness or completeness depends upon strong black men. [...] Black women playwrights bring to their works their vision, however, different of what black women are or what they should be. (qtd. in Brown-Guillory 206)

Alice Childress, Lorraine Hansberry, and Suzan-Lori Parks wrote about the same subject that of the African American male playwrights, but they differed in terms of perceptions. The central characters in their plays are generally female. These women are often found in key roles. In many plays, the husband is dead, or deficient in the family unit. The action for some of the parts takes place in a domestic situation. However, the effects of racism resonate in the house. They offered a multiplicity of options through African American characters that came from the heart of African American community.

Alice Childress dwells on the triple jeopardy and subjugation of African American women due to racism, classism, and also by the white and African American patriarchal social order. She uses a dramatic technique known as iconographic approach of representation which highlights the problems of ethnic identity. The icon functions as objects related to other objects on the stage. Photographs, masks, signs, and paintings also function as related elements, representing the blackness on the stage. Childress uses this iconographic method to structure *Trouble in Mind* and *Wine in the Wilderness*. In *Trouble in Mind*, this iconographic method is based on metadramatic device of the play within play. *Wine in the Wilderness* pictures the black womanhood through an elaborate painting called triptych. This metadramatic device of pictorial representation has become a major artistic tactic for dramatic representation of the identity in African American theater. Alice Childress has made significant and innovative contributions to the African American women's playwriting in America. She discovered new ways of expressing the old themes in the historically conservative theater that has opened the doors for other African American women playwrights to make dramatic advances.

In *Florence*, Childress delineates a young African American woman who finds it difficult to make a living in the theater as an actress, because the theater for too long remained locked into the stereotypical images of the African American women in the racist white society. She is a victim of these racist stereotyping even by a self-proclaimed liberal white woman who has a prejudiced opinion about Florence that she would not make it as a dramatic actress, because she is an African American woman. Nobody finds a profession of dramatic actress for her except as a maid. It is a racist white society which does not recognize her talent and capabilities of being an actress.

In *Gold through the Trees*, Childress draws out periods of struggle from the African continent to America and back to Africa from the time of the Middle Passage to the contemporary struggle of South Africa. In the play, the black women are subjected to triple patriarchy in which sexism under white colonialism subjugates the black women socially, economically, and politically. The colonial factor in black women's experiences subjects them to another form of patriarchal authority which is a foreign power, in addition to the one in their culture (Omofolabo 162). The new revolutionary images of ideal African and African American womanhood such as Harriet Tubman represent the liberation struggles to end racism in America and white colonial domination in Africa.

In *Trouble in Mind*, she explores the racism, sexism, and classism by using the melodramatic play-within-the-play structure through a theatrical audition the burial of black womanhood under its distorted white images. The racism, sexism, and classism do not provide the opportunities to the young African American women who are interested in pursuing a career in the theater arts. The play underscores the fact that there is a shortage of challenging roles for African American women actors in the contemporary American theater. The African American women in the play are the victims of discrimination on the basis of race, gender, and class. The play draws out that the African American characters in general and African American women characters particularly turn out to be the victims of not only the white dominance and egotism but also the African American insensitivity.

Wedding Band, an interracial tragedy, dramatizes the relationship between a colored woman and her white lover in the contemporary political and racist era. Childress has dramatized the political and racist attitudes introducing diverse ethnicity of characters. It examines the issue of discriminatory treatment among lower social groups within the African American society. The expression of subtle nature of segregation establishes the patriarchal norms that made living difficult for both black and white women alike. These norms prohibited legal miscegenation and divorced African American women from their property rights.

In *Wine in the Wilderness*, Childress has taken an aggressive stand toward the social, economic, and political rights of the African American women. She has artistically unfolded the problem of class discrimination, the problem of the educated African Americans adopting the white middle-class values and the consequent maltreatment of a poor African American woman. The African American men feel that African American women should learn to be more subservient to the black men in their lives.

Childress critically deals with anti-woman laws made by the white men to deny African American women's rights and to make their personal and social lives struggling. In *Wedding Band* and *Wine in the Wilderness*, she portrays a number of problems including interracial love, preventions against miscegenation, and patriarchal oppression encountered by African American women. The women characters—Florence, Harriet, Julia, Willeta, and Tommy—have been triply jeopardized in the white racist society. They, mostly belonging to working class, voice against their ruthless experiences of racism, gender inequalities, and class discrimination. They are not in the position to bring about any change in American society, but they are strong and powerful enough to obligate the African Americans to bring change in their lives.

Elizabeth Brown-Guillory has appreciated the black women characters that Childress created as, "The modern black woman ... no longer is she depicted as the overtly devout, hard-working, suffering matriarch, the prostitute, or the faithful (and/or dumb) servant; instead, she emerges as a real human being of dimension, having needs and desires." (231) These female characters have been marginalized in the American society. Olga Dugan accurately observes about Childress' plays saying that:

> Her commitment to writing plays that vindicate a race through themes of conversion and resistance, transformation and self-definition, political awakening and self-acceptance, and developing stages of self-love that represent truths about the daily situations and realities of black people's experiences, creates for Childress a critical platform in the African American dramatic and intellectual traditions. Not only did she write about a black self-determinist theatre in terms of theory, but she also wrote for one in terms of theme. (152)

Lorraine Hansberry explores the Africans' and the African Americans' social, economic, political, and cultural exploitation, deprivations, anger, history, culture, and segregation during the slavery era and even after the abolition of the slavery. She is the classic prototype of the evolution of a tradition that highlights the various branches of racial conflict and largely gloomy heritage in which the black womanhood denotes the triple subjugation.

A Raisin in the Sun is a milestone in the history of African American theater. The success of the play not only inspired a generation of young writers of many colors, but opened the door for more honest and authentic portrayals of African American experience in the pitch of the theater. It genuinely portrays the aspirations, anxieties, ambitions, and contradictory pressures of the white people affecting the poor African American men in general and African American women in particular. The African American women—Mama, Ruth, and Beneatha—dream as one of those triply oppressed by the white society: as African Americans, as women and as workers.

Their lives are the most traditional—the lives of sacrificing and being sacrificed for the survival of their family. They have the American dream in which they want to be free from the black ways of life. Therefore, they are committed to the African Americans by improving themselves and the black society through education, professions, social, and political action and a proud awareness of their black heritage. They have a strong sense of racial pride with humanistic commitment to seek freedom from racism, discrimination, and the unfinished business of slavery.

In *The Sign in Sidney Brustein's Window*, Hansberry protested against the suffocating reality of human existence and against a despair ingrained in man–woman relationship. The play embodies the solipsism of the intellectual, the oppression of women, patriarchy, betrayal, and the sexual double standard. At the center of the play are the three sisters who are the victims of race, gender, and class dominance. They are crushed under the burden of patriarchal social order in which women are measured as the objects of distorted sexual fantasy of men.

In recreating African colonial scene in *Les Blancs*, Hansberry advances the need for dialogue between the oppressed and the oppressor. Hansberry argues for humanism even as she directs her themes through African historical and socio-artistic experience. *Les Blancs* makes a strong statement about race by highlighting the intersectional oppression instigated by colonialism, racism, sexism, and patriarchy. The play explores the African quest for freedom from European colonialists. It is possibly viewed that the play is both about colonialism in Africa and as a commentary on race relations in the early 1960s America. Harold Clurman says,

> *Les Blancs* is not propaganda, as has been inferred; it is a forceful and intelligent statement of the tragic impasse of white and black relations all over the world, as well as of the complexity of motivation and effect where European nations colonize undeveloped lands inhibited by blacks. (Gunton 190)

Thus, the colonialism is linked with sexism and racism by suffering and humiliation of the blacks in general and black women in particular. *Les Blancs* is the only play of Hansberry taking place in Africa in which she uses symbols, African drums, music, dance, and sound of crickets, birds, and frogs as dramatic elements signifying the African and African American cultures. In the play, Hansberry does not depict African or African American struggle against oppression, but a struggle that must be put forth by anyone who is against oppression and in favor of liberation of the oppressed. She condemns African Americans and/or Africans who were not involved in this struggle for freedom.

The Drinking Gourd is an insightful exploration of American plantation slavery based on the exploitation of inexpensive labor in America. The play identifies the slavery system as the basis for American economic philosophy and capitalistic expansion and dramatizes the overwhelming psychological and physical impact of the slavery on the blacks. Robert Nemiroff observed in *A Critical Background*:

> What interested her in *The Drinking Gourd*, as to one degree or another in all her works, was the dissection of personality in interaction with society. [...] Her object was not to pose

black against white, to create black heroes and white villains, but to locate the sources of human behavior, of both heroism and villainy, *within* the slave society. (151–52)

The play introduces class with the gender and racial oppression and demolished the myth of the submissive and forgiving African American mother. Rissa epitomizes the evolving black woman who changes from mammy to an extremely independent, assertive, and revolutionary woman, when her family is threatened by the white master. She is a perfect black mother who tries to save and protect her children from being killed in the hands of white masters and overseers. She possesses virtues such as tolerant, long suffering, devoted, heroic, and loving black mother, but she is not forgiving. The most vigorous strength in her life is her high regard for her children and grandchildren.

What Use Are Flowers? is about the destruction and/or survival of the human race. Human beings have some destructive inner drives such as violence and jealousy within themselves from the beginning of the history of humanity and the two World Wars in the twentieth century have observed it. The play brings out the sources of such destructive inner forces in the hearts of small children which bring about the ruin of the human race. The play also proposes the resolutions to overcome such negative impulses for the survival of human race by instilling the small children with human values such as virtues, sympathy, kindness, compassion, morality, truth, reason, innate goodness, beauty, and love.

Hansberry, through these plays, brings the subaltern and marginalized people to the center of the stage. Her characters—black men, black women, and white women—convey the truths that they have perceived from the edges of society. She proves that the truth of blacks' lives could command audience—both the black and the white. She also speaks in her plays for women who were chafing at the restrictions placed on them by the patriarchy. Hansberry's plays characterize a significant step in the way of African American theater which has emerged as an instrument of African American power and assertion without causing any embarrassment to the whites. She has created manifold and multidimensional voices for African American women in American theater. She shapes her plays on the inherited traditions of the dramatists from earlier years of the twentieth century. She was cherished rationally and artistically in Harlem's cultural organizations. However, unlike her predecessors, she became a flame in the track for African American women's entry into the off-Broadway and Broadway stage.

Both Alice Childress and Lorraine Hansberry embrace the theater, because they were indebted to speak against the inequality between black and white, women and men, and poor and rich. Like Childress, Hansberry also believes that the African American artists have a responsibility to tell the truth about the sufferings of the African American people. Each one has carved for herself a distinctive place on the American stage. They serve as a vital link in the evolution of African American women's theater. The theatrical advances made by Alice Childress and Lorraine Hansberry compelled the African Americans to struggle together in order to accomplish social, economic, and political gains. Alice Childress' pioneering spirit and Hansberry's vision encouraged the young African American women dramatists of the later period such as Suzan-Lori Parks.

Suzan-Lori Parks focuses on the attempts to the African and African American men and women to gain self-awareness and self-identity by rewriting their history and culture. Her plays throw light on the plight of African American men and women who face racism, sexism, and poverty in America. Through her plays, Parks underscores the reshaping of African American identities in questioning dominant ideologies that perpetuate racism, sexism, and classism in America. *The America Play* deals with the suppressed cultural representations of African Americans in the mainstream history of America, because many events in the history of African Americans have been ignored and wiped out from the consciousness of Americans, especially African Americans. The Great Hole of History figures racial memory as a wound in black consciousness. The effects of ignored experiences of the African Americans from the national history of America propagates the beliefs, experiences, understandings, and achievements of the natives who are powerful elites in America.

Venus offers a picture of the patriarchal social system in which a black woman is treated merely as an object of sexual pleasure. It demonstrates the objectification of a black woman who has been renounced her humanity by being treated as an animal or a thing by the reigning powers on the basis of her race, gender, and social class. Her body is used as a commodity without any respect of her dignity. The black men and women are objectified and degraded by the European colonial powers, but the black women in comparison to black men are the most common victims of this objectification. The black women have dehumanized grades due to the European colonial powers and racial constraints. The delineation of Venus exposes a lamentation for all the suffering humanity across the world. The play also explores the anger at the human oppression especially black women at the hands of oppressors in every face having the power.

In the Blood captures troublesome experiences in the life of Hester La Nigrita, a black woman living in isolation from society, who is brutally victimized by the social system. She is oppressed by the evils in the society, such as discrimination, sexual harassment, hypocrisy, and violence. The vultures in the society—Reverend D and the Welfare Lady: African Americans representing social institutions of religion and social welfare, respectively, as well as the Doctor and Amiga Gringa: the whites representing the health agency and prostitution, respectively—are the oppressors of Hester who ostracize her as the other. Hester is the epitome of a black mother portrayed in the history of African Americans. She is a self-sacrificing mother devoted to her children's survival, protection, nurturing, and caring at any cost. She works insistently to establish a new life for herself and for her homeless family. She is at war everywhere with poverty and the society which has no mercy for poor. Thus, she is a tragic character for whose downfall all the other characters are liable. She has been sexually exploited by everyone whom she knows. These people have taken advantage of her body as a commodity. She suffers because of the poverty and the rigidity of patriarchal social system. Throughout the play, she wants to get up but every time she is pulled down by the social system.

Fucking A clearly marks the severe consequences of race, gender, and class on the African American men in general and African American women in particular. The play deals with sexuality and fertility of women which is dominated by white patriarchy and power politics. The modern social standards are the roots of the oppression and suffering of subordinate classes in American society. The suffering of Hester and Monster, her son, signifies the tragic stories of African Americans who are victimized by the racist white society. In this society, the black women were denied the status of the motherhood of their own children. The marginal status of Hester and Monster in the society clearly reflects the interrelationship between race and gender.

The class and racial consciousness lead toward the destruction of the notion of womanhood. The woman of higher class (white) shows less interest in the concerns of women in the lower class (both black and white). As a result of this, the lower-class women like Canary (white) and Hester (black) generate negative perceptions about the rich women like the First Lady (white). Mother's excessive love is much powerful than the bond between two women. The notion of womanhood is sacrificed for the sake of the notion of motherhood. Thus, the play focuses on the intersectional conflict of race, class, and gender. Throughout the play, human bodies such as higher-class white women, poor white women, black men, and black women are objectified.

Topdog/Underdog reveals the question of identity of two African American brothers who have no links to family or any other member in the community. Deborah Geis says, "Here, Parks creates her own version of a trope that appears frequently in African-American literature: that African-American identity almost inevitably involves disguise and role-playing as part of the effort to function in a hostile culture" (114). Both the brothers fail to maintain their relationship with the women in their lives. Lincoln was also unable to have his wife Cookie, due to his inability to sustain and maintain wife and family. In the slavery system, the African American men were wiped out of their masculinity. Their family life was destructed due to racial slavery. The African American men were made effeminate to keep their wives with themselves physically.

In *The America Play* and *Topdog/Underdog*, Parks intentionally casts her characters as African Americans whose racial identities become dramatic devices. Parks rarely uses stage directions to transform the form and contents of her plays. For her, stage directions become old-fashioned as she states, "the action goes in the line of dialogue instead of always in a pissy set of parentheses. *How* the line should be delivered is contained in the line itself" (Parks, *From Elements of Style* 15–16). This creates a real challenge for the stage director and actors. Parks uses slightly unconventional theatrical elements to give back this lack of stage directions. In *From Elements of Style*, Parks offers her readers, actors, and directors some guidelines in which she explains the significance of these theatrical devices. She defines her theatrical devices as below:

a (rest)
Take a little time, a pause, a breather; make a transition.
a spell
An elongated and heightened (rest). Denoted by repetition of figures' names with no dialogue. Has sort of an architectural look.
LUCY.
BRAZIL.
THE FOUNDLING FATHER.
LUCY.

BRAZIL.
THE FOUNDLING FATHER.

and

LINCOLN.
BOOTH.
LINCOLN.
BOOTH.
LINCOLN.
BOOTH.
This is a place where the figures experience their pure true simple state. While no 'action' or 'stage business' is necessary, directors should fill this moment as they best see fit.
The feeling: look at a daguerreotype; or: the planets are aligning and as they move, we hear the music of their spheres. A spell is a place of great (unspoken) emotion. It's also a place for an emotional transition. (16–17)

In Parks' plays, "Spells" provide the performers with some options. Here, the performers are free to choose how to fill in the blank spaces. The use of the Spells helps the performers to fill the gap with their own interpretations. Rests and Spells create short and long silences.

One of the ways to challenge the white historiography is Parks' use of a technique of "Repetition and Revision." It is based on the basic structure of jazz, where a motif is repeated and varied. Parks uses it "to create a dramatic text that departs from the traditional linear narrative style to look and sound more like a musical score" (Parks, *From Elements of Style* 9). Suzan-Lori Parks has used these dramatic techniques to give tone and texture to the themes of her plays, because these techniques are inseparable from the language of the text. She uses these techniques to transform the social reality into theatrical reality.

Thus, Alice Childress, Lorraine Hansberry, and Suzan-Lori Parks used the theater to educate African Americans to protest against the injustices on the African American race and to uplift the race. The folk culture is given dignity on the stage through the plays of African American women. They carried out the African Americans' voice on the African American theater by telling the story of their race and gender. The common topics of their plays are poverty, miscegenation, passing for whites, and lynching. The protagonists in their plays revealed the strength of the African American race, gender, and class in America. The color of one's skin complexion is an implicit topic of their plays.

Through their experiences, Alice Childress, Lorraine Hansberry, and Suzan-Lori Parks have made a precious contribution to the dramatic movement of African American women. They have transformed and reinvented American theater by writing plays for African American theater which focused on African Americans concerns. The themes of their plays include delineation of blackness, challenging the racial and gender authorities, projection of black womanhood, and production of African American history. They have expressed their own experiences and feelings to an audience both black and white.

They have occupied their place as the leaders of the American theater, creating their own theatrical space, history, and myths. These three women playwrights have fought against the racial prejudices as African Americans, women, and servants. They have also strengthened their probing for their own independent identities. Thus, the dramatic movement of African American women unlocks the doors for the mainstream American theater to understand and feel these voices of racial groups in the United States.

Works Cited

Brown-Guillory, Elizabeth. "Contemporary Black Women Playwrights: A View from the Other Half." *Feminist Theory and Modern Drama*. Ed. Taisha, Abraham. Delhi: Pen Craft International, 1998. Print.
Dugan, Olga. "Telling the Truth: Alice Childress as Theorist and Playwright." *The Journal of African American History, The Past before Us* 87. (Winter, 2002).
Geis, Deborah R. *Suzan-Lori Parks*. Ann Arbor: University of Michigan Press, 2008. Print.
Gunton, Sharon R. *Contemporary Literary Criticism 17*. Detroit, Michigan: Gale Research Company, 1981. Print.
Nemiroff, Robert. "A Critical Background." *Lorraine Hansberry: The Collected Last Plays*. Ed. Nemiroff, Robert. New York: New American Library, 1983. Print.
Omofolabo, Ajayi-Soyanka. "Black Feminist Criticism and Drama: Thoughts on Double Patriarchy." *Journal of Dramatic Theory and Criticism*. (Spring, 1993).
Parks, Suzan-Lori. "From Elements of Style." *The America Play and Other Works*. New York: Theatre Communications Group, 1995. Print.

BIBLIOGRAPHY

Primary Sources

Childress, Alice. "Florence." *Wine in the Wilderness: Plays by African American Women from the Harlem Renaissance to the Present.* Ed. Elizabeth Brown-Guillory. New York: Praeger, 1990. Print.

———. "Gold through the Trees." *Selected Plays: Alice Childress.* Ed. Kathy A. Perkins. Evanston, IL: Northwestern University Press, 2011. Print.

———. "Knowing the Human Condition." *Black American Literature and Humanism.* Ed. R. Baxter Miller. Lexington: University Press of Kentucky, 1981. Print.

———. "Trouble in Mind." *Plays by American Women: 1930–1960.* Ed. Judith E. Barlow. New York, London: Applause, 1994. Print.

———. "Wedding Band: A Love/Hate Story in Black and White." *Selected Plays: Alice Childress.* Ed. Kathy A. Perkins. Evanston, IL: Northwestern University Press, 2011. Print.

———. "Wine in the Wilderness." *Selected Plays: Alice Childress.* Ed. Kathy A. Perkins. Evanston, IL: Northwestern University Press, 2011. Print.

Hansberry, Lorraine. "A Raisin in the Sun." *Eight American Ethnic Plays.* Eds. Griffith, Francis and Joseph Mersand. New York: Charles Scribner's Sons, 1974. Print.

———. *"A Raisin in the Sun.* New York: Random House, 1959. Print.

———. "Les Blancs." *Lorraine Hansberry: The Collected Last Plays.* Ed. Nemiroff, Robert. New York: New American Library, 1983. 37–128. Print.

———. "The Drinking Gourd." *Black Theatre, USA: Forty Five Plays by Black Americans, 1847–1974.* Ed. Hatch James V. New York: The Free Press, 1974. Print.

———. "The Drinking Gourd." *Les Blancs: The Collected Last Plays of Lorraine Hansberry.* Ed. Nemiroff, Robert. New York: Random House, 1972. Print.

———. *The Sign in Sidney Brustein's Window.* New York: Random House, 1964. Print.

———. "What Use Are Flowers?" *The Best Short Plays.* Ed. Richards, Stanley. Radnor, PA: Chilton Book Company, 1973. Print.

Parks, Suzan-Lori. "An Equation for Black People Onstage." *The America Play and Other Works.* New York: Theatre Communications Group, Inc., 1995. Print.

———. "From Elements of Style." *The America Play and Other Works.* New York: Theatre Communications Group, 1995. Print.

———. "Fucking A." *The Red Letter Plays.* New York: Theatre Communications Group, Inc., 2001. Print.

———. "In the Blood." *The Red Letter Plays.* New York: Theatre Communications Group, Inc., 2001. Print.

———. "Possession." *The America Play and Other Works.* New York: Theatre Communications Group, Inc., 1995. Print.

———. "The America Play." *The America Play and Other Works.* New York: Theatre Communications Group, Inc., 1995. Print.

———. *Topdog/Underdog.* New York: Theatre Communications Group, Inc., 2001. Print.

———. *Venus.* New York: Theatre Communications Group, Inc., 1997. Print.

Secondary Sources

Books

Abramson, Doris. *Negro Playwrights in the American Theatre: 1925–1959.* New York: Columbia University Press, 1969. Print.
Allen, Thomas B. *Harriet Tubman: A Secret Agent.* Washington, DC: National Geographic Society, 2006. Print.
Anderson, Lisa. *Black Feminism in Contemporary Drama.* Urbana and Chicago: University of Illinois Press, 2008. Print.
Andrews, William et al. *The Concise Oxford Companion to African American Literature.* New York: Oxford University Press, 2001. Print.
Bigsby, C. W. E. *Confrontation and Commitment: A Study of Contemporary American Drama 1959–66.* Columbia: University of Missouri Press, 1967. Print.
Brodhead, Peter. *Life in Modern America.* London: Longman Group Limited, 1970. Print.
Burke, Sally. *American Feminist Playwrights: A Critical History.* New York: Twayne Publishers, 1996. Print.
Carter, Steven R. *Hansberry's Drama: Commitment amid Complexity.* Urbana and Chicago: University of Illinois Press, 1991. Print.
Cheney, Anne. *Lorraine Hansberry.* Boston: Twayne Publisher, 1984. Print.
Christy, Gavin. *African American Women Playwrights: A Research Guide.* New York: Rutledge, 2011. Print.
Dakorwala, N. K. *Contemporary African-American Drama: From Cultural Nationalism to the Poetics of Resistance.* Jaipur, India: ABD Publishers, 2004. Print.
Faludi, Susan. *Stiffed: The Betrayal of the American Man.* New York: William Morrow, 1999. Print.
Franklin, John Hope. *From Slavery to Freedom: A History of Negro Americans.* 5th ed. New York: Knopf, 1980. Print.
Geis, Deborah R. *Suzan-Lori Parks.* Ann Arbor: University of Michigan Press, 2008. Print.
Sinha, M. P. *Research Methods in English.* New Delhi: Atlantic Publishers and Distributors, 2004. Print.
Thernstrom, Stephan. *Harvard Encyclopedia of American Ethnic Groups.* Cambridge, MA: Harvard University Press, 1980. Print.

Articles in Books

Ashley, Leonard R. N. "Lorraine Hansberry and the Great Black Way." *Modern American Drama: The Female Canon.* Ed. Schlueter, June. London and Toronto: Associated University Presses, 1990. Print.
Barlow, Judith E. "Foreword to Trouble in Mind." *Plays by American Women: 1930–1960.* Ed. Judith E. Barlow. New York and London: Applause Theatre Book Publishers, 2001. Print.
Brown-Gillory, Elizabeth. "Contemporary Black Women Playwrights: A View from the Other Half." *Feminist Theory and Modern Drama.* Ed. Taisha, Abraham. Delhi: Pen craft International, 1998. Print.
Bush, Jason. "Who's Thuh Man? Historical Melodrama and the Performance of Masculinity in Topdog/Underdog." *Suzan-Lori Parks: A Casebook.* Eds. Wetmore, Kevin J. and Smith-Howard, Alycia. Oxon: Routledge, 2007. Print.
Carter, Linda M. "Ira Aldridge." *African American Dramatists: An A to Z Guide.* Ed. Emmanuel S. Nelson. Westport: Greenwood Press, 2004. Print.
Cleage, Pearl. "Artistic Statement." *Contemporary Plays by Women of Color: An Anthology.* Eds. Kathy A. Perkins and Roberta Uno. New York: Routledge, 1996. Print.
Frazier, Franklin. "Motherhood in Bondage." *Black History.* Ed. Melvin Drimmer. New York: Doubleday and Company, 1968. Print.

Gray, Christine R. "Discovering and Recovering African-American Women Playwrights Writing before 1930." *The Cambridge Companion to American Women Playwrights*. Ed. Murphy Brenda. Cambridge: Cambridge University Press, 1999. Print.
Hatch, James V., and Ted Shine. "Modern Black Women." *Black Theatre USA: Forty-Five Plays by Black Americans, 1847–1974*. Eds. James V. Hatch and Ted Shine. New York: The Free Press, 1974. Print.
Halloway, Karla F. C. "Cultural Narratives Passed on: African American Mourning Stories." *African American Literary Theory: A Reader*. Ed. Napier, Winston. New York: New York University Press, 2000. Print.
Jennings, La Vinia Delois. "Alice Childress." *Twayne's United States Authors Series, 652*. New York: Twayne Publishers, 1995. Print.
Kanakaraj, S. "The Prophetic Vision of Lorraine Hansberry." *Modern American Literature*. Eds. Mutallik–Desai A. and T. S. Anand. New Delhi: Creative Books, 2002. Print.
King, Martin Luther Jr. "I Have a Dream." *Speeches That Changed the World*. Ed. Alan J. Whiticker. Mumbai: Jaico Publishing House, January 2015. Print.
Malkin, Jeanette. "Suzan-Lori Parks and the Empty (W)hole of Memory." *Memory-Theater and Postmodern Drama*. Ann Arbor: The University of Michigan Press, 1999. 155–82. Print.
Nemiroff, Robert. "A Critical Background." *Lorraine Hansberry: The Collected Last Plays*. Ed. Nemiroff, Robert. New York: New American Library, 1983. Print.
Shine, Ted. "Foreword to Black Theatre U. S. A." *Black Theatre U. S. A.: Forty-Five Plays by Black Americans 1847–1974*. Eds. Hatch, James V. and Ted Shine. New York: The Free Press, 1974. Print.
Shyama, D. P. "Black Symphony: A Study of Lorraine Hansberry's Plays." *Critical Essays on American Literature*. Ed. Bal Chandra, K. New Delhi: Sarup and Sons, 2005. Print.
Tannenbaum, Frank. "The Negro in the Americas." *Black History*. Ed. Drimmer, Melvin. New York: Doubleday and Company, 1968. Print.
Thompson, Debby. "Digging the Fo'-Fathers: Suzan-Lori Parks's Histories." *Contemporary African American Women Playwright: A Casebook*. Ed. Kolin, Philip C. New York: Routledge, 2007. Print.
Turner, Darwin. "Introduction." *Black Drama: An Anthology*. Eds. William Brasmer and Dominick Consolo. Columbus, OH: Charles E. Merrill Publishing Company, 1970. Print.
———. "The Black Playwright in the Professional Theatre in the U. S. A., 1858–1959." *The Black American Writer*. Ed. Bigsby, C. W. E. Florida: Everett/Edwards, 1969. Print.
Wetmore, Kevin J. "It's an Oberammergau Thing: An Interview with Suzan-Lori Parks." *Suzan-Lori Parks: A Casebook*. Eds. Wetmore, Kevin J. and Alycia Smith. Howard, Coxon: Routledge, 2007. Print.
Wilkerson, Margaret. B. "From Harlem to Broadway: African-American Women Playwrights at mid Century." *The Cambridge Companion to American Women Playwrights*. Ed. Brenda, Murphy. Cambridge: Cambridge University Press, 1999. Print.
Wood, Jacqueline. "Shaking Loose: Sonia Sanchez's Militant Drama." *Contemporary African American Women Playwrights: A Casebook*. Ed. Collin, Phillip C. New York: Routledge, 2007. Print.
Young, Harvey. "Choral Compassion: In the Blood and Venus." *Suzan-Lori Parks: A Casebook*. Eds. Wetmore, Kevin J. and Alycia Smith-Howard. Oxon: Routledge, 2007. Print.

Articles in Journal

Abell, Joy L. "African/American: Lorraine Hansberry's Les Blancs and the American Civil Rights Movement." *African American Review* 35. 3 (2001). Print.
Achilles, Jochen. "Allegory and Iconography in African American Drama of the Sixties: Imamu Amiri Baraka's Dutchman and Alice Childress's Wine in the Wilderness." *American Studies: A Quarterly* 45. 2 (2000).

———. "Postmodern Aesthetic and Post-Industrial Economics: Games of Empire in Suzan-Lori Parks's Topdog/Underdog." *South Atlantic Review* 75. 3 (Summer 2010). Print.
Anderson, Mary Louse. "Black Matriarchy: Portrayal of Women in Three Plays." *Black American Literature Forum* 10. 3. Ed. Tasker, Witham W. Terre Haute: Indiana State University, 1976. Print.
Bernstein, Robin. "Inventing a Fishbowl: White Supremacy and the Critical Reception of Lorraine Hansberry's *A Raisin in the Sun*." *Modern Drama* 42. 1. Ed. Bluestein, David A. Ontario: University of Toronto Press (1999): 16–27.
Bigsby, C. W. E. "Black Theatre." *A Critical Introduction to Twentieth-Century Drama (Beyond Broadway)* 3. Cambridge: Cambridge University Press (1985): 375–415. Print.
Brown-Guillory, Elizabeth. "Black Women Playwrights: Exorcising Myth." *Phylon* 48. 3 (1987).
———. "Images of Blacks in Plays Black Women." *Phylon* 47. 3 (1986).
Burrell, Julie M. "Review: Childress Alice Selected Plays." *Theatre Journal* 65. 2 (2013).
Carter, Steven R. "Commitment amid Complexity: Lorraine Hansberry's Life in Action." *Multi-Ethnic Literature of the United States* 7. 3. Ed. Newman, Katharine. Los Angeles: University of Southern California, Fall 1980. Print.
———. "Images of Men in Lorraine Hansberry's Writing." *Black American Literature Forum* 19. 4 (1985). Print.
Cooper, David D. "Hansberry's A Raisin in the Sun." *Explicator* 52. 1 (Michigan State University, 1993). Print.
Curb, Rosemary. "An Unfashionable Tragedy of American Racism: Alice Childress's Wedding Band." *MELUS* 7. 4. *Ethnic Women Writers of II of Dwelling Places* (Winter 1980).
Dawkins, Laura. "Family Acts: History, Memory, and Performance in Suzan-Lori Parks's The America Play and Topdog/Underdog." *South Atlantic Review* 74. 3 (Summer 2009). Print.
DuBois, W. E. B. "Krigwa Players Little Theatre." *Crisis* 32. 2 (1926).
Dugan, Olga. "Telling the Truth: Alice Childress as Theorist and Playwright." *The Journal of African American History* 87, *The Past before Us* (Winter 2002).
Effiong, Philip Uko. "History, Myth, and Revolt in Lorraine Hansberry's Les Blancs." *African American Review* 32. 2 (Summer 1998). Print.
Farley, M. Foster. "A History of Negro Slaves Revolts in South Carolina." *Afro-American Studies* 3. Ed. Richard Trent. London: Gordon and Breach Science publishers Ltd., 1972. Print.
Foster, Verna. "Suzan-Lori Parks's Staging of the Lincoln Myth in the America Play and Topdog/Underdog." *Journal of American Drama and Theatre* 17. 3 (Fall 2005). Print.
Frank, Haine. "The Instability of Meaning in Suzan-Lori Parks's The America Play." *American Drama* 11. 2 (2002). Print.
Gies, Deborah. "Hawthorne's Hester as a Red-Lettered Black Woman: Suzan-Lori Parks's In the Blood and Fucking A." *Journal of American Drama and Theatre* 16. 2 (2004). Print.
Gill, Glenda. "Techniques of Teaching Lorraine Hansberry: Liberation from Boredom." *Black American Literature Forum* 8. 21. Eds. Hedrick, Hannah and John F. Bayliss. Terre Haute: Indiana State University, 1974. Print.
Gourdine, Angeletta. "The Drama of Lynching in Two Black Women's Drama, or Relating Grimke's *Rachel* to Hansberry's *A Raisin in the Sun*." *A Modern Drama* XLI. 4. Toronto: University of Toronto Press Incorporated, 1998. Print.
Gunton, Sharon R. *Contemporary Literary Criticism* 17. Detroit: Gale Research Company, 1981. Print.
Guran, Letitia. "Suzan Lori-Parks: Rearticulating the Laws of Race and Gender in African American History." *South Atlantic Review* 76. 2 (Spring 2011). Print.
King, Woodie Jr. "Black Theatre: Present Condition." *The Drama Review* 12 (Summer 1968).
Krasner, David. "Review of In the Blood." *Theatre Journal* 52. 4 Women/History (December 2000). Print.

Kurahashi, Yoko. "Review of Deborah Geis's Suzan-Lori Parks." *African American Review* 43. 4 (Saint Louis University, Winter 2009). Print.
LeMahieu, Michael. The Theatre of Hustle and the Hustle of Theatre: Play, Player, and Played in Suzan-Lori Parks's Topdog/Underdog." *African American Review* 45. ½ (Spring/Summer 2012): 33–47. Print.
Matuz, Roger. *Contemporary Literary Criticism* 62. Detroit, New York, London: Gale Research Inc, 1991. Print.
Mendelman, Lisa. "Resonant Silence: Love, Desire, and Intimacy in Suzan-Lori Parks's Venus." *GRAMMA* 17. 1 (2009). Print.
Omofolabo, Ajayi-Soyanka. "Black Feminist Criticism and Drama: Thoughts on Double Patriarchy." *Journal of Dramatic Theory and Criticism* VII. 2 (Spring 1993).
Rayner, Alice, and Harry Elam, Jr. "Unfinished Business: Reconfiguring History in Suzan-Lori Parks's Death of the Last Black Man in the Whole Entire World." *Theatre Journal* 46 (1994). Print.
Schafer, Carol. "Staging a New Literary History: Suzan-Lori Parks's Venus, In the Blood and Fucking A." *Comparative Drama* 42. 2 (Summer 2008). Print.
Shafee, Syed Ali. "Probing the African-American Psyche: A study of the Protagonists of *Funnyhouse of a Negro* and *Les Blancs*." *Indian Journal of American Studies* 24. 2. Ed. David Harrell. Hyderabad: A. S. R. C., Summer 1994. Print.
Warner, Sara L. "Suzan-Lori Parks's Drama of Disinterment: A Transnational Exploration of Venus." *Theatre Journal* 60. 2 (May 2008). Print.
Washington, J. Charles. "A Raisin in the Sun Revisited." *Black American Literature Forum* 22. 1. Ed. Weilxlmann, Joe. Terre Haute: Indiana State University, 1988. Print.
Wilkerson, Margaret B. "The Sighted Eyes and Feeling Heart of Lorraine Hansberry." *Black American Literature Forum* 17. 1. Terre Haut: Indiana State University, 1983. Print.
Willis, Robert J. "Anger in Contemporary Black Theatre." *Negro American Literature Forum* 8. 2 (Summer 1974).
Worthen, W. B. "Citing History: Textuality and Performativity in the Plays of Suzan-Lori Parks." *Essays in Theatre* 18. 1 (1999). Print.
Young, Jean. "The Re-Objectification and Re-Commodification of Saartjie Baartman in Suzan-Lori Parks's Venus." *African American Review* 31. 4 (Winter 1997). Print.

Articles in Magazine

Als, Hilton. The Show-Woman: Suzan-Lori Parks's Idea for the Largest Theatre Collaboration Ever." *The New Yorker* 2006. Print.

Articles in Newspaper

Siegel, Ed. "Ambitious Blood Enriches an Old Tale." *Boston Globe* 28 March 2002, D3. Print.

INDEX

365 Days/365 Plays (Parks) 126

A
Abell, Joy L. 101
Abolitionists 4
Abramson, Doris 10
Achilles, Jochen 58
African American bourgeois 11
African American community 11, 13, 18, 22, 24, 29, 30, 34, 41, 43, 73, 75, 77, 80, 164, 169
African American culture 13, 17, 33, 127
African American heritage 6, 129, 167
African American history 19, 26, 29, 32, 34, 127, 161, 163, 176
African American theatre 9–13, 15, 19, 20, 26, 27, 29, 31, 34, 42, 170, 171, 173, 176
African American women ix, x, 7, 8, 12, 21–27, 29–31, 33, 34, 37, 42, 45, 47, 52, 73, 78–81, 160, 167, 169–71, 173, 174, 176
African Folk-culture 9
African Garden, The (Childress) 26, 42
African Grove theatre 9
Afro-American Authorship 9
Aftermath (Burrill) 24
Ain't I a Woman (Truth) 22
Aldridge, Ira 14
Alexander Plays, The (Kennedy) 28
Allen, Thomas B. 4
Allison, Hughes 15
Amen Corner, The (Baldwin) 18
America Play, The (Parks) 37, 125–32, 174, 175
American economy 2
American professional theatre 9, 11
Amos and Andy 41
Anderson, Garland 10, 32, 87
Andrews, William 58
Anemone Me (Parks) 124
Anna Lucasta, (Yordan, Philip) 42
Another Show, (Peterson) 17
Antar of Araby, (Hare) 25
anti-miscegenation law 27, 68

Appearances (Anderson) 10
Artistic Statement, (Cleage) 32
Ashley, Leonard R. N. 84–86
Atkinson, Brooks 85
autonomy, Denial of 22, 133

B
Baccalaureate: A Drama in Three Acts (Branch) 17
Bad Man (Esmonds) 16
Bailey, Peter 13
Baldwin, James 18, 123
Ballad of Dorie Miller, The (Dodson) 16
Baptism, The (Baraka) 18
Baraka, Imamu Amiri 12, 13, 18
Barlow, Judith 42, 47, 58
Bartman, Sartjie (Character) 133, 134
Barton, Andrew 13
Bayou Legend (Dodson) 16
Bayou Relics (Brown-Guillory) 35
Beast's Story, A (Kennedy) 28
Beauvoir, Simone de ix
Begin the Beguine (Collins) 31
Betting on the Dust Commander (Parks) 123
Big White Fog (Ward) 11, 16
Bigsby, C. W. E. 11, 16, 18, 20, 29, 94
Black Arts Movement 12, 13, 20, 29, 33, 43
Black consciousness 12
Black Doctor, The (Aldridge) 14
Black Drama 12, 35
black identity 78, 98, 125
Black Mass, A (Baraka) 19
black matriarch 59, 80
Black Nationalism 6, 84
Black Panther Party 6
Black Pride 6
Black Revolutionary Theatre 12
Black Theatre 20
Black Woman Speaks, A (Richards) 25
black womanhood 46, 61, 74, 75, 78, 80, 121, 170, 171, 176
Blood 145

Blue Blood (Douglas Johnson) 24
Blue Vein Society, The (Kelly) 20
Blues for Alabama Sky (Cleage) 33
Blues for Mr. Charlie (Baldwin) 18
Bonner, Marita 23, 25
Bontemps, Arna 15
Boogie Woogie Landscapes (Shange) 29
Booji Wooji (Molette) 30
Bournbon at the Border (Cleage) 33
Branch, William Blackwell 17
Breath Boom (Corthron) 35
Broadway 9–11, 14, 15, 19, 27, 42, 43, 50, 52, 58, 59, 85, 123, 173
Brodhead, Peter 2
Broken Banjo: A Folk Tragedy, The (Richardson) 14
Bronx Is Next, The (Sanchez) 29
Brotherhood (Ward) 18
Brothers: A Play in Three Acts, The (Collins) 31
Brown, William Wells 9, 14
Browne, Theodore 15
Brown-Guillory, Elizabeth 9, 10, 23, 25, 29, 35, 46, 171
Brownskin Melody 58
Brownsville Raid, The (Fuller) 19
Bubbling Brown Sugar (Mitchell) 17
Bullins, Ed 12, 13, 20
Burke, Sally 23–25, 29, 42, 43, 83
Burrill, Mary 23, 24, 37
Bush, Jason 164

C

Cage Rhythm (Corthron) 35
Caleb the Degenerate (Cotter) 14
Carroll, Vinnette 27
Carter, Steven 14, 83, 102, 116, 118
Ceremonies in Dark Old Men (Elder III) 18
Chain (Cleage) 32
Chaos in Belleville (a fictional play) 58, 63
Checkmates (Milner) 21
Cheney, Anne 84, 85, 98, 103
Chiaroscuro: A Light and Dark Comedy (Rahman) 34
Childress, Alice ix, x, 26, 27, 37, 41–81, 169–71, 173, 176
Chip Woman's Fortune, The (Richardson) 10, 14
Christophe (Easton) 14
Christy, Gavin 25
Civil Rights Act 6
Civil Rights Movement 12, 26, 32, 52
Clara's Ole Man (Bullins) 20

class ix, 2, 6, 7, 14, 17, 18, 20, 24, 27, 30, 31, 33, 36, 37, 43, 61–65, 73, 75, 78, 80, 81, 83, 86, 87, 89, 92, 95, 98, 123, 124, 127, 132, 133, 147, 153–56, 160, 170–76
classism 13, 22, 27, 30, 32, 81, 167, 169, 170, 174
Cleage, Pearl 30–33
Clurman, Harold 172
Collins, Kathleen 30, 31
Color-Struck (Hurston) 26
Coloured American, The 4
Come Down Burning (Corthron) 35
Compromise: A Folk Play (Richardson) 14
Constitutional Convention 4
Conversations with Julie (Collins) 31
convict-leasing system 2
Cool Dip in the Barren Saharan Crick, A (Corthron) 36
Cooper, 15, 22, 30, 85, 93
Corthron, Kia 30, 35, 36
Cotter, Joseph 14
Crazy Horse (Peterson) 17, 35
Crisis, The (magazine) 10
Cross: A Play of the Deep South or Mulatto (Hughes) 15
Cruz Brothers and Mrs. Malloy, The (Collins) 31
cultural hegemony x
Curb, Rosemary 64

D

Dakorwala, N. K. 9, 10, 13, 15, 17, 20
Davis, Ossie 19
Dawkins, Laura 125, 129, 166
Day of Absence (Ward) 18
Deacon's Awakening, The (Richardson) 14
Dean, Phillip Hayes 19
Death of the Last Black Man in the Whole Entire World (Parks) 37, 123, 124
Deavere Smith, Anna 30
Democratic Party 7
Dent, Thomas Covington 19
Dessalines (Easton) 14
Devotees in the Garden of Love (Parks) 125
Dickerson, Glenda 34
Digging Eleven (Corthron) 35
Dirty Hearts (Sanchez) 29, 30
Disappointment: or, The Force of Credulity, The (Barton) 13
Divine Comedy (Dodson) 16
Dodson, Owen 16
dominant ideology x

INDEX

Don't Bother Me, I Can't Cope (Carroll) 27
Don't You Want to be Free? (Hughes) 11
Douglas Johnson, Georgia 23, 24
Douglass, Frederick 4, 17
Douglass, Sarah Mapps 4
Dr. B. S. Black (Molette) 30
Drama of King Shot Away, The (Brown) 9
Dramatic Circle, The 28
Dramatic Movement ix, 8
Drinking Gourd, The (Hansberry) 27, 84, 109–15, 172
DuBois, W. E. B. 5, 10, 14
Dugan, Olga 171
Dulane (Character) 11
Dunbar-Nelson, Alice 23, 25
Dutchman (Baraka) 18, 19

E

Easton, William 14
Eel Catching on Setauket: A Living Portrait of a Community (Dickerson) 34
Effiong, Philip Uko 101
Elam Jr., Harry 125
Elder III, Lonne 12, 18
Electronic Nigger and Others (Bullins) 20
Elements of Style (Parks) 175, 176
Eli Whitney's cotton gin 3
Elliott, the Reverend Stephen 4
Emancipation Proclamation 5, 6
enslaved Africans ix, 1, 2, 9, 52, 53
Entertain a Ghost (Peterson) 17
Equation for Black People Onstage (Parks) 124, 126
Escape: or A Leap for Freedom, The (Brown) 9, 10, 14
Esmonds, Randolph 16
Evans, Donald T. 43
Everybody Join Hands (Dodson) 16
Exit, An Illusion (Bonner) 25

F

Faith, Hope, and Charity: The Story of Mary McLeod Bethune (Kelly) 21
Famous Orpheus (Gordon) 21
Farley, M. Foster 2, 3
Farrison, Edward 109
Features and Stuff (Dent) 20
Federal Theatre 11, 15
Film Club, The (Kennedy) 28
Flight of the Natives, The (Richardson) 14
Florence (Childress) 26, 42–50, 170

Floyd, George 7
Flying West (Cleage) 33
folk-drama 9
For Colored Girls Who Have Considered Suicide/ When the Rainbow is Enuf, (Shange) 29
Force Continuum (Corthron) 35
Foreword to Black Theatre U. S. A. (Shine) 13
Forrest, Thomas 13
Fortune of the Moor (Molette) 30
Foster, Verna 129, 166
Foundling Father (Character) 127–32
Frank, Haike 33, 86, 104, 132
Franklin, John Hope 5
Frazier, Franklin 7
Frederick Douglass Paper, The 4
Freedom Aint Free (slogan) 126
Freedom Drum, The (Childress) 42
Freedom's Journal 4
Fried Chicken and Invisibility (Gordon) 21
From Slavery to Freedom (Franklin) 5
Fucking A (Parks) 37, 125, 152–60, 174
Fugitive Slave 14
Fugitive Slave Acts 4
Fuller, Charles 19
Fungibility 133
Funnyhouse of a Negro (Kennedy) 28

G

Gaines-Shelton, Ruth 23
Garden of Time (Dodson) 16
Garnet, Henry Highland 4
Garrett, 12
gender ix, 7, 14, 22–25, 29, 30, 33, 34, 37, 43, 45, 61, 63, 81, 88, 123, 133, 155, 157, 160, 170–76
Gentlemen Caller, The (Bullins) 20
Getting Mother's Body (Parks) 124
Gies, Deborah 144
Gill, Glenda 90
Girl 6 (Parks) 124
Go Down Moses (Browne) 15
Gold through the Trees (Childress) 26, 42, 170
Gordone, Charles 19
Gordon, Charles F. 21
Gordone is a Muthah (Gordone) 19
Gourdine, Angeletta 23
Graham, Ottie 25
Grandy, Moses (former slave) 7
Granny Maumee (Torrence) 10
Graven Images (Miller) 25
Gray, Christine R. 23, 25

Great Migration 3
Green, Paul 11
Grimke, Angelina Weld 23, 26, 37
Guinn, Dorothy C. 26
Gullah (Childress) 42
Gunner, Frances 26
Gunton, Sharon R. 84, 93, 95, 109, 172
Guran, Letitia 127, 142

H
Halloway, Karla 131
Hansberry, Lorraine ix, x, 9, 11, 12, 26, 27, 37, 42, 43, 83–91, 93, 94, 96–121, 169, 171–73, 176
Happy Ending (Ward) 18
Hare, Maud Cuney 25
Harlem (Rapp William J. Wallace Thurman) 6, 10
Harlem Renaissance 6, 10, 15, 24, 25, 32
Hatch, James V. 35, 80
Hawthorne, Nathaniel 126, 152
Hero Ain't Nothin' But a Sandwich, A (Childress) 42, 43
Hewlett, James (actor) 9
Hill, Abraham 11, 28
Holiday (Graham) 25
Hopkins' Colored Troubadours, The 10
Hospice (Cleage) 32
House of Shame, The (Richardson) 15
How Do You Do (Bullins) 20
Hughes, Langston 10, 11, 15, 26, 42, 85, 86
Hurston, Zora Neale 10, 26, 34, 124

I
I am a Man (Gordon) 21
I'm Black When I'm Singing, I'm Blue When I Ain't (Sanchez) 29, 30
Ibsen, Henrik 16
Idle Head, The (Richardson) 15
Images of Black Women in the Plays by Black Playwrights (Miller) 169
Imperceptible Mutabilities in the Third Kingdom (Parks) 37, 123, 124
In Living Color (Gordon) 21
In Splendid Error (Branch) 17
In the Blood (Parks) 37, 125, 142–51, 174
In the Midnight Hour (Collins) 31
Inertness 133
Instrumentality 133
intersectional oppression 172

J
Jennings, La Vinia Delois 73
jeopardy ix, 81, 169
Jericho Jim Crow (Hughes) 15
Jim Crow 5, 41, 44, 64
Johnson, Hall 11, 37
Johnson, James Weldon 27
Just a Little Simple (Childress) 26, 42

K
Kanakraj, S. 94, 95
Kelly, Samuel L 20
Kennedy, Adrienne 12, 26, 28, 37, 43
King Jr., Martin Luther 6, 21
Knowing the Human Condition (Childress) 41
Kurahashi, Yoko 156

L
Lady Day: A Musical Tragedy (Rahman) 33
Land beyond the River (Mitchell) 11
Last Chord, The (Gordone) 19
Les Blancs (Hansberry) 27, 84, 100–8, 172
Let Me Live (Gordon) 21
Liberator, The 4
Life by Asphyxiation (Corthron) 35
Light of the Women (Gunner) 26
Light Raise the Roof (Corthron) 36
Like One of the Family (Childress) 42
Lincoln, Abraham 5, 6, 37, 127, 128, 132, 161–63
Little Ham (Hughes) 15
Livingstone, Myrtle Smith 23
Locke, Alain 10
Look at the Contemporary Black Theatre Movement, A (Bailey) 13
Looking for Jane (Collins) 31
Losing Ground (Collins) 31
Louisiana (Smith, Augustus) 11
lynching 2, 7, 23–25, 37, 58, 89, 124, 176
Lyon, the Reverend James A 4

M
Malcolm Man Don't Live Here No Mo (Sanchez) 29
Mam Phyllis (Brown-Guillory) 35
Margaret Sanger's Progressive Birth Control Review 24
Marry Me, Again (Brown-Guillory) 35
Matter of Color: Documentary of the Struggles for Racial Equality in the U. S. A., A (Hansberry) 84

Matuz, Roger 88, 91
Mau Mau Revolution 101
McKay, Claude 10
Medal for Willie (Branch) 17
Megastasis (Corthron) 36
Mendelman, Lisa 133
Miller, May 23, 24, 37, 169
Milner, Ron 21
Mine Eyes Have Seen (Dunbar-Nelson) 25
Miralda or *The Beautiful Quadroon* (Brown) 9
Mitchell, Loften 11, 17
Mojo (Childress) 26, 42
Mojo and the Sayso (Rahman) 34
Molette, Barbara 30
Moms (Childress) 42
Moot the Messenger (Corthron) 36
Mortgaged, (Richardson) 15
Motion of History 19
Movement: Documentary of a Struggle for Equality, The (Hansberry) 84
Mulatto, Hughes 11, 15

N

National Era, The 4
Native Son (Green, Paul and Richard Wright) 11
Natural Man (Browne) 15
Negro Ensemble Company 12, 18
Negro Playwrights Company 16
Negro Study No. 34A (Dent) 20
Negro theatre 10, 11
Negro Theatre Guild 11
Nemiroff, Robert 83, 84, 93, 103, 109, 118, 172
New Lafayette Theatre 12, 20
New Negro Movement 6
New World A-Coming: An Original Pageant of Hope (Dodson) 16
Newton, Huey 6
No Place to Be Somebody (Gordone) 19
Noah's Ark (Molette) 30
North Star, The 4, 109
Nussbaum, Martha 133

O

Obama, Barack 7
Objectification 132
Off-Broadway 42
Ohio State Murders, The (Kennedy) 28
Omofolabo, Ajayi-Soyanka 170
On Strivers Row (Hill) 11

Only in America (Rahman) 34
Only the Sky is Free (Collins) 31
Our Lan, (Ward) 11, 16
Out of the Dark (Guinn) 26
Owl Answers, The (Kennedy) 28
Ownership 133

P

Panyared (Allison) 15
Parks, Suzan-Lori ix, x, 30, 36, 37, 123–76
Paul Robeson (Dean) 19, 83
Peer Gynt (Dodson) 16
Peterson, Louis 11, 14, 17
Pill Hill (Kelly) 20
Pillar of the Church, A (Richardson) 14
Plumes (Douglas Johnson) 24
Pollard, Edward A 4
Poor La Patrie (Corthron) 36
Possession (Parks) 126, 161
Pot Maker, The (Bonner) 25
Proclamation of Independence 5
Prosser, Gabriel 3
Puppet Play (Cleage) 32
Purlie Victorious (Davis) 19
Purple Flower, The (Bonner) 25

R

race ix, 3–5, 7, 8, 14–16, 20–27, 33, 36, 37, 61 63, 65, 71, 74, 76, 77, 83–85, 91, 93, 101, 102, 104, 105, 117, 119–21, 124, 132, 133, 141, 157, 160, 162, 163, 170–76
Rachel (Grimke) 23
racial segregation 2, 44
racism ix, 12, 13, 17, 22, 23, 25, 27–30, 32, 42, 43, 45–47, 50, 55, 58, 61, 64, 68, 72, 73, 81, 85, 92, 98–101, 104, 108, 123, 124, 165, 167, 169–72, 174
Rahman, Aishah 30, 33
Raisin in the Sun, A (Hansberry) 9, 11, 12, 27, 80, 83–85, 87–91, 93, 171
Rapp, William J. 10
Rats Mass, A (Kennedy) 28
Rayner, Alice 125
Re/Membering Aunt Jemima: A Menstrual Show (Dickerson) 34
Reading, The (Collins) 31
Real Negro theatre 10
Reckoning, The (Ward) 18
Repetition and Revision 176
rest 129, 130, 146, 148, 157, 159, 175

Resurrection of Lady Lester, The (Gordon) 21
Richards, Beah 25
Richardson, Willis 10, 14
Riders of Dreams, The (Torrence) 10
Riding the Goat (Miller) 25
Riot Duty (Dent) 20
Ritual Murder (Dent) 20
River Nigger, The (Walker) 18
Rosalee Pritchett (Molette) 30
Run, Little Chillun, (Johnson) 11

S

Safe (Douglas Johnson) 24
Safe Box (Corthron) 36
Sam's Coming (Corthron) 36
Sanchez, Sonia 29, 30
Scarlet Letter, The (Hawthorne) 152
Schafer, Carol 126
Sea Island Song (Childress) 42
Seale, Bobby 6
Second Sex, The, (Beauvoir) ix
Seeking the Genesis (Corthron) 35
sexism ix, 13, 22, 25, 27–30, 32, 42, 43, 61, 101, 123, 167, 169, 170, 172, 174
Shafee, Syed Ali 28, 84
Shange, Ntozake 13, 26, 28, 29, 37, 43
She Talks to Beethoven (Kennedy) 28
Shine, Ted 13
Short Walk, A (Childress) 42
Shyama, D. P. 12
Sign in Sidney Brustein's Window, The (Hansberry) 27, 83, 84, 94, 172
Simon the Cyrenian (Torrence) 10
Simple Speaks His Mind (Hughes) 26, 42
Sinha, M. P. 8
Sinner's Place, The (Parks) 123
Sister Son/Ji (Sanchez) 29, 30
Slave, The (Baraka) 19
Slave Ship (Baraka) 19
Slave Trade Act 136
slavery ix, 1–6, 8, 10, 11, 13, 17, 20, 22, 23, 26, 27, 31, 32, 36, 44, 52, 55–58, 78, 84, 85, 92, 109–16, 121, 123, 124, 129, 136, 138, 162, 166, 171, 172, 175
Slaves' Escape: or the Underground Railroad (Hopkins) 10
Slingshot Silhouette (Corthron) 36
Smith, Augustus 11, 26
Snapshot (Dent) 20
Snapshots of Broken Dolls (Brown-Guillory) 35
Soldier's Play, A (Fuller) 19

Souls of Black Folks, The (DuBois) 5
Spell 175, 176
Spell #7 (Shange) 29
Spence, Eulalie 23
Splash Hatch on the E Going Down (Corthron) 35
St. Louis Woman (Bontemps) 15
Star of Ethiopia, The (DuBois) 10, 14
Star of Morning: Scenes in the Life of Bert Williams (Mitchell) 17
Steven R., Carter 86
Stewart, Maria 4
Stowe, Harriet Beacher 13
String (Childress) 26, 42
Sty of the Blind Pig, The (Dean) 19
subjectivity, Denial of 133
Sunday Morning in the South, A (Douglas Johnson) 24

T

Take a Giant Step (Peterson) 11, 17
Tale of Madame Zora (Rahman) 33
TALK 156
Tannenbaum, Frank 2
Tap the Leopard (Corthron) 36
Tate, Claudia 88
Tell the Pharaoh (Mitchell) 17
Their Eyes Were Watching God (Parks) 124
Thernstrom, Stephan 2, 6
They That Sit in Darkness (Burrill) 24
Those Other People (Childress) 43
Thruway Diaries: Driving While Black, (Kelly) 20
Thurman, Wallace 10
Titus Andronicus (Aldridge) 14
To Be Young Gifted and Black (Hansberry) 27, 84
Toilet, The (Baraka) 19
Topdog/Underdog (Parks) 37, 123, 124, 126, 160–66, 175
Torrence, Ridgely 10
Toussaint (Hansberry) 84, 85
Trial of Dr. Beck, The (Allison) 15
Trickle (Corthron) 36
Trouble in Mind (Childress) 26, 42, 43, 58, 169, 170
Trumpets of the Lord (Carroll) 27
Truth, Sojourner 4, 22
Tubman, Harriet 4, 15, 25, 52, 56, 170
Turner, Darwin 9, 62

INDEX

U

Uh Huh, But How Do It Free Us (Sanchez) 29, 30
Unborn Children, The (Smith) 26
Uncle Tom's Cabin, (Stowe) 13
Underground Railroad 15, 25, 109
Unfinished Women Cry in No Man's Land While a Bird Dies in a Gilded Cage (Rahman) 33
Urban Transition: Loose Blossoms (Milner) 21

V

Venus, (Parks) 36, 37, 123, 125, 132–42, 174
Venus De Milo Is Armed, The (Corthron) 36
Village: A Party, The (Fuller) 19
Violability 133

W

Wake Up Lou Riser (Corthron) 35
Walker, David 4
Walker, Joseph A 18
Walker's Appeal 4
Ward, Douglas Turner 11, 12, 16
Warner, Sara 133
Warning: A Theme for Linda, The (Milner) 21
Washington, Booker T. 5, 14, 93
Weales, Gerald 13, 20, 93
Wedding Band: A Love/Hate Story in Black and White (Childress) 26, 27, 42, 43, 64–72, 170, 171
Wetmore, Kevin J 134, 139
What the Wine-Sellers Buy (Milner) 21

What Use Are Flowers? (Hansberry) 27, 84, 116–20, 173
Where the Mississippi Meets the Amazon (Shange) 29
While Older Men Speak (Collins) 31
White Chocolate (Kelly) 20
white patriarchy 22, 25, 42, 152, 174
Who's Got His Own (Milner) 21
Wilkerson, Margaret B. 28, 43, 84, 109
William and Ellen Craft (Douglas Johnson) 24
Williams, Peter 4
Willis, Robert J. 12
Wine in the Wilderness (Childress) 26, 27, 42, 43, 73, 75, 77, 78, 80, 169, 171
Woman Playwright Speaks Her Mind, A (Childress) 42
Wood, Jacqueline 29
World on a Hill, The (Childress) 84
Worthen, W. B. 142
Wright, Richard 11

X

X, Malcolm 6

Y

Yeamans, Sir John 1
Yordan, Philip 42
Young, Harvey 125
Young, Jean 134

Z

Zooman and the Sign (Fuller) 19

Ingram Content Group UK Ltd.
Milton Keynes UK
UKHW012207220623
423877UK00003B/11